C0 AYR 387

Wars and Peace

Wars and Peace

The Memoir of an American Family

Rory Quirk

PRESIDIO

Copyright © 1999 by Rory F. Quirk

Published by Presidio Press
505 B San Marin Drive, Suite 300
Novato, CA 94945-1340

All rights reserved. No part of this book may be reproduced or utilized in any form or by any means, electronic or mechanical, including photocopying, recording, or by any information storage and retrieval systems, without permission in writing from the publisher. Inquiries should be addressed to Presidio Press, 505 B San Marin Drive, Suite 300, Novato, CA 94945-1340.

Library of Congress Cataloging-in-Publication Data

Quirk, Rory F., 1943–
    Wars and peace : the memoir of an American family / Rory F. Quirk.
      p.   cm.
    Includes index.
    ISBN 0-89141-683-8
    1. Quirk, James T. (James Thomas), 1911–1969 Correspondence. 2. Quirk, Elizabeth, 1909–1962 Correspondence. 3. Quirk, Rory F., 1943–   . 4. World War, 1939–1945—Personal narratives, American. 5. Korean War, 1950–1953—Personal narratives, American. 6. Soldiers—United States Biography. 7. Publishers and publishing—United States Biography. I. Title.
CT275.Q557A4 1999
940.54'8173—dc21   99-20095
                                CIP

Printed in the United States of America

Contents

In memory of
James T. Quirk (1911–1969)
and
Elizabeth Wolstencroft Quirk (1909–1962)
and for
Clare, Christopher, and Elizabeth

Author's Note

About the Letters

James Quirk and Elizabeth Wolstencroft corresponded almost daily throughout World War II and the Korean War. The one extensive gap, during the Battle of the Bulge in the winter of 1944–45, I attribute to my father's lack of time to write. Elizabeth preserved all of James's letters in a large crate along with other World War II materials. Only a small number of Elizabeth's letters survived the war; they were similarly preserved. The crate and its contents somehow survived numerous moves as well as a small basement flood in 1951.

I was aware of the existence of the letters for a number of years but never read any of them until my father's death in 1969, when they passed to me. When I returned from Vietnam in the spring of that year, I read all of them, saved most, and discarded others. The letters were recrated and again survived my myriad moves.

In 1993, I sought to house the letters in a safe, permanent repository where they might be used as a resource by historians and scholars. They were placed at the Harry S. Truman Library in Independence, Missouri, where they are part of the library's permanent collection.

In selecting letters and memoranda for publication in this book, I excluded some (thus the jump in dates), chose some for publication in their entirety, and edited others for reasons of space and relevance. In the latter instance, portions were omitted and/or condensed without ellipses. I sought always to preserve the context and my father's intent.

The words are entirely those of James and Elizabeth Quirk except for my occasional explanatory words, which are in brackets. I added punctuation for clarity, spelled out abbreviations, broke up large chunks of text into shorter paragraphs, and corrected typographical errors. James and Elizabeth were so-so typists but excellent spellers; I owed them that. The dating of entries and the location of the writer have been standardized.

I decided to keep end notes to a minimum, utilizing them only when necessary to facilitate the reader's understanding. My reasoning was that the value of the letters is as one soldier's diary of contemporaneous impressions of war, not a definitive history. For example, my father concluded erroneously in his letter of April 1, 1945, that General Patton, having attended Catholic Mass on Easter Sunday, was a Catholic; he was in fact an Episcopalian.

Preface

The book that I set out to write was a wartime diary of my parents' letters from World War II and the Korean War, with historical references to give the reader a sense of place and perspective. It is not the book that I wrote. Although this book does draw heavily from my parents' letters, which make up the two largest sections of the narrative, they are only part of this story.

In sharing the letters with friends who were familiar with the personalities and the events described and recounted there, I got a number of reactions. The first had to do with the sweep and literary quality of the letters themselves. Intended by my parents as ephemeral, on-the-fly communications between a man and a woman separated by war, their letters reemerge a half century later as finely etched, contemporaneous observations of extraordinary times and people. They combine the miniaturist's eye for detail, the historian's sense of context, and the writer's ability to distill the swirl and chaos of war into vignettes of crystalline clarity. The second reaction had to do with my parents' prewar past: Who were these letter writers James and Elizabeth Quirk? Where had they come from? What influences and events had shaped them before James went to war? The third reaction had to do with my parents' postwar lives. James and Elizabeth talk often in their letters of life after the war—the words *plans* and *dreams* and *reunion* recur. They were ill-defined plans and dreams, melding the material and the spiritual: a house of their own; an end to forced separation; curling up on a big couch on a rainy Sunday afternoon with their respective books; raising their infant son and giving him things that family setbacks and the Depression had denied them.

What had become of those dreams and hopes? The answer to that question is complex. James and Elizabeth attained much of what they had hoped for. Following his military career, James went on to one of the greatest successes in the history of magazine publishing. By any quantitative, material measure, their dreams came true. At a qualitative cost. Their much-anticipated reunion and the hopes of lazy, rainy Sundays ended up among the casualties—spiritual intangibles absent from the material cornucopia. That story became part of this book.

In editing the letters, I also came to realize that although James was initially just an eyewitness to history, he ultimately helped shape it—in significant ways during World War II, then in major ways in Korea. The awed junior officer who came ashore at Normandy in the wake of D day ended up with the best of America's World War II generals, and the most controversial. George S. Patton's military genius was in constant danger of being undone by his careless tongue. The image sent home to the American public accentuated his warrior strengths and excised his unadmirable faults. It was a misleading image to be sure, but the alternative was to permit Patton to verbally self-destruct. James helped craft that image, sanitizing the outrageous Pattonisms—censored them, to be blunt—thereby saving a gifted commander from himself and forestalling the inevitable career-ending implosion until the Thousand-Year Reich was itself in ruins.

Recalled to active duty in Korea five years later, to work for a general he didn't know in a war that the American public didn't understand, James again played a significant role. In his time with the extraordinary Matthew Ridgway, they collaborated to make sense of the "why" of Korea for a confused public while simultaneously suppressing an explosive issue: Ridgway in Korea was relentlessly undercut and recklessly upstaged by Douglas MacArthur, his superior in Tokyo. Had that friction come to public view, had MacArthur prevailed, a critical, perhaps pivotal chapter in the Cold War would have ended differently. Those events too became part of this book, along with my own Korean War research, which explains, I believe, why the Communists abruptly and inexplicably abandoned any hope of winning the war and came instead to the armistice table.

Although James shaped events, the wars shaped him. The thirty-four-year-old lieutenant colonel who came home at the end of 1945 didn't look appreciably different from the thirty-two-year-old captain who had shipped out for England at the end of 1943. He was a little thinner, and the forehead was a little higher. But he was not the same person. There was a confidence, a sense of impatience that had not been there before. Those qualities were intensified when he returned from Korea. Like Grant in Galena, he was waiting for a break, and when it came he seized the once-in-a-lifetime opportunity with a vengeance.

The wars changed Elizabeth as well. She had juggled a job, a son, and a household budget while James was gone in World War II, then found herself a single parent again when James went to Korea. The absences gave her confidence. After Korea, she chafed at the constraints of what today is called the "glass ceiling," and she sought to find creative outlets that accentuated her considerable abilities. In fact, they were to woefully underutilize them. Like so many talented, ambitious women of her generation, she too was mired in Galena, but for her there would be no Sumter. So that became part of this book as well.

Finally, I came to realize that the wars and the intermittent peace had affected me, too, shaped what I would become in subtle yet fundamental ways, silently dictating my career choices and how I would relate to my own family. James missed my birth, my first birthday, then my second. In my first eight years, he was away at war, twice, for three of them. Throughout the next decade, he was gone a great deal, pursuing his career, exploiting the opportunity he had finally gotten. Then I was away—off to college, off to war (our family's third). When I came home at last, James and Elizabeth were dead. I was left with my memories and their letters. So I became a part of this story, too.

In "Four Quartets," Eliot writes, "We shall not cease from exploration / And the end of our exploring / Will be to arrive where we started / And know the place for the first time." And so it has been for me.

That exploration is this book.

The greatest obstacle to being heroic is the doubt whether one may not be going to prove one's self a fool; the truest heroism is to resist the doubt.

In youth men are apt to write more wisely than they really know or feel.

—Nathaniel Hawthorne

Prologue

19 January 1969: Mekong Delta

We're heading north out of the delta, with the late afternoon sun on its downward run over the miles and miles of paddies to the west. The helicopter in which I am riding casts a clearly defined shadow on the ostensibly tranquil green and brown landscape below.

There are six passengers on the northbound Huey: me, and five dead grunts in body bags stacked lumpily at my feet. Riding the KIA chopper out of Dong Tam with a cargo of the recently dead, I am thinking about my father, himself recently dead of a heart attack in the Philadelphia airport at the age of fifty-seven. I know this because the major told me about an hour ago. Actually, he told me he had some bad news from home. When you are an only child and single, and your mother is dead, it all comes into focus unsaid. I am going home to bury my father.

There is a terrible irony to my homeward journey. My father had served his country in two wars—World War II and Korea—and had survived them both. The dead men against which my jungle boots rest gingerly are—were—not much younger than my twenty-five years, and they did not survive their first war.

Two generations of soldiers, all dead before their time.

My father's life—short, but much longer than that of my traveling companions this day—was shaped in the crucible of war. He served with three of the greatest combat commanders America has produced: Omar Bradley and George Patton in Europe, and Matthew Ridgway in Korea. He was a participant and an eyewitness to the memorable events of his time: the destruction of Nazi Germany, the horror of the torture-murder factories that were the linchpin of Hitler's vision, the miraculous turnaround of a thoroughly defeated army by Ridgway in Korea, and the relief of the American icon Douglas MacArthur, who had nearly brought the world to Armageddon on that frozen peninsula.

I am on this day only dimly aware of those events, my father's role in them, or their lasting impact on him (and on my mother and me). They would not become clear until I sat down with the vividly detailed letters that he sent to my mother on an almost daily basis, recounting and reliving those experiences. Those letters, saved faithfully by my mother, would become this book.

What I am aware of, as our death ship begins its descent to the mortuary outside Saigon, is that my father's experiences imbued him with altered horizons and a self-confidence that propelled him from a prewar career in local radio to a postwar career of a sweep and scale that would have been as unimaginable as it was unattainable before his wars.

His was an optimism, a certitude born of wartime experience. There was nothing that he and his generation, and the United States of America, could not do. I and the members of my generation are the children of the apogee of the American century that my father and his generation had wrought. We are the beneficiaries of that optimism; we share that certitude.

It was an optimism that saved western civilization from ice-cold Nazi barbarism. It was a certitude that, with the benefit of hindsight, decided the Cold War at mid-century, in Korea, long before the wall came down in Berlin and the statues of Lenin were toppled in the village squares.

But the optimism is foundering on the shoals of Vietnam. The certitude is beginning to crack. The bags at my feet are the latest daily installment in the growing shadow of national self-doubt.

The chopper lands, and the mortuary staff approach in a semicrouch, fighting the rotor wash. It is reminiscent of a scene that a later generation will see at the beginning of each episode of the television series M*A*S*H, except the doctors and nurses in those episodes are lifesavers, healers. We are well beyond that here.

"How many?" one of the mortuary crew mouths, the sound of his voice lost in the whap-whap of the rotors. The crew chief holds up four gloved fingers and a thumb. We off-load the body bags one by one into the waiting arms of the mortuary detail, who move them inside with practiced dispatch.

Airborne again, the pilot tilts the chopper on its side, trying to rid the ship of the stink of death.

As we continue farther north to the air base where I will board a plane for home, I reflect on the balance sheet of my father's life: his considerable achievements, the material benefits they afforded my mother and me, and the corresponding toll occasioned by his absences. He had gone off to his wars, come home, then gone off again to make his fortune. We warred at his absences. We were a family at war with the zero-sum nature of his success.

The Huey hovers just off the airstrip, and I jump the short distance to the ground. As the aircraft climbs again, I give the pilot an appreciative thumbs-up on this decidedly thumbs-down day. He returns the signal, banks hard into the sunset, and heads back to the war that has no back or front.

I sling my rucksack over my shoulder and jog across the airstrip. Heading home to bury my father next to my mother, I am the sole survivor of a family at war beginning a long search for an elusive inner peace.

Chapter One: Before War
1909–43

On September 24, 1943, at Fort Leavenworth in Kansas, army captain James T. Quirk received a telegram advising him that his wife, Elizabeth, had given birth that morning in Philadelphia to their first child, a son.

James and Elizabeth had been married for nine years and, like many childless couples entering their thirties, had all but given up hope of having children. During a visit to Canada in 1940, they had visited the birthplace of the Dionne quintuplets. There, in the last-chance saloon of the childless, James and Elizabeth had been photographed plucking a "stork stone" from a bin at the Dafoe hospital, where the quints lived. Childless women, the accompanying news story reported, carted away two tons of the good-luck stones every week. The amulets were garden-variety stones brought from the quarry out back. Still, Elizabeth had given it a shot. That had been three years before. Now they had a son, born three weeks prematurely and nicknamed Jackson (though in later years no one could recall why).

At the time he received the news, James had just returned from five months of wartime service in North Africa, where Axis forces had for the first time surrendered to the Allies. When James finished Command and General Staff (C&GS) School at Leavenworth in November, he would have an opportunity to peek in on his wife and son before sailing for England, where the Allies were preparing for the make or break invasion of Hitler's Europe.

• • •

James Quirk was born in West Philadelphia in 1911, the third of six children of John Quirk, a diminutive Irishman with twinkling blue eyes, and Kathryn McAvoy, an imposing Scotch Presbyterian who stood a head taller than her husband. John graduated from Roman Catholic High School in 1894 (his longevity—he died in 1966—would give him the distinction for much of the last ten years of his life of being the oldest living graduate of the nation's oldest Catholic high school). He went on to the University of Pennsylvania, where he was the coxswain of the Penn crew. Following his graduation in 1899, he pursued a career in real estate development and made a brief foray into Philadelphia politics, winning election to the post of school director in 1901. He prospered, married Kathryn, built a substantial house off Pine Street in West Philadelphia, and provided a comfortable existence for James and his siblings. But with the onset of the Depression, the Quirks experienced a lasting financial setback. An ambitious housing development in the Mayfair section bellied up, impoverishing John and his partner.

When James was in eighth grade, he was confined to bed for much of the next year with the only serious illness of his life. His mother, a teacher by training, tried to keep James abreast of his studies by tutoring him. Denied visitors throughout his convalescence, James was forced to communicate with school chums through an intricate basket-on-a-pulley system, which he rigged in a bedside window, the better to ferry candy and other contraband into his sickroom. At the conclusion of the school year, the authorities opted not to repeat him, and sent him on to high school with only seven years of elementary education.

At LaSalle High School, James excelled academically and athletically. An imposing six foot three, he was a good basketball player and an excellent cross-country runner. He could hit a baseball, although his fielding (as evidenced by the broken and badly reset index finger on his throwing hand) was another matter. Keeping intact his record of nongraduation, James skipped his final year at LaSalle and entered nearby Saint Charles Sem-

inary, where he began studies for the priesthood. After two years there, he reconsidered his career choice and entered Villanova University. With the Depression deepening and finances an issue, James sought (unsuccessfully) to accelerate his studies; he left school short of graduation, again without a diploma.

After bouncing about, he landed in broadcasting, on the bottom rung of the ladder at a twenty-five-watt station in the Frankford section of Northeast Philadelphia. There he produced, directed, and occasionally starred in dramatic presentations with casts drawn from out-of-work actors and actresses, of which there were many during the Depression years. Throughout the 1930s, James made a steady ascent in local radio and eventually landed an announcer's job. When he interviewed for the position, he was told that his name was a problem: Listeners would hear it as James Squirk, and Squirk simply wouldn't do. So he became James Allan.

In 1932, while riding the trolley home from work, James met a tall young woman with a striking mane of thick red hair. They struck up a conversation, then saw each other frequently throughout the spring. Her name was Elizabeth Wolstencroft.

Elizabeth Wolstencroft was born in the Frankford section of Northeast Philadelphia in 1909, the older of two children of William Percey Wolstencroft and Bessie Duffy. The Philadelphia Wolstencrofts, family lore had it, were somehow distantly related to the eighteenth-century English writer and feminist Mary Wollstonecraft (and thus to Mary Wollstonecraft Shelley, who wrote Frankenstein *at age nineteen).*

Elizabeth's grandfather, Bill Wolstencroft, was the president of the Wolstencroft Felt Manufacturing Company and a nationally acclaimed marksman ("the fastest man with a shotgun in America," according to his obituary). He appeared in shooting competitions throughout the country, won numerous prizes, and was a personal friend of sharpshooters Buffalo Bill Cody and Annie Oakley. (Annie, family lore had it, wasn't the crack shot she was cracked up to be; in an exhibition, Bill Wolsten-

croft allegedly tanked his performance to allow the off-center
Annie to win.)

Elizabeth's father, William P., followed his father, Bill, into the
family business. When Elizabeth was fourteen, the Wolstencrofts
experienced a lasting setback: Fire destroyed the Wolstencroft
factory, and it was never rebuilt. Her father, in reduced circumstances, took work at the nearby Frankford Arsenal, where he
worked until he retired.

Elizabeth's childhood (and lifelong) loves were books and animals. In the earliest existing family photograph (taken in the
spring of 1918), Elizabeth, age nine, dwarfed by a gigantic hair
bow restraining her cascading auburn tresses, is seated on the
front stoop with her mother, brother, and a stray pup.

Elizabeth graduated in 1926 from Frankford High School,
where she was a top student, starred in the spring play, and delivered the class prophecy on Class Day. She gave the prophecy
from memory, mentioning each classmate (in a class numbering
nearly a hundred) without benefit of notes. But there was a problem. She inadvertently omitted one student from her presentation. The student's family noted the omission; being relative new-
comers to America, they interpreted it as an intentional nativist
slight. When word got back to Elizabeth, she was crushed. On
her own initiative, she went to her classmate's house, apologized,
and presented the entire speech again from memory, rectifying
the omission. The classmate and his family seemed appeased,
although she found it difficult to tell from their silence. Years later
when Elizabeth got ready to attend her twenty-fifth high school
reunion, she wondered if the classmate would be there and fretted that he might still harbor ill feelings toward her for the long-
ago oversight. No one was harder on Elizabeth than she was on
herself.

In the graduation yearbook under the entry "Destination,"
most students duly listed the next academic rung (Penn, Drexel,
Normal School). A more expansive Elizabeth wrote: "Planting
noble thoughts in receptive(?) minds." In her graduation picture,
the set of the jaw, the piercing green eyes, and the Niagara of

red hair conveyed a seriousness of purpose beyond her seven-
teen years.

Following graduation, Elizabeth pursued her education at
Temple University. Money, tight from the outset, dried up dur-
ing the Depression. Forced to leave school, she got a job and
eventually moved into social work. She was a few months shy of
her twenty-third birthday when she met the tall ex-seminarian
on the Philadelphia trolley.

They were married in July 1934 (over the ill-disguised, silent
objections of the local parish priest, who bore no animosity to-
ward the bride other than her religion, which was Episcopalian).
James and Elizabeth moved to an apartment on Walnut Street.
Their major pastime was books; both of them read voraciously.
Their summer vacation each year was an extended motor trip.
Destinations varied: They toured the Civil War South one year;
in others, they headed north to New England and Canada (with
the side trip to the Dionne quints). In the final years before World
War II, they drove a snappy 1940 Packard, which averaged fif-
teen miles a gallon (ten gallons of gasoline cost $1.67 then).

James continued his rise in local radio (first at WIP, later at
WFIL) as program director and also established himself as a pop-
ular sports announcer. He was the voice of Penn football on Sat-
urdays and provided blow-by-blow descriptions of professional
boxing matches. He also covered the 1936 Democratic Con-
vention at Franklin Field, which figured prominently in local
broadcasting annals because of the near-death experience of one
of the station's engineers. Shortly before Franklin Roosevelt
gave his acceptance speech to a crowd of more than 100,000,
James heard a clicking sound in his microphone. Suspecting a
faulty connection somewhere down on the field, he dispatched
one of the station's engineers to locate the problem. While Roo-
sevelt was chastising "economic royalists" in his speech, the en-
gineer crawled under the speaker's platform. Groping about in
the dark, he bumped into a Secret Service agent, who forthwith
smushed him facedown in the turf and told him not to move a
muscle. All of this was unknown to the irate announcing crew,

which couldn't understand why the clicking persisted. After the president departed, the engineer reemerged from under the platform with what everyone agreed was an untoppable "the dog ate my homework" explanation.

As 1941 came to a close, James and Elizabeth, like millions of other post-Depression Americans, were living comfortable, modest, unspectacular lives. The Depression was behind them (though the memories lingered indelibly). On December 6, their horizons began and ended at the Philadelphia city line. December 7 changed that for them and for a generation.

In the spring following Pearl Harbor, James took the army physical exam and was found to be in good health except for a slight astigmatism. In reality, his vision was terrible. Family scuttlebutt (never confirmed by James but never expressly denied by him, either) had it that he memorized the cardboard eye chart, then correctly identified enough letters from memory to squeak through. He was commissioned as a first lieutenant in May and was stationed in Washington, D.C.

Wartime Washington (in the words of historian Doris Kearns Goodwin) "was pretty much like any other boomtown during the war—its population had doubled since 1940, decent housing was impossible to find, uniforms were everywhere, gasoline was scarce, buses were overcrowded, and living costs were high." James and Elizabeth considered themselves fortunate to find an apartment on New Hampshire Avenue out near the Maryland border.

During the next nine months, James found himself doing familiar tasks and thoroughly unfamiliar ones. He helped coordinate The Army Hour on the NBC-Red radio network. With remote pickups from London, Moscow, North Africa, the Pacific, and other points around the globe, the Sunday evening program brought the war home to listeners through first-person accounts by soldiers stationed overseas—an account of a Tokyo bombing raid, for example, or Gen. Claire Chennault describing the missions of the Flying Tigers in China. In addition to this relatively familiar territory, James was thrown into new areas, such as war bonds. With taxes paying only a portion of the cost of the war, the U.S. Treasury was hopeful that bonds could finance the lion's share. James spent time in towns around the country, including Denver and Wheeling, West Virginia, promoting bond drives. Bond sales raised a handsome $10 billion in the first nine months of 1942 while serving as a conduit for home-front support of the war effort. (The cost of the war was so staggering, however—$160 billion during the same nine-month period, $304 billion overall—that bonds eventually financed less than 10 percent of the total war cost.)

James's Washington duty ended in May 1943, when he, now a captain and junior staff officer, was posted to North Africa (as the Axis forces trapped in Tunisia were surrendering to the Allies). The following month, Elizabeth, five months pregnant, returned to Philadelphia and moved in with her parents. James remained in the Mediterranean through the summer as the Allies launched a seaborne assault on Sicily, which was liberated in mid-August. He returned to the United States and Leavenworth in early September, prior to the Allied landings in southern Italy. When his C&GS class of 111 officers (106 men, 5 women) finished in mid-November, he returned to Philadelphia for a short visit with Elizabeth and their infant son.

Four days before Christmas, James was off again, headed to England and back to the war.

Chapter Two: A Family at War
1944–45

January–June 1944: England

In his New Year's message, Adolf Hitler attacks the "Jewish-Bolshevist" alliance fighting against Germany and vows that Germany will continue to fight because war is infinitely preferable to the fate the German people would suffer in the event of defeat.

Darling,

Things are looking up and I am getting to be a busy little man. One of my jobs at the moment entails a lot of research and I have been running around into a lot of odd places and agencies asking searching questions and getting very unsatisfactory answers. I have even ventured so far as to brave the Cloak and Dagger boys in their den and have now worked up so much prestige that one of them is actually coming to see me. The job is interesting and not too wearing but it keeps me busy enough. This afternoon I was handed a two-day job that had to be finished in two hours and I was dashing about like an announcer on his first special event. I beat the deadline easily but I haven't told them that someone had already completed the thing and that I had only to pick it up and copy it. The colonel was surprised when I came back with the answer but I just looked smug.

Every day I meet someone new that I have met somewhere or other in the world. I really feel that I have been here a long time but my military roots aren't actually holding on to anything. I do miss Rory and you so very much and I hope I shall just get so terribly busy that I shan't have too much time to think about it. I think that I shall feel a little better when I begin to hear from you and know that you are faring well. John is trying to get me a flat in his building and that will help a little, too. So will having my baggage which is still un-delivered. All of those things add up to a black total but I shall have to get over it. I have so many plans for our life after the war and they all look good to me. You make a lot too.

England is a little shabbier and a little tireder but all the British have a tough core that no fatigue can ever reach. I was talking yesterday to an officer who was stationed down in the country just after Dunkirk when the Germans were expected to invade any minute. There were queues at the shooting galleries, and the widows of retired British officers turned out with forty-year-old pistols to practice marksmanship. The country women sharpened up kitchen knives to fight the Germans with. In the towns women kept great tubs of hot water on the coal grates in the second floor rooms so that they could dump them on the heads of the invaders. One middle-aged woman, so badly crippled that she could walk only on crutches, had her gardener tear up her beautiful garden and bring the boulders up to her bedroom. She had a pile made at each window so that she could throw them on the heads of the Germans as they came by. Some of the boats that went to Dunkirk were little outboard motorboats that came pouring down the canals and streams to make the run across the Channel. Old men and children strung pitiful little bits of barbed wire across the road and poured concrete roadblocks. I'm inclined to think that the Germans are lucky that they didn't invade.

Waiting for your letters. Best love. (4 January 1944, London)

In mid-January, Dwight Eisenhower arrives in England to assume duties as Supreme Commander, Allied Expeditionary Force (SHAEF). His mission: "You will enter the continent of Europe and undertake operations aimed at the heart of Germany and the de-

struction of her armed forces." His principal U.S. ground com-
mander, Omar Bradley, has set up First Army headquarters at
Clifton College in Bristol in Southwest England, where American
invasion forces will muster.

Darling,

In the course of one of my travels I passed through a little country town called Clun which is near the Welsh border and sixteen miles from the nearest transportation. The people are so isolated that they know very little about the war and had probably never seen an American soldier before in their lives. They are farmers and speak with an extremely difficult accent. Just as I came out of the inn after lunch, I saw two men walking down the road that made me think I was ready for a Section Eight. They were dressed in cotton stockings, knee britches, doublets, long capes and turned-up hats. I asked about them and learned that they were two of the "Twelve Old Men of Clun." It seems that a native of Clun went up to London in Elizabethan times and made his fortune. When he died he left money for a home for twelve old men of good character and included that they should be allowed so many pairs of hose, so many doublets, so many capes and so on. They still draw those outfits and wear them without comment. We went out of our way to see where they live. It is a large building shaped like an E and has twelve doors leading to twelve separate little houses where each man can have privacy on his own. There is a staff to take care of them and they have a lovely time. The regulation says that they must be over fifty which was really old age in Stuart times.

Someday we must come back to England. (10 February 1944, London)

Darling,

I had just about started toward my bus when the sirens went. It was a clear black night with no moon but the stars were brilliant. Since bus travel was uncertain I decided to duck down into the tube and make my ten-minute trip home that way. It was my first experience with the underground during a blitz.

The trains were not crowded but the stations were jammed with people. Along the walls running the whole length of the platform were double-decker bunks with metal straps as springs. About half of these are filled with people who have come to spend the entire night there, mostly women and children. They make little attempts to try to fix up the bunks in some attractive manner. Many of them drape curtains of chintz or colorful cotton across the front as a kind of curtain. A great many have lovely quilts, nicely covered pillows, and green blankets although they are the poor of the city. In spite of the crowding and the noise of the people and the trains, many of the full-time shelterers seemed to be sound asleep as a result of long habit. The rest of the bunks have whole families sitting along them. Momma and Poppa bring along a book or a newspaper or a small suitcase with things for the baby and sandwiches for the family. In general they stay down only for the duration of the raid. There is not too much noise and no confusion at all. The bobbies in steel helmets stand about the entrances but I am certain that they never have anything to do. Children play and eat and some cry but there is no overtone of suffering or crisis. Costumes are apt to be a bit bizarre but the people seem friendly and quite unafraid. It is the safest place in London and they have very good sense to go there. The papers keep pointing out that there are only rare instances that anyone who has taken proper shelter ever gets injured. The consistency of the raids is probably beginning to have a little effect on the people. There are no signs of nerves cracking or any of that sort of thing but it is more a topic of conversation everywhere. As each day goes by, someone comes in with a story of a friend who was hurt or a house that is gone. (24 February 1944, London)

Darling,

This is a clean, cold, bright, sunshiny day that reminds me more of winter at home than winter in England. It has been cold here the past month and there has not been too much fog or too much rain either—or am I just in an optimistic mood?

Today has been a busy one with a lot of talk and not too much work. The colonel is a tough guy and I go to meetings so that I can nod my head in the right places after he tells everybody what to do. I took part of the morning writing a report on a meeting I attended yesterday and got that through to the boss. We have more meetings than CBS or a good advertising agency. We'll have to murder the Germans with minutes. It probably all adds up to something important after all but it is sometimes difficult to recognize the importance of some of the things.

This place is so utterly different from America yet the differences aren't readily apparent. If you ask directions here, you are always told to go to the top of the street or the bottom of the street. I have asked several people how one distinguishes between the top and the bottom of the street and have never gotten an explanation that makes any sense. There probably is some intuitive distinction because I find myself referring to the top of the street myself. I still don't know how you tell the difference.

Joe Smith says that the great market here after the war will be for a mop factory. The omnipresent person in England is the char down on her hands and knees scrubbing the floor. It is probably the largest British industry. I am told that the chars know about mops but they just don't put any faith in them. On second thought I am inclined to believe that there are more people who watch fires than who scrub floors. We could do wonders over here with synthetic kindling.

That's a brief dissertation on that Empire you have heard so much about. (4 March 1944, London)

Darling,

We stopped off at a part of Westminster School for tea in the Dean's Yard of the Abbey where we sat on a lovely stone terrace soaking in the sun, drinking our tea and reading names that almost three centuries of small boys have carved in the doors and walls of the school.

We went then into the Cloister and so into the Abbey itself. We could easily have spent hours there and I shall some day when I get back again but we really stayed only a short time. It is wonderfully aged and the tombstones seem to be a roster of all the greats of the ages. The Abbey was not too crowded, and it was very relaxing for a moment to look down the long leaps of the Gothic arches. This I copied from a little chapel and I must have been in the mood because it moved me very much: "TO THE GLORY OF GOD AND TO THE MEMORY OF ONE MILLION MEN OF THE BRITISH EMPIRE WHO FELL IN THE GREAT WAR, 1914 TO 1918. THEY DIED IN EVERY QUARTER OF THE EARTH AND ON ALL ITS SEAS AND THEIR GRAVES ARE MADE SURE TO THEM BY THEIR KIN. THE MAIN HOST LIE BURIED IN THE LAND OF OUR ALLIES OF THE WAR WHO HAVE SET ASIDE THEIR RESTING PLACES IN HONOUR FOREVER." (30 March 1944, London)

In April, to mask invasion preparations, SHAEF imposes a no-visitors ban throughout a ten-mile coastal strip and suspends diplomatic correspondence out of England by non-Allies. Later in the month, the Americans conduct dress rehearsal beach assaults at Slapton Sands, on the coast of Devon.

In early May, Eisenhower sets D day for June 5. He has 3 million troops under his command (1.7 million U.S. troops, 1 million British Canadians, 300,000 Free French and others). At mid-month, the senior staff conducts its final review of the cross-Channel invasion (Overlord). In late May, the invasion forces are sealed in their marshaling areas, the crews of the invasion fleets are sealed in their vessels, and mail is impounded. On May 30, the loading of the D-day invasion force will begin.

Darling,

We started out on the road about ten o'clock when the day had already become a glorious one and struck off toward the South Coast of England. The country is so lovely at this time of year with the chestnut candles still in bloom and the pink and white of the May trees everywhere. The stone walls of England are overgrown with all kinds of ivies and creepers and the pattern of the fields from the hills seems to offer a blend of every shade of green. The farms and the houses in the small towns are neat and trim and the whole tempo of life seems to have a kind of subdued gaiety. The colonel was hungry, as he always is, so we stopped in the first shop that we came to and got ourselves some buns to go with one of your packages of cheese. We laughed at ourselves at the complete lack of dignity of a very senior and moderately junior officer bowling along in an open car munching on huge buns spread with cheese.

The first part of the route we followed lay through the south of England, climbing over and alongside the rolling hills. By lunch time we had gotten to Southampton and ran along Southampton Water down to the bay that separates England from the Isle of Wight. This is the Whitsun holiday and all of the small boat owners were working on their boats and the youngsters were swimming. The countryside was so lovely that war seemed incredible. We both tried to relax but the camps are everywhere, and the roads full of heavy transport, tanks, and huge guns were a constant reminder that the peaceful scene was only an illusion and that we still have our job to do.

We passed through Southampton, the great port of the transatlantic liners before the war, now scarred with the terrible effects of the great blitz of 1940 and '41. It's a busy, crowded town of a definite naval flavor and has the general air of a port and the sea. The air has the smell of salt water and outside it are great flats that remind me for all the world of the causeway into Atlantic City. Because it is so close to Europe it is one of the ports that Jerry worked on most during the blitz and it will take years to repair the scars that he made. But like any blitzed city, life goes on with an air of complete normality.

We also passed through Portsmouth which was a great port of the Royal Navy before the war and still has much of the illusion of a naval town. On a hill behind the town stand great forts that were built a hundred or more years ago and have long since passed their usefulness. The western bastion was built by the great Duke of Marlborough and was known through the decades as Marlborough's Folly because all of the guns pointed inland. A British officer told me that no one uses that name for it since the fall of Singapore, where none of the guns pointed inland.

We started out to the North and then swung off across Salisbury plain toward Stonehenge. I had always envisioned Stonehenge as standing stark out of some bleak moor like those in *Hound of the Baskervilles* or *Rebecca*. Instead it stands in a fertile plain with the fans green all around it. You come upon it rather abruptly standing all alone with a low fence around it and one of the typical swinging self-closing gates. We wandered about it for about half an hour rather quietly, everyone thinking his own thoughts about it. My principal thought was a phrase of Winston Churchill's that kept running through my mind, "What kind of people do they think we are?" They are the same dogged, stubborn people who dragged these mighty stones across miles of country, floated them down the slow-moving shallow streams, hacked away at them with the horns of a deer, and then by sheer strength managed to lift them into place. We don't know why they did it and I think that they probably were not sure what made them do it, either. The British haven't changed too much from those people but they still go about many of their missions with a determination to get it done but no real reason ever expressed for it.

We drove back through the long evening with the sun getting lower over the hills. It cools rapidly as the sun sinks and it was a little chilly toward dark. We finally arrived home at

about eleven thirty and the last traces of twilight still showed
in the sky. I found that the Jameses were still awake and we
had some tea and talked until after one before I went to bed.
(28 May 1944, Bristol)

With Bradley

Omar N. Bradley was born in 1893. He graduated from West Point
(Class of 1915) near the top quarter of his class and was assigned to
the infantry (as was classmate Dwight Eisenhower). Much to his regret,
Bradley missed the fighting in France during World War I.

As an instructor at the Infantry School at Fort Benning in the early
1930s, Bradley favorably impressed the commandant, George C. Marshall. When Marshall was named Army Chief of Staff in 1939, he tapped
Bradley for duty at the War Department, and in 1941 Marshall named
Bradley commandant of the Infantry School at Fort Benning (where he
worked with Col. George S. Patton).

With the outbreak of World War II, Bradley was named commander
of the newly reactivated 82d Division (where his assistant division commander was Matthew Ridgway, who succeeded him). Posted overseas
in 1943, Bradley served in North Africa and Sicily under Patton.

In the fall of 1943, he was named to the most important combat job
in the U.S. Army—command of U.S. First Army, the American component of the D-day invasion force. On June 9 (D+3), Bradley moved his
First Army headquarters ashore on Normandy. Among the troops who
would land within the next two days was a recently promoted major in
the Publicity & Psychological Warfare (P&PW) section. The major
would become Bradley's public relations officer (PRO) responsible for
handling the correspondents traveling with the army.

On August 1 (D+56), Bradley would step up to command 12th Army
Group (which comprised First Army and George S. Patton's newly activated Third Army) and would take the major with him as his PRO. Major James Quirk would remain with Bradley until the Battle of the Bulge.

June 1944: Normandy

On June 6 (D day), the Allies launch Overlord, the cross-Channel invasion of Hitler's Europe. Night bombing opens the as-

sault. Airborne troops are dropped inland at midnight. The first troops are put ashore at 0630.

Dear James—

D-Day is almost over and I hope you are safe. I heard the first SHAEF flash at 3:30 this morning. I thought of all those swell young GIs in those 4,000 ships and those 11,000 planes and all the LCs and the chutists and the Navy gun crews and the hell that had come to them and the Norman peninsula.

I heard the first German communique at 12:37 a.m. on the Dawn Patrol and I stayed up just to hear it called "stuff" and it was three hours later that I learned it was the real Mc-Coy. The enormity of it was dreadfully hard to take. I was so keyed up that I never went to bed at all and just stuck with WIP and Mutual til dawn, then showered and dressed, and went to church to offer my little aimless prayer for all the guys—most especially my own.

I went to the office, driving past home after home with radios pounding and every car radio was blaring too, and people everywhere were serious and quiet. An aura of sadness, of full realization of the dread meaning of the day misted everything. I am one of seven women in my office with someone in England—two other wives and four mothers—and I was the only one in today. This was not at all true at defense plants. Absenteeism was at a new low and production was up everywhere. I dreaded American shoddiness on D-Day but there was none. People were quiet and restrained, children in the street were quiet. There was no display of the sort you would have expected—only in isolated spots were whistles blown at 3:30 a.m. when confirmation came.

Today was a day of prayer, a day of quiet supplication, a day of recognition of the pain that must be. Churches over the country were open and crowded. Today America found God. It would have been most reassuring to you who has always hated the Hollywood in your countrymen. (6 June 1944, Philadelphia)

D-day elements of U.S. First Army land on Omaha and Utah Beaches; on Omaha, V Corps meets stiff resistance ("a bloody chaos," in Bradley's words), forcing him to consider evacuating Omaha Beach. On Bradley's left, Gen. Bernard Montgomery's British Canadian force advances inland. Germans fail to commit their reserves in anticipation of an illusory "main" attack by Patton farther north at the Pas de Calais. By sunset, 175,000 Allied troops are on the beaches. By D+4 (June 10), 325,000 Allied troops are ashore.

Darling,

Sitting in the wardroom of a British LST [landing ship, tank] headed for the war. I have just been out on deck watching the other ships of the convoy sliding along a fairly smooth sea under a low, gray sky. We can hear airplanes above us but in the air we can see only the barrage balloons of which each ship has two for protection against strafing. In the wardroom here most of the officers are asleep in chairs, and on the deck are really only a few men dozing in their vehicles or scanning the horizon. This is quite different from a transport—no card games, no music and most of the men spending more time on their weapons than on horseplay. Even the two dogs aboard are lying quietly. It is a calm and peaceful Sunday morning but the war is only a few hours away and the calm and the peace will be shattered.

The last two days (or is it three?) have been a nightmare. We spent one evening getting ready and then pushed off in a long motor convoy at 0300. It was raining steadily and since we were moving tactically we had to keep the tops down on our vehicles and let the rain pour down. The most cheering thing was to see the people in every town and village turning out to watch us pass. Some of the older people were in tears but most of them just waved to us and called "Good luck lads." Many of them came out with cups of tea but we didn't stop long enough for everyone to get a cup. The roads were jammed with military transport and the atmosphere of war was inescapable.

We finally arrived at the embarkation camp at 2100 hours and the British had a hot meal ready for us in long mess tents. Daylight lasts almost until midnight fortunately, and the activity was intense. There was a series of briefings and then I had to round up the men and vehicles and get them organized for loading. It was daylight at 0430 and we realized it was going to be a sunny day. We finally arrived at the harbor dock and in front of the open gaping jaws of the LST.

Our ship was to carry a varied cargo of heavy trucks, jeeps, ambulances, half-tracks, armored cars and heavy bulldozers. My jeep fortunately won a spot on the upper deck where we have air and light. My jeep driver is a Mexican from San Antonio, Rudolfo Garcia, who speaks broken English although his father fought in France in the last war. We checked over our weapons and then mess was ready at 1830. Our principal diversion from our work was watching LSTs unload several hundred Jerry prisoners. They look young and tough.

I took off my shoes, leggings and trousers, rolled my combat jacket for a pillow, wrapped a blanket around myself, and slept for 12 solid hours without batting an eye. When I got up this morning I ate two of your chocolate bars for breakfast and am now waiting for dinner which I need badly.

Much later

Going ashore on a long low coastline with a ridge of low hills. No trouble except that a craft about 200 yards from us went up with a mighty roar and we all became a bit white-faced as we ducked the wreckage. A big ship is firing monotonously off to our right.

I can only say that I love you very much and shall be home to you safely. I hope that Rory will be proud of his father and you of your man.

All my love and good night, darling. Think of me.

(11 June 1944, English Channel, at sea)

On June 12, U.S. troops from Omaha and Utah overrun Carentan and link up. On June 15, Bradley holds his first press conference and announces that First Army has suffered 15,000 casualties in the first ten days, far below anticipated losses. On June 17–18, U.S. forces (VII Corps) drive twenty-five miles west to the Atlantic coast, seal off the neck of the Cotentin Peninsula, then wheel north to attack the German-defended port of Cherbourg. On June 19–22, "The Great Storm," with thirty-five-mile-per-hour winds, rips through the Channel, closing down Omaha Beach, slowing the buildup, and causing shortages and ammunition rationing.

Darling,

Yesterday I went up to the fall of Cherbourg but it didn't fall. The road to the front is over Route 13 (shades of Philadelphia to Washington) and it is a trail along one ruined city after another. Isigny, which was smashed up rather badly in the early days, has a normal life now. Much of the debris has been piled and the people have returned to the unruined homes. The blackened shells of the other places will have to wait for some other day in order to be homes again. On to Carentan, where the airborne troops fought so bitterly and died so bravely. Carentan still gets shelled every day but much of the town is standing and the people stay. Everywhere though is ruination and destruction. It gives you a little bit of a start to see the rough little sign with an arrow on it pointing to "American Cemetery." Beyond Carentan across the River Douve the swamps and fields are full of the broken and wrecked gliders in which our men landed and surprised the Jerries so thoroughly.

Then into Montebourg which our men were in and out of a half-dozen times. The town is well-scarred from the bitter battles that were fought there and life seems to have disappeared. A thin trickle of refugees are coming back into town but there is little there for them. The church steeple is pockmarked with shell holes but the clock still runs and marks the proper hours. Here I saw the first of the French who hope to fight the Germans but their sole uniform is a rifle in one hand with the Cross of Lorraine around their arms. Because they are not in uniform they look like cutthroats or

brigands and they have a rather sheepish look as they give us
a smiling and most unmilitary salute. The gendarmes seem
to have them in tow and they probably perform some useful
service in preventing the other people from looting.

As you go north along the road there are ruined farmhouses at every little crossroads and more shell-marked
church steeples. The sides of the road are littered with
burned and broken guns and vehicles, and there are slit
trenches and pillboxes everywhere. Quite suddenly you come
upon a farm or a little village that bears not a single scar because war seems to strike with the blind, unreasoning force
of lightning. People stand outside and smile you along your
way either with the V sign or just a wave of the arm. The children are the friendliest but the adults seem to welcome you
also. You pass lines of refugees now plodding their way back
to the towns that lie behind. A soldier in a truck or a jeep will
stop and pick up a tiny family and their belongings and try
to dump them out on the sidewalk in a place where their
houses used to be. There are a few horses or carts but most
of their pitifully few belongings are in a small hand cart or
baby carriage. Theirs is not a lack that comes from poverty
because these farmers are the wealthiest in all of France and
their peacetime homes are generous and well-filled. It's just
that the tide of war made them select the few small things
that they considered the most precious and now they are
trundling them back to the place where they rested before.
It's a sight that we haven't seen in America for eighty years
and I hope that we never see again. You come into the shambles that is Valognes and the war is right in front of you.

We cut off the main road to the division CP [command
post] and made our way down a narrow lane until we came
to a bridge that Jerry had blown out. The engineers had simply taken a dozer and piled earth over the narrow stream up
to the level of the road so that we could go through. The
signs read "Road Cleared" but you know that the engineers
haven't had a chance to do the shoulders yet and you drive
dead center on the road. The artillery is all around you ham-

mering away steadily and you hear the rolling crump of Jerry's stuff hitting.

The infantry moves up in small units in a single file on each side of the road and the ambulances come down the center in a fairly heavy stream. Two MPs [military police] pass you herding some Jerry prisoners and they look dirty and dishevelled but rather cheerful. Traffic is a very thin trickle and the country seems desolate and empty. Smoke rises around from shell bursts. We ducked once into a pillbox to find that the dead Germans were still there to keep us company. The only occupants of the road are the scattered MPs and the division engineers working away.

Their two principal jobs are to clear the mines and to fill in the shell holes. We caught up with the mine sweepers and stopped to ask about going on ahead. We started down the road until another engineer waved us down. He had a special plea to make in behalf of his engineers—"Sir, would you please have your driver hold it down to about five miles an hour. If you go faster than that, you kick up a lot of dust. Jerry zeroes in on the dust cloud and whams some 88s right on us. He's been doing it all day. It's all right for people passing through but goddam it, sir, we gotta stay here." It made good sense and we complied while the engineers worked away.

We finally found the regimental forward CP which was staffed only by a captain, a lieutenant and a couple of enlisted men. It was located in a little dell surrounded by semicircular cliffs about twelve feet high. People came in to see him and he carried on a series of profane conversations on the phone directing a lot of people forward of us and around us. The artillery was in the three fields around us and the place was bedlam. He showed us the map and told us it was probably all wrong but that people were in approximately these locations. A young doctor had a long wrangle with him about trails that could be used to reach some wounded and they dispatched the aid men in an ambulance and a jeep to see if they could haul some wounded out of the woods. The drivers couldn't read a map but he explained the location to them and they assured him that they would find it. They looked young and eager and unafraid as they set off.

A minute or two later a jeep arrived with three wounded Germans aboard. The drivers were breathless with their experience but not a little proud of themselves. They had been driving down a trail and were captured by a German patrol who made them load some German wounded on the vehicle and start for Cherbourg. They ran into an American patrol who captured the Germans that they didn't kill and set the ambulance back on the route to our line. About that point the 88s opened up on us and the conference broke up abruptly. We flattened ourselves against the wall of the cliff and I noticed that the more experienced hands seemed to be trying to burrow their way in it. There was no word spoken and no expression on anyone's face as the shells smacked all around us and the rocks and pieces of earth flew. I scanned their faces carefully and hoped that my own face was as calm and expressionless as theirs. There came a lull in the fire and someone finally said, "they're all ours now." There was a moment's hesitation and then everyone slowly unpeeled himself.

It's dark now and the tents are shadowy in the new moon. The guns are thundering heavily tonight and there must be a big action down below. They have been going all day and their rolling is earth-shaking and ominous. We can see the flashes across the horizon and listen plainly to the irregular, deep-throated rumble. It makes you think of the men that are up there dug in and sweating it out. It will be wonderful to get home to peace and security again. (24 June 1944, Normandy)

June 26–27—Cherbourg falls, opening a major resupply lifeline to the Allies.

Darling,

It's a little chilly with the sun down, and the desultory settling shots of the AA guns sound lonesome like a far-off train whistle. Our orchard's green looked a little dark against the lowering late sky and I am seeing portents that aren't there.

Yesterday I went up to give some quite unnecessary help to the troops that were taking Cherbourg. I arrived along the main highway at the final sign which actually read "Cherbourg" and knew that we were in the town. The road climbs over a hill mass and then snakes in sweeping curves down the hill into the flat of the seacoast on which the port is situated. The road is flanked on either side by two great rocky cliffs about 250 feet high, the one on the left covered with trees and hedges and the one on the right a sheer rocky mass. The infantry had already cleared up the left-hand hill, and the constant explosions and sudden flares of flame and plumes of smoke came from a burning Jerry ammunition dump on the top of the hill. The mass on the right is the famous Fort du Roule and that was an entirely different story.

As we rolled down the hill we ran into a company of engineers who had arrived to begin cleaning up the outskirts but the town wasn't ready for that yet. The sea was visible about a thousand yards ahead but it was impossible to get to it. The dozers started working on the rubble where we were standing but seventy-five yards ahead men were being killed. Just ahead of us was the first cross street of the town and the Jerries on the hill to the left had two concealed machine guns zeroed in on the crossroad. We stood and watched while three patrols tried to get across but each one took casualties and had to pull back. The whole operation was stopped but infantry patrols took off around the hill to try to locate the guns from the rear and silence them with grenades. We watched the patrols start and saw them slide into the hedge. We waited quite awhile and then heard the crack of rifles, the stutter of the machine guns and the blast of the grenades. The infantry patrol came back triumphant.

The fort on our right was part of the coastal defense of Cherbourg and the fighting there was the first bit of vertical warfare that I have heard of by ground troops. The place is honeycombed with tunnels and passages, and our men fought their way in from the top of it and began to fight the

Jerries out of it, chasing them down from level to level. Meanwhile another group had gotten into the bottom level. There was one great room filled with literally thousands of cases of Three Star Hennessy cognac. The men lugged the cases of cognac out, standing beside dead Germans to whom they paid no attention at all. The war took on a momentary atmosphere of a grisly picnic but that was short-lived because the fighting was still going on inside.

It was really a miniature of the big war brought down to scale. The street and the side alleys were filled with German vehicles, military equipment and personal belongings. The men, completely oblivious to booby traps, pawed over everything with a kind of childlike curiosity and unfailing amazement at the high quality of the German equipment. Some men were setting up the range-finding equipment trying to figure out how it worked. Others had German machine pistols and Mausers and Lugers; some were wearing German goggles; and some were fumbling through packs and vehicles to see what they could find. These were men who had fought and stormed their way all the length of the peninsula and they had been through this same routine before. The pitiful thing is that each time they go forward they have to leave behind their souvenirs. As a result each time they take another objective they have to go for the souvenir hunting again.

The only thing that they avoided like sin was a dead German by the side of the road. He had fallen backward with a grenade clutched in his hand. No one could be certain when that grip would relax and they all gave him a wide berth. I got back to Corps HQ to see there the general and the admiral of Festung Cherbourg who had surrendered after giving an order to the troops to die to the last man. Sort of a vignette of war. (27 June 1944, Normandy)

Darling,

Cherbourg has safely fallen. These are the days when the papers simply report that there was patrol activity and limited artillery activity along the front, and that phrase covers a multitude of small but bitterly fought actions among small units of troops—and each one produces its toll for the burial squads and the hospitals. They are unspectacular even for the men who fight them but they are highly personal, close combat contests that quickly make men out of boys. It's rather a pity to see kids who ought to be making plans for their return to their sophomore year in college in the fall now living in slit trenches, eating iron rations, ignoring the wind and the rain, finding it impossible to keep clean, and thinking only of trying to kill Germans and not get killed themselves.

It's a brutalizing business and I think that all of us become startled at our reactions to stories that would have been either horrible or unthinkable a short time ago. These troops of ours have convinced me that the tough spirit of the pioneers isn't lost in America. They are very brave, amazingly aggressive and wonderfully trained. The most satisfactory thing is the fine record that has been made by units in their first experience with combat. They have met Jerry in ground that has been well and carefully prepared and have beaten him every time. I think that Jerry's had it and the next several months will prove it.

My thoughts turn to you constantly and I get more homesick every day. In England I was only one step removed from home but now I feel that I am one step removed from England; and home and the idea of getting there seems remote. I carry your picture folder in my shirt pocket. You look so lovely and Rory looks so happy and so cocky that I sometimes just get sick for the sight of both of you. I think that I now know more and more how much I love you and how much I want to get back to you. We are just short of our tenth anniversary and it would be wonderful to be together for it.

Take care of our son for me and take care of yourself until I get home again. These have been the six longest months of my life and every day gets longer. Keep loving me, darling, and don't worry about me. (29 June 1944, Normandy)

On June 29, Rommel and Rundstedt, senior German generals in the West, confer with Hitler at Berchtesgaden and urge withdrawal from Normandy. Hitler orders Normandy held.

July 1944: In the Hedgerows

Since D day, the Allies have landed 920,000 troops, 600,000 tons of equipment, and 177,000 vehicles. On July 3, the Battle of the Hedgerows begins: First Army kicks off south in bad weather through marshlands toward the St.-Lô–Coutances road, which is to serve as a springboard for the breakout east across the shoulder of the Normandy Peninsula. The following day at noon, First Army fires all of its artillery pieces on German targets to celebrate the Fourth of July.

Darling,

You remember my pictures of Marrakech in French Morocco and how completely fascinated I was with the place. Most of them were taken by me with a camera that I borrowed from a little fellow named Pete Parris who was a corporal with YANK. I learned just a few days before D-Day that Pete was with one of the divisions. When I came ashore I learned almost immediately that Pete had been killed on the beach while coming ashore and that he lay sprawled at the high tide mark with his camera equipment around him. As soon as we had a break, I took Sam Brightman and we found the grave where he had been rather hastily buried during the early days when there was no time for much ceremony. We found the rude grave marked with his name and the date of his death and we arranged to have the body moved along with a few others to the quite lovely American cemetery beside the shattered steeple of the church in Carentan where he lies with the airborne troopers who fought and died there.

I told you about the fall of Cherbourg. There are one or two little things that make you realize the complete ridiculousness of being killed in a war and bring you to a silly conclusion that so many people die needlessly and without much purpose. One of the less pleasant sights of the place where I went in was a young German who had died from three bullet wounds. Someone had propped him up so that he was sitting on the steps of a house with his rifle lying at his feet and with his back braced so that he seemed to be resting. He was rather young and looked tired so that the sight of him was more pathetic than grisly. While I was there, two Frenchmen came to tell me in French a long story of which I could gather practically nothing except that they knew the locations of some mines. I took them along to the engineers and they repeated the story to a sergeant who understood French. They told him that the Germans had hooked some mines to one of the utilities but that the Frenchmen had disconnected them and wanted the engineers to come and take them away. As we went back up the street the [Frenchman] pointed to the dead German on the step. "It's too bad that he's dead," he said. "He showed us how to disconnect the mines." (7 July 1944, Normandy)

Darling,

The whole drama of the thing is so intense because it is so real and because the actors in the thing are so completely unconscious of the heroic role they play. The dogfaces in the line fight so well and suffer so silently that I feel at a complete loss in their presence. These kids have no superman cult to sustain them and they have no fanatical belief in some outrageous doctrine on which to pin the hope of a future Valhalla. They are sustained only by a grim and inarticulate belief that there is something essentially right about what they are doing and that the silly beliefs of Hitler and his minions are as ridiculous as the fact that Germany thinks it can win. They are so courageous and so strong that I am proud that I am from the same country as these wonderful kids.

Yesterday I set up a ceremony in which General Montgomery gave British decorations to ten of our men and it was a wonderful spectacle in its sheer simplicity. We set up in a

field about 200 feet square surrounded by the hedgerows of
Normandy and with the camouflage nets of the tents for our
background. The recipients were to stand in a line with the
general facing them. Two of the men are in the hospital, one
is dead, and one just failed to be present. The Chief of Staff
stepped forward and called "Attention to Orders" and he
proceeded to read the citations. They were stories of valor
too incredible for any fiction. As he finished each citation
the man stepped forward and Monty pinned the ribbon on
his chest with only a few quiet and serious sentences. There
were no theatricals and pompous speeches because these
men would only have mocked at them. The ceremony was
over finally and General Bradley had a word to say to each
man.

The thing that touched me most was a sergeant out of one
of the other divisions. He came up to one of my officers and
said, "Sir, I was supposed to report here to get some kind of
medal." I found out that he was the missing member of the
party. I reported to the Chief of Staff and the whole party re-
assembled. General Montgomery came back out of his tent,
the Chief of Staff came out with a copy of the order, we all
stepped back and the sergeant stood very straight and fine
before them. He had an M-1 rifle in his hand, his clothes
were dirty and wrinkled, his beard was two days old but his
shoulders were square and his eye was clear, and he stood
very straight and calm. The General read the citation and
Monty pinned the medal on his breast. We crowded in then
and he spoke to the Chief of Staff very respectfully but quite
straightforwardly, "I'm sorry to be late, sir, but our outfit
jumped off this morning and they needed me in the line."

The stories of these men are a saga all their own. The first
was a major general Taylor of an airborne division. They
landed before H hour in the swamps behind Carentan and
so disrupted the German forces that they never got organized. The general landed with them and fought his way
back into town in one of the bloodiest battles of the war. He
is six feet tall, this side of 40, handsome, straight in his well-

worn paratrooper's coverall, with fine brown eyes and straight brows.

The second went to a 59 year old brigadier who is the assistant division commander of one of our outfits. He is about five feet nine, slight, and looks like a well-preserved 60 year old. He rallied his outfit on the bad beach on D-Day and got them started inland. His rallying cry was, "We're getting killed here on the beaches. Let's go on inland and get killed." And they did—and a lot of them did get killed but they took their objectives. (8 July 1944, Normandy)

By mid-July, the First Army advance has bogged down in bloody hedgerow-to-hedgerow fighting, seldom advancing more than five hundred yards a day. On July 17, Rommel is wounded and evacuated. The following day, St.-Lô is taken in bitter fighting, concluding the Battle of the Hedgerows. On July 20, an attempt by dissident German generals to assassinate Hitler fails.

Darling,

Rain is the ruination of an army and I saw that so clearly today. The hard surfaced roads become covered with the muck of the side roads and the pace of all the vehicles is greatly slowed. The side roads are little more than cart tracks that have been widened by the dozers and they become pools of thick muck. The shoulders are filled with the rubble of the shattered houses but in the rain they give way under the weight of the heavy vehicles in spite of the busy and dripping engineers working with their picks and shovels. The paths here are really sunken roads like defiles through the hedgerows. On a rainy day like this everything just goes to hell. Along the roads heavy vehicles are tilted at precarious angles with their wheels in the ditches, and the great ten-ton wreckers are busy hauling them out.

We went up to the CP of one of the divisions and it was the same dreary sight. The ground is the heavy red clay of Northern Georgia and the thick mud clings to everything. The

men are dispersed under the trees and most of them are trying to keep dry by huddling in their shelter tents. They are
one of our very best divisions and have fought well on a lot of
dirty jobs and always seem to get selected for them. I heard a
good piece of philosophy on that subject today from a corporal up there: "Who the hell wants to be the best division? The
way I figure, one division is just as good as another and they
can start using them. If it would be any help I'll go around
and make speeches to raise their morale so they can do some
of these jobs. I'll tell them that they are just as good as we are
even though I know it's a goddamned lie. As a matter of fact,
all this Army's got is this division and ten million replacements." (21 July 1944, Normandy)

*On July 25, Cobra—combined First Army air-ground opera-
tion—marks the start of the St.-Lô breakout from the Normandy
Peninsula. Carpet-bombing aircraft dump 4,000 tons of bombs
on German positions (and inadvertently kill 111 GIs and wound
490 as bombs fall short). Stunned Germans hold, barely. On July
27, First Army breaks through the enemy line and prepares to
pursue the disorganized Germans.*

Darling,
    Today I made the trip up through the land of the dead.
The armor broke through today and I followed in its wake. It
was a trip through a devastated land where nothing lived except the soldiers along the road. The Army had passed this
way, and the countryside, which should be lovely in the fertil-
ity of full summer, was blasted and quiet. The houses were ruined with only bare walls or walls gutted with gaping holes to
mark the places where people had lived two days ago. The
rich farms were growing without the aid of man or standing
pockmarked with the holes of shells and with the air stinking
of dead cattle lying obscenely bloated everywhere. Dough-
boys were sleeping or resting in the sun and the smell of
burning wood and the stench of death was over everything.
The engineers were toiling in the hot sun to fill the cratered

road and the dozers were busy shoveling the burned out vehicles off the road and pushing earth over the bloated bodies
of the dead cattle. It was a scene of death and destruction
and ruin and blight and there was little cheer even in victory—and the victory is a great one.

We pulled down into the town of St. Gilles on the road to
Coutances. It is really only a crossroad with a bare score of
houses and the inevitable French school standing across the
road from the lovely Norman church. The church was a
shambles with overturned chairs covered by the rubble of the
walls and ceiling that had been blasted by the artillery. High
up in the chancel the wooden beams were burning and the
smoke was curling lazily up through the holes in the roof.
The stained glass windows were shattered and the shimmering pieces of colored glass were spread everywhere through
the dust and the debris. Beside the ruined altar stood a
statue of the Sacred Heart and under it was written in Latin,
"Come to me and I shall give you peace." Where the choir
usually sat, German prisoners were sitting in solemn rows
with fear and shock on their faces while MPs kept their rifles
trained on them as they leaned against the dust-covered pulpit. No peace here.

Across the road was the school recognizable only by the
ruins of the children's desks and the shattered blackboards
still hanging in their frames. In the heavy dust of the street
where the tanks were rolling by were the pitiful copybooks of
children with their letters and simple sentences written in
large childish characters. Where the children had gone, I
don't know.

I went on down to the crossroad where a dozer was throwing the wreckage of a burned out Jerry tank out of the road-
way so that the waiting columns of troops could pass up to
fight. Amid the desolation was a gray Normandy donkey
standing among the broken walls and the smoking timbers
apparently oblivious to his surroundings. He finally walked
out into the road, pawed the dust for a moment then laid
down for a good roll in the dust. The long column of half-

tracks rolling up to kill Germans stopped for the foolish gray
donkey that lay in their path. They couldn't kill him. The two
dust-covered MPs at the crossroad came along and shooed
the donkey into the field out of the way and he kicked his
heels as he dashed off. The grim faced men on their half-
tracks loosened their grips on their rifles or stepped back
from their machine guns long enough to smile faintly at the
whole performance. Then their eyes looked forward again
and the column started rolling down the dusty road. It all
seemed human and decent for a moment but the basic
wickedness of the war went on again. (27 July 1944, Normandy)

July 28—Coutances falls.

Dear James—
    Today I received the following lovely letter from Mr. James
written on June 22nd:

> It was our pleasure and privilege to entertain your
> husband during his short stay in our city. Mrs. James
> and I became very attached to him in the few weeks he
> was with us and I promised him I would write to you,
> because we are sure that you will be pleased to know
> that he was very fit and cheerful when last we saw him.
> He showed us with pride the beautiful photographs of
> yourself and baby son, and may I say that he has good
> reason to be. We like to think that he is a typical Ameri-
> can gentleman, whose stay with us will always remain a
> pleasant memory.
>   Our own two boys are away in active service and your
> husband reminded us so much of our elder boy, hence
> our attachment to him.
>   Mrs. James joins me in conveying to you our sincere
> wish that your husband will return to you fit and well
> when this business has been completed, and may you
> enjoy together many years of peaceful happiness.

Your husband said frequently that he would return to
England when the war was over. If you do so, please do
not fail to visit us. We would be delighted.

May I say God bless you and my best wishes for the
future.

Yours faithfully,

T. E. James

Isn't that a lovely letter? (30 July 1944, Philadelphia)

*As the month closes, there are 900,000 Americans in Normandy
facing 750,000 Germans. With the German left flank in the air,
the road east to Paris is open.*

August 1944: Envelopment and Breakout

*Patton's Third Army is activated to exploit the breakthrough.
Bradley turns over First Army to Gen. Courtney Hodges, and it
overruns Mortain. The Germans counterattack. In response, the
Allies launch a double-pincer envelopment: Third Army's southern pincer advances to Argentan, but Montgomery's northern
pincer stalls, leaving the eighteen-mile Falaise Gap, through
which 40,000 troops of the nearly encircled German Seventh
Army escape ("a shattering disappointment," in Bradley's assessment). At midmonth, Patton splits his XV Corps at Argentan
and overruns France northeast to the Seine.*

Darling,

I have travelled over nearly all of France that we hold.
General Ike's announcement of the new commands over
here probably gives you a full explanation of why I made the
change of headquarters, and the new job is excellent.[1] I have
been in most of the towns that you have read about—
Coutances, Granville, Avranches, Fougeres, Vire, Laval, Le
Mans, Chateaudun and Chartres. The war moved very
rapidly through most of those places and some of the towns
are virtually untouched. I had gotten so accustomed to the

razed towns of Normandy that towns look good to me just because there are still some buildings standing.

The people in the interior still have a tremendous enthusiasm for the Americans. They stand along the roads to watch the really thrilling sight of the endless stream of American equipment rolling up to the front. It is the most impressive parade that the world has ever seen. The people all wave or give the V sign and your arm is tired returning them. The men and women and children stand along the road with bottles of wine or cider and baskets of the small sweet green apples and press them on you as your vehicle slows down. Many of them have great bunches of flowers and they fling them at you as you pass. I saw a whole company of colored troops yesterday working on the road and every one of them had a rose stuck in the camouflage net of his helmet. As we made the turn to cross the Mayenne River at Laval yesterday, a woman handed me three eggs. I was so surprised that I took them and moved off before I realized what they were. We had them for dinner.

The war goes on apace and I think that we may see the end this year. It has been a brilliant campaign. Everyone is confident and anxious to get on with it. (19 August 1944, Normandy)

Germans retreat east beyond the Seine, ending the seventy-five-day Battle of Normandy. They have sustained 450,000 casualties; the Allies 210,000. Third Army forces the Seine north and south of Paris. On August 25, Paris is liberated. Third Army is across the Seine at Troyes, 150 miles from the German border.

Darling,

I have not written for well over a week and this will begin to tell you the reason why. I am in Paris and have been since the day before the fall of the city was announced. It has been an incredible experience.

Colonel R. and I were given the job of organizing the P&PW part of the Paris Task Force and we had come to the

Chateau Montingny as our assembly point. We had a small force and our only mission was to wait for word that Paris had fallen and then to proceed. In spite of rash claims by the French and the BBC, the city had not fallen and we were waiting for the official go-ahead. The Chateau was pleasant and lovely and we did nothing there but sit. The rest of the story I want to tell you while it is still fresh in my mind.

Wednesday, August 23, Chateau Montingny
[The courier] gave us the message which said that Paris had surrendered and that we were to proceed at once. It was a shock to me because I felt that I was hours late in my mission; I was supposed to get into Paris immediately and here I was almost sixty miles away with a slow convoy of vehicles. We left our meal unfinished and began to get organized for the move. I decided not to wait for the convoy but set Longchamps Race Track as the rendezvous point and started for Paris alone.

The engineers had repaired the blown bridge that morning so we slid down the hill behind the chateau and crossed the Loire into Cloyes. We swung north through the rich flat farm land—through Chateaudun and north on the road to Chartres. There were no signs of war here because the war had moved so fast. The land was yellow after the harvest, the sun was warm, and the fields were dotted with the bound sheaves like a Millet painting. The land is gently rolling here but we could see the spire of the great cathedral a long way off. We came into the traffic circle at Chartres and the whole town turned out to watch the French armored division move through. They were headed for Rambouillet but we were to continue on north to Dreux and then go into Paris by way of Versailles.

The armor was moving fairly rapidly in a column miles long. This was not a tactical move but the triumphal move to Paris. The equipment was entirely American—half-tracks, tanks, armored cars and trucks—but the French had marked them all with the Cross of Lorraine and had named their

vehicles for French cities and departments just as our
men name their jeeps for their girls. The French soldiers
wore American uniforms but with minor identification for
their Gallic souls. The men were all on top of their tanks
and vehicles, and most of them had taken off their helmets
and substituted kepis, the red caps of the revolution; the
marines in the outfit wore their sailor caps with the red
pompoms.

We went through town after town where the Germans had
been early this morning and the towns were mad with joy.
There were flags everywhere, appearing from God knows
where. Everyone in the towns was on the street and flowers
were flung at us as we passed. The French soldiers were busy
hurling their cigarettes and rations to the people along the
way. We moved fairly rapidly through one hysterical little
town after another and finally came to Rambouillet.

We headed out of town on the road to Trappes but were
able to get only about four miles when we came under German fire from 88s and mortars. The Germans were pulling
back but it was obvious that we would not be in Paris that
night. We turned back to Rambouillet to the most remarkable sight we had yet seen.

It's a small town, probably eight to ten thousand, and it
was loaded to the gunwales. In every street were the tanks of
the forward elements of the French armor, and the towns-
people were clambering all over them. In the main street was
every press vehicle in the American armies, and the entire international press corps of more than 200 were gathered in
the little hotel on the main road from Chartres to Paris. I
scrounged rooms in the hotel, then got the mayor of the
town over and in the next couple of hours they found billets
for all the press. Behind us was the French armor, before us
were the Germans, and in Rambouillet was all the American
press working like mad and drinking like crazy. The triumphal march on Paris was much bogged down. G-2 told us
that the number one German capability was a counterattack
on the town because General de Gaulle had arrived. The
whole scene was very confusing.

Hemingway had organized a little French army in the town but he had run out of money and the men had given up. In the course of the evening he had smacked another correspondent who was too drunk to defend himself. We found that the hotel had some very good Reisling so we ordered a few bottles. A very pretty little femme de chambre delivered it when de Gaulle hit town. She looked out the window and with tears rolling down her face kept repeating, "General de Gaulle, General de Gaulle," very softly to herself. I felt rather bad that he doesn't stir the same emotion in me.

Thursday, August 24, Rambouillet

Two hundred correspondents with hangovers awoke to find the town drenched with rain. The armor had moved out of the town during the night and was supposed to move up early in the morning—but it didn't. It was late in the afternoon before the armor really got on the move. I made three visits to their headquarters during the day and learned that Paris was not to be ours that day, either. The French division was badly confused, and was asking for information that I didn't have either. General Leclerc had said that Paris was an egg that had been sucked dry but which still had a shell of Germans around it. That was pretty true.

The correspondents were all writing color pieces, but most of them were more deeply concerned with the fact that the liquor supply had run out and that they were reduced to drinking vin ordinaire. We had urged every man to bring rations but many of them had neglected to. The rains came. The French armor had gone forward but was meeting some opposition at Trappes and Palaiseau.

We knew that the breakthrough was definitely coming because just about twilight the army artillery, 8-inch howitzers and the Long Toms began to roll through in quantity and the French stood goggle-eyed at their size and number.

Friday, August 25, Le jour de la liberation

The day started quietly enough. I went over to the French HQ and learned that patrols were at the gates of Paris. We were just about to leave when word came that we would probably not get in today.

Colonel R. sent me off with Bill Drake of Third Army to pick out a bivouac at Longjumeau. We picked a route we believed to be free of Germans and drove as fast as we could. We were in the flat plain of the Seine now and rolled through lovely little towns. We were on the trail of the French armor—we thought—but we suddenly came across American MPs and recognized the clover leaf of the Fourth Division. It was obvious now that we were going to Paris with the Americans.

We finally swung into Longjumeau where we found one regiment of the Fourth forming up to go into Paris. The snafu of our intelligence and our plan was getting no better. We stopped at a blacksmith shop on the narrow main street, draped one of our press bags on a chair on the sidewalk as a sign, and went into business taking copy from the correspondents who were writing on the hoods of jeeps, on the curbs, and on the anvils and forges of the smithy. We had just gone into business when Bill B., PRO of the Fourth Division, came along.

I got the story from him. One regiment of the Fourth was moving into Paris immediately. He wasn't sure of the precise starting time but figured it would be soon. He suggested that we go to the head of the column and talk to the colonel in charge. Before we were able to reach the head of the column, which was about two miles long, it started to move. We speeded up trying to find the colonel but no one had seen him. We were rolling for Paris, passing the troops on their way there.

We finally caught the foremost vehicle and learned that we were on the point of the Third Battalion and that nothing at all was ahead of us. We stopped and talked with the commander and he said he was definitely going to fight his way into Paris. We ran our jeep at convoy speed paralleling the lead jeep of the column.

We were on the main road now rolling at ten miles an

hour. We were right on the point, and strung out behind us were the reconnaissance and cars and jeeps loaded with machine guns. The streets were lonely and littered with German vehicles that our air had caught. We passed an airdrome that was completely destroyed and suddenly arrived at a point in the road where we could see a great section of the city of Paris lying in the saucer of the Seine below us. The Eiffel Tower stood out above everything and we seemed to be on a level with it, looking down on the city. We paused for a moment while the colonel peered at the barriers that we could see across the road ahead of us and we then pushed on rather cautiously.

We were joined suddenly by a civilian car carrying three members of the FFI [French Forces of the Interior] and they agreed to lead the column to Notre Dame. They said that the Germans were all around us but not in any strength. The column started to roll again with the colonel slouched nonchalantly in his jeep, making us feel better because he seemed so unworried.

We came up to the first barricade and stopped to look it over. The FFI and the people of Paris had fought their fight in the traditional manner. The barricades were made of torn-up paving blocks, iron bedsteads, radiators, boilers, and felled trees that they had erected across the road. There were literally thousands [of barricades] in Paris and we were to see them on every street and at every corner. Men and women and children had built them faster than the Germans could tear them down and had really crippled the Germans so that they could never get a real force into action in Paris.

The realization that we were the Americans seemed to come to the people in a flash and they came running and screaming from every direction. They flung themselves on us and stopped the column from moving. Everyone from babies to old ladies insisted on kissing us and in a few moments we were all smeared with lipstick. The American Army entering Paris covered with lipstick is a horrifying sight. The colonel shooed them off and the people flung themselves on the barricade, tearing it apart so that we could go through. The scene was repeated at every corner and along every street. They thrust flowers and wine and bread and jam into our jeeps as we passed. Every window was full, the streets were jammed and more people were coming every second. Ironically we were headed down the Boulevard Marechal Petain. The long-awaited triumphal march on Paris had finally come through.

We forced our way through the milling crowds and finally arrived at Notre Dame, where our battalion halted. The one thing I remember most is the look of absolute incredulity and hysterical joy that crossed every face when they first realized the Americans had come. A fine old gentleman brought out a bottle of champagne he had saved for four years and we opened it and drank it on the street. The firing became heavy and the crowd scattered but not very far.

My mission was to take over the Hotel Scribe near the Place de l'Opera as soon as possible. The French told me I couldn't possibly get there because the Germans were still there. Bill B. and I picked up an FFI as a guide and decided to try it. We tried one route and got considerable rifle fire. We tried another route and got machine gun fire. We decided to believe we couldn't get there. There wasn't anything for me to do except hold tight and wait for someone to clean up the Germans around the Hotel Scribe. My own party was hours behind me, there was firing everywhere in Paris and there was nothing to do but wait.

[Later] I decided to make one last effort. I picked up two members of the FFI who said that they could get me there. I told Barnes to drive as fast as he could and we took off. We went through the deserted streets with the shots ringing everywhere but in our jeep, and the FFI frantically signaling directions as we tore along. Suddenly we arrived at the Hotel Scribe. I dashed in, while the French bystanders cheered wildly, and requisitioned the place.

The next few hours were sheer madness. In about two hours some correspondents and some of the officers began to arrive out of breath. The bar was open and the correspondents began to hammer out their stories and get drunk simultaneously.

In the middle of it, one of the drivers came in to tell me that the French were about to kill a bunch of German prisoners that had been rounded up in the Place de l'Opera. I don't know why I objected but I did. I got into a jeep and forced my way through the crowd. The Germans were huddled there under guard of some of the French soldiers from the Armored Division but the civilians had gotten at some of them and had kicked a couple to death. There were vehicles there to take the prisoners away but the French captain in command wasn't making much of an effort to get them on the trucks and I was afraid the crowd would tear them to pieces. I got up on a half-track and kept waving my arms with a pistol in my hand and screaming "Ces sont prisonniers." The crowd finally began to relax a little and the French guards began to push them back. It was a kind of hammy performance but it worked. I ordered the French captain to take the frightened whitefaced Germans away at once and he began to load them, none too gently, on the trucks.

The crowd's hatred of the Germans hit me in waves. Suddenly they began to pick up a refrain in the manner of a football crowd yelling "Hold that line." Someone started the cry and then they were all shouting in a chorus with a heavy accent, "Kaput, kaaput, kaaaput." The trucks rolled away and the incident was over—except for me. I was a lone American, the first this crowd had seen, and they mobbed me. The same routine of kissing and mauling, and I was being literally carried along by a hysterical crowd. I was finally rescued by the FFI who surrounded me and escorted me back to the Scribe, thrusting the crowd aside with their rifles.

The rest was bedlam. By midnight there were two hundred correspondents and assorted writers in the hotel. The correspondents were getting drunker and all the whores in Paris had arrived and were doing a thriving trade. I was too exhausted to sleep well and there was firing everywhere through the night.

Saturday, August 26, Paris

By noon things were fairly under control. The Rue Scribe was filled with vehicles, and a few thousand civilians were flocked around them. The endless kissing and singing of the Marseillaise went on all day while the FFI went racing up and down the streets in cars bristling with rifles, chasing down the Germans and the French they don't like. There was desultory fire all day. The crowds were streaming toward the Place de la Concorde for the parade. I went down to see a minute or two of it but had to get back to the hotel. As a result I missed the attempt to assassinate de Gaulle.[2] In midafternoon, in spite of the parade, there were still a couple of thousand people around our hotel since we were the only headquarters in Paris.

The hotel was a madhouse all day. Correspondents were dashing in and out, every one with a hair-raising story. The bar was running like a Klondike saloon, and the place was overrun with women. The colonel ordered the hotel cleared of women and the FFI did the job for us. In the evening we made a check of the identity cards in the bar amid the protests of the correspondents. They all insisted that the little girl was either a very old Parisian friend or a former fiancee. At eleven the colonel and I went up to our room and proceeded to drink the manager's best champagne when the raid started.

I never knew an air raid that scared me like this one. There was absolutely no antiaircraft in Paris and it was a bright night. The planes came flying in with impunity and they really came in low. There was nothing to stop them at all. We went down into the street to try to get our vehicles dispersed. The planes were coming in at rooftop height, bombing and strafing, and the men were firing at the planes with rifles. Fires were beginning to light up the sky and we felt we were really in for it. I don't think there were so many planes but the raid lasted for a very bad hour. It was over and we went to bed.

Thus endeth the saga of Paris. (26 August 1944, Paris)

The Germans have collapsed west of the Seine. The Allies have pushed north beyond the river. On August 27, elements of Third Army cross the Marne. By month's end, elements of Third Army are across the Meuse, thirty-five miles from Metz, fifty miles from the unmanned pillboxes in the West Wall (Siegfried line) at the German frontier. The lightning Allied advance is weeks ahead of schedule, but supply lines are lengthening daily.

September 1944: Slowdown

Eisenhower orders Montgomery and a major portion of First Army to strike up the Channel coast, eliminate V-bomb launching sites, seize Channel ports and Belgian airfields, and secure bridgeheads over the Rhine in preparation for seizure of the German industrial heartland of the Ruhr. Third Army, firmly across the Meuse, is to push toward the Moselle in the vicinity of Metz and Nancy in preparation for occupying the Saar Basin. On September 4, Montgomery takes the critical port of Antwerp (the largest in Europe), but the Germans keep a grip on the seaward shipping passages, barring Allied resupply.

Darling,

Paris is the loveliest city in the world, I think. It glitters, but there is an unwholesomeness and unhealthy air about it now. On the great boulevards the people are sleek, beautifully dressed, with elaborate hairdos and wonderful makeup. The German occupation rested very lightly and most of the French fared well under it. We walked through Montmartre to Montparnasse this afternoon and there are long bread queues in the side streets and the people look underfed and shabby. Most of the barricades were here. The contrast is sharp and not very pleasant.

As far as the Parisians are concerned the war is over and the French won it. They are celebrating a victory that hasn't come yet and in which they played virtually no part. Their walls are full of proclamations from General de Gaulle saying that the French have liberated France and that the French

division liberated Paris. There is no word in any proclamation of the Allies, and the Parisians apparently never heard
of them. The proclamations point out that France will be
present at the peace conference "in great force" and that
they will have their rights. It all gives me a pain and I am just
a little bitter about it.

The French are very charming and that's about all. They
are overwhelmed with self-pity for their sufferings. These suffering people are certainly the best dressed people in the
world. The shops are jammed with merchandise, clothing,
furs, perfume, jewelry and everything else. (5 September
1944, Paris)

Darling,

The metamorphosis of Paris is amazing. On Friday and
Saturday two weeks ago it was the front line but by Sunday
the war had left it far behind. There is no more racing about
the streets by the FFI but there are sinister undercurrents
and I greatly fear that trouble will break out on a grand scale
and soon. There are too many people with guns and too
many conflicting elements. De Gaulle is trying to form a government that will please all elements but I don't think he will
ever have the wholehearted support of the left. The communists within the Resistance have insisted that they are non-political until the war is over but there are too many things taking place for them to remain passive very long. While the
French are convinced that they beat the Germans single-
handedly, there is some difference of opinion among the
French as to which Frenchmen did it.

All of the elements of a terrible inflation are here. The spi-
ral is getting very bad. The worst sign is that they would
rather have any kind of money instead of francs. The black
market is an institution and will get worse. The rich get
richer and the poorer go hungry.

None of the services are restored just because of lack of
coal. There is no electricity or gas and the great Paris Metro
is not running. As a result everyone walks miles to work. The

Bois de Boulogne is full of people cutting wood against the bitterness of the coming winter. The armies are moving so fast that their own supply problems are difficult and we are not able to do much toward alleviating conditions. The French are helpless and useless and I don't think that they will do much toward solving their own problems.

The city of Paris is a city of bicycles. There are thousands of them here and the boulevards literally swarm with them four times a day at nine, noon, two and five o'clock. There is every type that you have ever heard of, and everyone has one. Dignified gentlemen pedal along with their wives clutching the seat behind. Women go to market with babies and small children in special seats in front of the handlebars. The French girls, all beautiful (or have I been away too long?), ride bicycles with reckless abandon. They pedal away with their long legs, and their flimsy skirts fly into the air.

I keep missing you badly and wanting you very much. I have a lot of dreams of after the war but they really are just desires for our life before the war. My thoughts are always built around you and the big chair and the radio and a quiet drink. I love you very much, darling. Keep loving me. (7 September 1944, Paris)

Darling,

The war moves well but we shall have to keep pushing hard to get the war over before winter comes. If we aren't able to, I fear that it may drag on until spring. We have lovely golden afternoons and the leaves on the chestnut trees over the boulevards are still green. I wish that I could think of it as a lovely fall instead of as the precursor of a terrible winter. (9 September 1944, Paris)

By midmonth, 2 million Allied troops are ashore. Elements of First Army have reached the city of Luxembourg and crossed the German border south of Aachen. Except for a strip of land along the German border, Belgium and Luxembourg are liberated.

Darling,

On the 12th we got a message that some 20,000 Germans south of the Loire wanted to surrender.

The bridges across the Loire are all gone but I finally found a little GI ferry that the engineers had in operation. It consisted of three assault boats side by side with a short ramp across it and an outboard motor for power. We eased down the bank and skidded across to the far shore, up the bank, through a path in the woods and out to the highway. The land south of the Loire is very different from the fertile fields on the north side. It just misses being swamp but it is sterile and dead-looking with scrub woods like South Jersey and only a few scattered small towns. The few people that we saw seemed stony faced and unfriendly and we couldn't quite figure that out.

Romorantin is a dirty little French town with a dirty and dishevelled looking town square, a few streets of dirty white flat-walled houses and two foul little hotels. The Intelligence and Reconnaissance [I&R] Platoon was established in one of the hotels of which the proprietor was also a lieutenant in the FFI. The hotel is built around a small central courtyard with a long balcony along the second floor off which the rooms open. There was some pale electric light in the place and some running water. Some Senegalese with great long rifles were guarding the gate of the place and I couldn't imagine where they came from. I scraped off a little dust and went down to dinner with a fantastic collection of people.

There were eighteen of us who were Americans and we represented the entire American army south of the Loire. The commander of the troops was a Lt. Magill, who used to be a cornet player in Ashtabula, Ohio, and he had made the contacts with the Germans to arrange the surrender. His men were a fine bunch with plenty of experience in I&R and they had seen plenty of action. There was nothing exotic looking about them, but their mere presence in such a place seemed a little crazy since they were the only opposition force to 20,000 Germans.

Across the table were two members of the FFI in strange uniforms they had scrounged from varying sources but which were largely American olive drab. They both spoke about as much English as I do French so we got along quite well. They had been working with the FFI for some time and had most of their value to us in their knowledge of the territory. On my left was Mr. Van, who speaks fluent and voluble French with exaggerated Gallic gestures but who is really a Dutchman. He landed in France about a year ago and has been working with the FFI ever since. He had lived in the small towns, passed easily as a Frenchman, and had done a pretty valuable job for the Resistance. The other character was a British major who had come to France several weeks before to work with the Maquis [French Resistance] and he proved to be one of those mysterious figures. Also at the table was a rather beaten-up looking French girl who had been an interpreter for the Gestapo and had been captured by the FFI. They had worked her over and beaten her up pretty badly. The waiters at the table and the help were the same Senegalese that I had seen guarding the gate of the hotel. No one seemed certain of their status but they did make pretty good waiters. The whole scene and the unbelievable collection of characters presented one of the most fantastic sights.

Magill was in constant contact with the Germans and was working out the movement of the German columns north to the Loire where they were to lay down their arms before they crossed the river and made their way into the cages. I worked out the details of press coverage and we sat around and chatted a little while before going to bed.

I had asked the hotel proprietor-lieutenant to have someone call me at seven o'clock in the morning. I fell asleep right away and slept soundly until I felt a hand clutching at my shoulder. I opened my eyes in the gray light and looked up at two big German soldiers who were staring down at me. We just looked at one another and then one of the Germans leaned over me, held out his wrist and pointed to the watch to indicate it was seven o'clock. It seems that the night before they had neglected to tell me that they had four German prisoners as orderlies. I ate a hearty breakfast.

I finished up a few details and made my way back to Paris about a hundred miles away. Back through the deserted countryside, back over our little GI ferry and then on the broad highways that run everywhere in France. It was pouring rain and was a really foul, chilly and filthy day. We were a little slowed by the rain but we stayed off the main routes as much as possible so as to miss the endless convoys of trucks rolling up with food and petrol and ammunition. The roads were still filled with refugees making their way back to their old homes or away from their wrecked homes. Every civilian food truck had families sitting on top of it making a long journey in the cold driving rain. Families moving on bicycles were huddled under trees for protection from the weather. It was a dismal sight but a familiar one.

I spent the 13th and 14th in Paris and took off early on the 15th to go back for the surrender. We checked in at the CP and then went back to Orleans. Orleans has taken a terrific beating, starting out with the original bombing by the Italians in June 1940. They came over for no particular reason and sowed the center of the city with incendiary bombs and levelled most of the Place Jeanne d'Arc. There is now no single reminder of the girl of Orleans except the equestrian statue that still stands in the center of the place in spite of a shell that hit the base of it. The other parts of the town were hit by our bombers aiming at the bridges over the Loire, and one section of the town was knocked down by shell fire when Jerry put up considerable resistance there about five weeks ago.

We got up the next morning and took off for Beaugency, about 18 miles below Orleans on the north bank of the Loire. Beaugency is a lovely old town distinguished mostly by the fact that it has a bridge over the Loire. The bridge is about two hundred yards long, very low and with round Roman arches. The bridge was built hundreds of years ago and the abutments are of solid stone eight to ten feet thick. In spite of repeated bombings, only two of the arches were knocked out. The bridge was not yet repaired but a footpath had been laid over the knocked-out arches.

The surrender was scheduled for three o'clock. The whole thing was like a Hollywood opus with the newsreel cameras all set up, microphones to record the actual surrender, and the site selected so that the ruins of the ancient bridge would give a picturesque background for the performance. The thing built itself up very well. First arrivals on the scene were Magill's platoon. Then the MPs arrived and took up their station along the bridge. Across the river plainly visible were the new posts and the fresh wire of the stockade that had been prepared. A little later a platoon of infantry arrived and took up their position as the formal guard.

We could see the guards begin to stiffen down the right-hand road and knew that General Elster and his staff were coming for the surrender. They pulled up in their tired-looking German staff cars and dismounted. All of them were in the full splendor of their Wehrmacht officer's uniforms. General Elster spoke briefly and stated that he desired to surrender his entire force to the American army. General Macon's reply was brief and to the point. General Elster took his pistol out of his holster and handed it to General Macon, who took it and passed it back to one of his staff. The German general saluted formally and then turned around and marched off with his glum looking, grim faced staff, and the surrender of 20,000 Germans was complete.

The press was clamoring to go down and see the German columns who were only a few miles down the road making their way north. I spoke to the regimental commander and he told me to do what I pleased. I finally promised to go down and see what kind of reception I got before bringing the others down. Mac and I set off in the jeep to drive down and visit a column of 20,000 fully armed and bitter Germans who felt that they had been sold down the river by their officers. This wasn't the war as I had come to know it. (18 September 1944, Beaugency)

Dear James—

Yesterday I got your cable and today I got your letter of 9/14/44. I've made a note of your Homecoming dinner menu and it will all just be like you said—today that dinner seems farther off than it did when you wrote; it wasn't "tomorrow" at any point but the rain and the better Nazi troops inside Germany seem to have postponed things awhile, didn't they?

Rory had a lovely party on Sunday complete with a luscious cake and one tiny red candle and it said "Happy Birthday, Rory." He ate his usual Pablum and junk, and we had chicken salad and potato salad and devilled eggs, and hot rolls and coffee and cake—also what few drinks my liquor ration could provide. The guest list was strictly family and we drank a toast to you—all of us—your parents and Kath and Bill, and my parents and Doris and Bud. Jackson got a lot of nice gifts—two suits and a pair of scarlet fleece-lined slippers, a tiny chair, a big ball, a cuddly panda (which he adores) and $2 from Aunt Mattie. Everyone left by 11 p.m. Sunday night and then I sat down and got quietly tight. It was a lot of work and I was nervous and exhausted and lonely for you so I drowned my sorrows. It doesn't take much. Needless to say, I got up on Monday with a hangover of historic proportions and will stick to beer for another six months. (26 September 1944, Philadelphia)

With Montgomery given supply priority to open the port of Antwerp, First Army goes over to the defensive along most of its line. Third Army, short of gasoline, is ordered to sit down on the Moselle River and assume the defensive ("the momentous error of the war," in Patton's view).

October 1944: Running on Empty

The breakneck Allied advance along a five-hundred-mile front has sputtered and soon will run out of gas and supplies. Bad weather will cause flooding, which will further slow the Allies short of the German border. With the onset of the "October

Pause," First and Third Armies will be immobilized for six weeks until Antwerp is finally opened in November. The prospect of early autumn victory fades.

Darling,

You asked me what I wanted for Christmas and I said nothing. I want to change my mind. I would like a wallet, one that is strong rather than fancy. Buy another bond with the money you might have spent and we shall have enough to get ourselves a house after the war. We have a lot to do after the war.

The war is being fought bitterly but progress is not startling although the general news is good. The Germans have succeeded in two things, though, and that is their campaign against communism and their anti-Semitism. We find it all around us here. We get it from the people of the country and the German prisoners. When I was in one of the cages at the last surrender I got the pitch from several Germans about the trouble we are going to have with the Russians. I had a stock answer for them. We don't expect to have any trouble with the Russians because anyone that can lick the Germans like they did has our vote. Jerry doesn't like that very much. The French are more imbued with the anti-Semitic stuff and give us a lot of pitches about that. All of the French, except the communists, are worried to death about the communists. The communists claim that they are non-political until the war is over but they will be the potent force then. In any case, there will be some fun here in Europe after the war and I shall be very pleased not to be here to watch it. (1 October 1944, Northern France)

During the first week of October, First Army begins an attack against the West Wall at Aachen and encounters strong opposition. To the south, Third Army launches an attack on the Metz fortifications and makes limited progress at great cost.

Darling,

Today we had a little more excitement than we had bargained for. We went up to one of the armies to do a little business and decided to go forward. The regimental S-2 showed us the maps and told us what was cooking and we finally decided on an artillery OP [observation post] where we could get a good view of the war in that area.

We made our way in single file along the deserted road wishing that the trees were a little higher and a little thicker. We followed along the edge of the road and found our guide in a slit trench by the side of the orchard. We were actually in a little crossroads town that nestled on our side of the ridge with buildings running up and over the crest. Just beyond was a deep draw and across the draw in a large semicircle were the Germans. The town was deserted since it was under continuous fire and only a few cows remained of what must have been a thriving village. Our guide was a little on the sober side as he led us over a tortuous route to the farthest building in the village where we had a fine view of the draw and the heights on the other side.

We finally fetched up in a stone house that was not too badly hit. The ground around was all full of shell holes, and several of the buildings had been hit. We made our way through the house, through a hole in the wall into the barn and then climbed up two rickety ladders into the loft where there were two officers and four men with two field telephones and two BC scopes, which are used for artillery observation. One of the scopes was poked up through a hole in the roof like a submarine periscope and the other was directed through a slit in the forward wall. With their excellent magnification we had an excellent view for a long distance and we could see small details of the terrain across the way. There are probably two hundred such OPs across the front and as many on the German side.

We stretched out on the straw with our binoculars and proceeded to get ourselves oriented. Off to our right was another little crossroads town that had been badly hit and which was deserted. Straight ahead of us and for a long sweep to our left we could see the other side of the draw covered with thick woods except for a long open space in which a Jerry trench was plainly visible. Between us and them were two separate farms plainly marked on our maps, and through the glasses we could see the scattered haystack where a shell had hit, dead cows lying in the fields and the half-dug potato patch with the potatoes still lying on the ground. There were several places across the way that Jerry might be using for OPs, and our artillery was picking them out, with the observers in our position calling the fire. Jerry was carrying on the same process.

We were really in the midst of two or three operations. One lieutenant was trying to direct fire for a 90 millimeter AA gun which was trying to get zeroed in. Another lieutenant was alternating with a sergeant in calling the fire for two batteries a few miles to our rear, and everyone was trying to spot the Jerry guns across the way as was the Piper Cub flying over our heads. They decided to try to tear down one of the farmhouses across the way since Jerry might be using it for an OP, and they directed the fire until the guns found it and then proceeded to tear it to the ground with eight rounds right on the target.

Then Jerry got an idea, too. He picked out two houses in the next little settlement about three hundred yards to our left and put heavy fire on them. We all concluded that the fire was coming from a large woods across the way but we couldn't locate the source. They called for fire on the woods and we dropped some rounds in there but there was no way of knowing whether it was effective.

We had heard a lot of shells roaring over our heads and we had watched the bursts of a lot of his shells a few hundred yards one way or the other. Without any warning, there was a terrific explosion and right in front of our eyes a shell hit a telegraph pole across the road from us. We all hit the straw by sheer reflex. We had just straightened up when another round hit just behind us and we knew that we were bracketed and Jerry was on us. We started for the low door of the loft but before all of us could get through it, the whole building rattled and shook and the roof on the far end of the barn disintegrated in a great cloud of dust. A couple of us went down the ladder and the rest just jumped down to the floor below and then down into the basement. We dived into a small narrow cellar, where I put in the worst forty-five minutes of my life. The place had a heavy stone ceiling and thick generous walls with only two narrow doors. Those doors began to seem too wide after a while. Jerry had decided that the remaining buildings of the town had stood too long and he proceeded to tear them down. The seven of us sat on the floor with our backs against the wall and just waited it out. The ground shook, the explosions were all around us and we could smell the smoke after a few minutes. We would stick our heads out one door or the other and make sure it wasn't our building that was burning and then go back to another cigarette. After the first few minutes we achieved a sort of relaxation and began to tell stories about the war of one kind or another and tried to keep our minds off the artillery shells. It worked to some extent although we couldn't help stopping in mid-sentence when another round hit too close. It went on for forty-five minutes and then the fire just petered out. We waited a few minutes, then cautiously emerged.

The colonel and I had the job of going back that long thousand yards to the jeep and we walked back much less gaily than we had come up. Our little town was a sad sight, with most of the houses and barns badly beaten up. The fields around the road were pitted with shell holes and some of them were still smoking. We got back to our jeep and told our driver to take off. We were glad to be out of that. (7 October 1944, Northern France)

In the north, First Army halts its advance because of supply shortages. To the south, Patton abandons a new offensive against Metz because of ammunition and gasoline shortages.

Darling,

The war goes slowly. The fighting is very bitter on all sides and the Germans are well prepared for this defensive war that they are fighting. I'm still not too pessimistic and I think that old Omar will fool them yet and beat their brains out. Jerry is tough but our men are better soldiers. They always amaze me just by their sheer fortitude and the fact that they have become such canny fighters. They think that they can lick anybody and they can. (19 October 1944, Northern France)

October 21—Aachen is liberated by elements of First Army; it is the first German city to fall.

Darling,
        The army isn't going much of anywhere at the moment and all interest is centered on Aachen. I managed to get up there and get a look but I arrived just a couple of hours before the surrender and saw none of the fighting. It was quite a fight but our men just cleaned the city out slowly and methodically. It is a shame that so lovely a city with so much historic significance should be so badly beaten up, but there is some satisfaction in knowing that the Germans are now around to tearing down their own country. I suppose that there will be many more Aachens before the war is over.
        One little incident impressed me very much. One of the TD [tank destroyer] crews had a dog right with them in the town where they were set up at the corner of a building. The dog walked out into the street and a jeep ran over him and injured him badly but he wasn't dead. The company aid man looked him over and said he couldn't do anything for him and they ought to put him out of his misery. Not one man in the crew would shoot the dog. They finally sent one man dashing across the street (a really dangerous job) to bring back a soldier from another outfit to shoot the dog. Then they buried it in the rubble right beside their tank destroyer. They were all broken up about it. (22 October 1944, Aachen)

Darling,
        Today I was awarded the Bronze Star Medal for the Paris operation. Usually they have large ceremonies for a lot of

people but mine was the only award this month and I had mine all alone.

Colonel Fitzgerald led me into the office and the General [Bradley] waved us all in. The General had the medal on his desk and the citation lying beside it. He stood up and read the general order himself and then read the citation. He came over and pinned the ribbon on my field jacket. He just said, "That was a very fine job. Very fine. Congratulations."

It isn't the Congressional Medal of Honor but it is something to show that I did go to war once upon a time. It's a rather nice looking ribbon, too.

I'll be glad when we get to Berlin but I shouldn't like to guess when that will be. I am still optimistic and think that old Omar will knock them off when he is ready. He's always come through before when things seemed tough and I'm sure that he can do it again. He looks like such a sweet old soul and he speaks softly and gently but he is tough and ruthless. He has fired more generals than I can remember and he doesn't hesitate to do it. The United States must be full of generals and colonels he has fired because they didn't produce. I really think that his basic concern is for the men and he has no intention of carrying along an incompetent that will just get a lot of doughs killed. (26 October 1944, France)

Darling,

Sunday afternoon in France. I wakened and suspected that it would be a good day because there was a narrow streak of pale sunlight over my cot where the light was leaking in through my blackout screen. The sunshine still carries on and the day is lovely and fairly mild. It would be a wonderful afternoon to see Penn play Army at Franklin Field and have a big jug of hot buttered rum to go along. No sense in thinking silly things.

Went to church this morning in a barnlike former stable that has been fixed up somewhat. There was a small portable organ that played the hymns and we all sang them heartily. Nicest part of the mass was a WAC T/Sgt. in fatigue clothes and a helmet who sang "Mother at Your Feet Is Kneeling" in a sweet soprano voice. It was a little startling to us because we have almost forgotten what a woman's voice sounds like.

The war on our front is in a lull. The British and Canadians are carrying the ball at the present and are doing very well. The war will probably open up in full blast somewhere one of these days. (29 October 1944, France)

As the month ends, Bradley orders the three American armies (First, Third, and Ninth) to prepare for operations against the West Wall.

November 1944: War of Attrition

Resupplied at last, the Allies mount a two-pronged offensive north and south of the Ardennes Forest. The U.S. First Army north of the Ardennes is to force the Roer River beyond Aachen and move toward Cologne on the Rhine. The U.S. Third Army south of the Ardennes is to force the Moselle River north of Metz, leap to the West Wall, then break through the Saar Valley to Mannheim on the Rhine. Rain, swollen rivers, and muddy roads slow the advance.

Darling,

Just after dinner on a Monday night with the stars shining in spite of the fact that it rained all day.

I spent a couple of hours this afternoon talking with Bill Shirer, who has recently arrived from the States. Most of our questions were about the election tomorrow and he tells us that there is not much question that Roosevelt will be elected. We are all suddenly concerned about it and I hope that he is right. I think over here we all realize that America's prestige would be terribly damaged if Roosevelt were to fail of reelection. The election will decide it tomorrow and I don't suppose that there is much that I can do about it. (6 November 1944, France)

Darling,

The wind is howling tonight and the temperature is slowly

sliding down. We had a few flakes of snow this morning but the day was largely divided between a bright sunshine and a driving rain. We live in a perpetual state of mud, and the sun never has a real chance to do very much about it. We have no coal or firewood but we have a plentiful supply of green wood and cut down the young birches. It burns well and throws plenty of heat but the atmosphere is usually just about right for smoking a ham.

We get a chuckle out of reading the back issues of *Time* and *Newsweek* because we get them just in time to laugh at how wrong they are about almost everything connected with the war.

I have just seen an article in *Editor and Publisher* giving portions of a speech by Melvin Whiteleather before the Poor Richard Club. He describes in detail the sufferings and the difficulties of the early days in Normandy. The whole thing would have been very touching except for the fact that he was never in Normandy, at least during this war.

If you want to get the war straight, stick to Don Whitehead of AP [Associated Press], Bob Reuben of Reuters, Harold Denny of the *New York Times* and Bob Richards of the *Herald Tribune*. On the radio ignore practically everyone.

I suppose the advent of Thanksgiving and Christmas plus the approach to the end of another year fills everyone with thoughts of other years and other places. Men are always coming up with wild projects to get back to the States but they know it is only conversation. We don't have statistics but the constant statement is that there are millions of men at home who can serve overseas and that there should be some rotation policy. The hard military fact probably is that the men in the States are not adequate substitutes for the highly trained men and the battle-wise men that we have here. They say that replacements are men who take the place of other replacements. I think it is true, too, because the casualties actually do run lower in the more experienced units in spite of the fact that they are usually given the tough jobs to do.

(9 November 1944, France)

Darling,

Armistice Day just before lunch.

The war has blazed up again and the Third Army is moving very well. All the news that has come in so far has been encouraging and it may be that we shall get somewhere before we are through. There are still the two little matters of the Siegfried Line and the Rhine River.

The soldier vote for Roosevelt is a good sign because troops here, for some reason that I can't understand, felt that the war would be over sooner if Dewey were elected. They felt that he would make some sort of armistice or compromise peace. If, in spite of that belief, most of them voted for Roosevelt it is an amazing commentary on how thoroughly they believe that Germany should be destroyed. That's probably placing too much importance on the soldiers' attitude because most of them showed little interest in it, and only voted if a ballot were thrust into their hands. The army was so anxious to be impartial that there wasn't a tremendous quantity of news about it and there wasn't much stirring up of interest. Besides, soldiers never think beyond tomorrow, and long-range problems seem beyond their ken. They are too busy trying to stay alive today to worry about what may happen next week. (11 November 1944, France)

During the last half of November, First Army jumps off but stalls short of the Roer; the attack on a broad front in the Huertgen Forest results in heavy American casualties (21,000 by mid-December). To the south, Patton and Third Army begin the encirclement of Metz and drive to the Sarre River but are stopped by the Germans at the West Wall.

Darling,

The French are tremendously interested in Metz because it is the capital of Lorraine and because it is a great fortress that has never been taken by storm. The city is surrounded by twenty-four forts of some size and by a lot of little pillboxes and strongpoints. The building of the place was started long ago and has been improved by the French and the Germans alternately as they occupied it. The army is well past Metz on both sides but would like to reduce it.

We started out after a driving rain, which was beating down in the early morning, finally let up. We started on a good road making excellent time and there were only thin clouds in a bright blue sky. There was some bright sunlight but the wind was cutting. We finally arrived at corps headquarters and went on to find the division.

We were roughly west of Metz, and the Germans were between us so we had to make a swing around to approach from the north. The country here is very hilly and well-wooded but the basic industry is iron ore and smelting with an entirely different appearance from the agricultural France that we have become accustomed to. There are great ore piles and the chimneys and heavy machinery of the smelters but there was no smoke from the chimneys. The people seemed well fed and not unfriendly. We'd passed through the valley of the Meuse and then swung over the hills between to come down into the valley of the Moselle which marks the western boundary of Lorraine. The sun had disappeared and ahead were heavy black clouds.

The division headquarters was in a small town with more children than I have seen anywhere in France. This section missed by a couple of miles being incorporated into Greater Germany and the people are still French and the children more than friendly. We tarried there briefly because it was getting late and took off in a mad rush for Metz.

This was still France but the road signs and the lettering on the windows were in German and the people seemed to look somewhat different from the French. The farms were not the familiar three-sided squares. The architecture seemed to change too, and most of the houses appear to have been built in comparatively recent time since they must have all been destroyed in the last war. We began to come on the signs of recent battle with dead horses and an occasional cow, every building deserted and no sign of life in the land.

The farmhouses were riddled with holes. The land was flooded from the recent rains and there were a few lonesome cattle in some of the fields. Along the roads were the deserted foxholes of the Germans, most of them well dug in and well covered with only a firing lit [port] to cover the road.

We finally came into the war very suddenly when we rolled into the little town of Woippy, which is a suburb of Metz just across the river from the town itself. It is a pleasant looking community not very different from an American suburbia with neat gray stone houses fronted by small lawns on the wide road and with large vegetable gardens behind. The place was a shambles. There wasn't a window in the town, curtains and shades were flapping in the breeze through the windows, and the iron shutters, which you find everywhere in Europe, were banging back and forth. Some of the houses were knocked down by shell fire and some were burned out from the shelling. The people had fled with only a few treasured possessions and the houses were filled with nice furniture, carefully made beds, tables laid for meals, toys and bicycles strewn about the back yards and every sign of a sudden flight. The streets were strewn with German dead. The fighting had obviously been bitter here. We could hear steady firing ahead of us, and to the right there were three huge columns of smoke where the heavy German guns in some of the remaining forts had set part of the city afire.

As we came into the outskirts, we caught up with the regimental S-2. We were standing between two 88s that covered the road and which had presented a real problem to the tanks. They had been held up until the infantry moved forward and knocked off the crews so that the tanks could roll again. While we were talking, there came down the road a little column of bedraggled and shivering German prisoners freshly dug out of one of the houses. The troops were marching in the familiar pose with their hands locked on the tops of their heads like men about to lie down to pleasant dreams. They were a sorry looking lot and seemed thoroughly scared.

We were at the head of a well spaced out column of infantry waiting for the signal to move up. Most of them were taking a long look over their rifles; the mortar men, ammunition carriers and machine gunners were looking for a dry place to rest their equipment. They looked like men who had had two days of hard fighting but they began to move up when the order was given to go in. Just before they moved out, the intermittent hammering of the bursting artillery was marked by the sharp pings of sniper fire. The forward men of the column dropped to one knee and we moved around a corner to cover. When they got the "forward" signal they trooped off in their long uneven line apparently oblivious to the sniper fire which continued. One man went down and two aid men were beside him in a second and laid him out on the steps of a house to work over him. The rest of the column looked at him without any curiosity or apparent emotion and kept slogging on down the muddy road. (21 November 1944, Metz)

As the month closes, the first Allied convoy reaches Antwerp, eighty-five days after the capture of the port. A war of rapid movement and lightning advances has given way to a war of attrition along the West Wall.

With Patton

George S. Patton, Jr., was born in 1885. Hampered by dyslexia, he had to repeat his first year at West Point. He graduated (Class of 1909) in the top half of his class and was assigned to the horse cavalry.

Patton participated in the 1912 Olympic Games (finishing fifth in the pentathlon) and served in Mexico with Pershing in the campaign against Pancho Villa. He also served in World War I, where he became the American authority on the infant science of tank warfare, led troops with distinction, and was seriously wounded.

After the war, he remained with the Tank Corps (mentoring a young tank officer named Dwight Eisenhower). When the tank fell into disfavor between the wars, Patton returned to the cavalry, and his career went into eclipse. He was on the verge of retirement when World War

II broke out. His career took off during the 1941 Tennessee and Louisiana war maneuvers, where he distinguished himself.

Posted overseas in 1942, Patton led American forces in North Africa and Sicily, where he earned a reputation as a skilled and innovative battlefield commander. His career nearly ended in 1943 in Sicily when he slapped two soldiers whom he believed to be malingerers, but he was given a reprieve by Eisenhower. In the doghouse, he was posted to England in command of a phantom army intended to decoy the Germans at D day (it did), then was given the command of Third Army.

On D+56, Patton's Third Army was activated in Normandy as part of 12th Army Group, which was commanded by Patton's former subordinate Bradley.

In December 1944, with Third Army in the thick of the fighting during the Battle of the Bulge and Patton in need of a public relations officer (PRO), 12th Army Group detached Bradley's PRO to handle the increasing number of correspondents covering Patton and Third Army. The assignment was to be temporary.

"The morning of a move," Major Quirk wrote his wife, "I usually go crazy because men and vehicles are running in every direction but by nine o'clock the old quarters are absolutely bare and I take off down the road. When I arrive at the new place there is the same indescribable confusion but everyone knows precisely what he is doing and by five o'clock or a little later everything is in place and in operation. If you can imagine moving WFIL a hundred miles without ceasing operation you can imagine what our moves are like, except that the press camp is bigger than WFIL."

Major (later Lieutenant Colonel) Quirk would remain with Patton and Third Army through the end of the war.

December 1944–January 1945: The Bulge

At the opening of the month, First Army prepares to move against the Roer River dams, and Third Army prepares for an offensive against the Saar Basin. By midmonth, elements of both armies are encountering stiff German resistance.

On December 16, the Germans mount a surprise counteroffensive against the thinly defended center of the U.S. line in the

*Ardennes in an effort to regain the recently opened port of
Antwerp. The offensive creates a bulge in the crumbling U.S.
line as the Germans advance westward into Belgium. On December 22, Patton wheels Third Army to the north on slippery,
snow-covered roads and counterattacks the Germans ("one of
the most astonishing feats of generalship of our campaign in the
West," Bradley would write). On the day after Christmas, the
German penetration stalls fifty miles into Belgium, then grinds
to a halt.*

*In early January, Rundstedt requests to withdraw German
forces east of the Rhine. Hitler refuses. In the meanest winter
in memory, First and Third Armies mount a coordinated attack
on the Bulge. Their offensive spent, the Germans fight to ex-
tricate themselves and sustain heavy casualties.*

Darling,

I have had a long interview with General Patton which was
more than interesting. He is tall, baldish, with white bushy
eyebrows over penetrating eyes, a chin like a rock and a small
thin-lipped mouth which relaxes into sort of a grin when he
is pleased. The Chief of Staff, General Gay, told me that the
General just wanted to "chat" with me and that's just about
what he did. He didn't make any long inquiries about my
background or qualifications or experience and he did more
of the talking. I think that he was just trying to get the feel of
me and I don't know what the results of his conversation
were. He is quite interesting with a fine historical knowledge,
a real consciousness of the fact that he has his place in history. He talks well and easily and is really quite charming. He
seems to be very frank and open (he insists that his staff always be fully informed) and he radiates an incurable optimism. He wound up by telling me that I am to come see him
whenever I want anything.

Having broken the ice, I shall now probably develop into
a nuisance. Yesterday morning I was back in his office with
photographers in tow to make some pictures while he
pinned medals on General Middleton and General Eddy, two

of the Corps commanders who have done outstanding jobs. This afternoon at five I have a date with him to introduce for a brief session three representatives of the American Newspaper Editors Association who are over here on some sort of vague junket.

Later

Had a long talk with the General and he was his usual interesting self. The newspaper committee were a bunch of stupes and I think he was bored but he was charming to them.

I make at least one and sometimes two trips to headquarters each day and freeze myself to death in an open jeep although I wear enough clothes and my field coat has a built-in hood on it. We have learned the value of warm clothing and we don't hesitate about wearing it. (25 January 1945, Luxembourg)

As the month ends, Hitler's grand gamble has failed. All ground lost in the German counteroffensive has been retaken in grim fighting. American casualties total 76,000; German casualties are estimated at upward of 100,000.

February 1945: Advancing to the Rhine

Allies mount an offensive to break through the West Wall and defeat the Germans west of the Rhine. First Army prepares to move east toward Cologne. Third Army with four corps (III, VIII, XII, XX) prepares to move on Pruem and Bitburg to the south. Mud, rain, and impassable roads impede movement.

Darling,

All the papers are full of speculation about the Big Three and their meeting [at Yalta] and we are the recipients of some fine rumors, too. I suppose that there is a lot to be worked out but I am not sure that the whole thing will amount to much. I am sure that Uncle Joe has all his plans made and that there is little likelihood of his deviating from them. I am sure that Winston has a plan also but he is in the

unfortunate position of having to sell it to either Joe or
Frankie, and America has already indicated that they don't
see things his way. I suspect that Frankie expects to improvise
as he goes and smile his way charmingly through the entire
thing.

I personally feel, and so does everyone else here, that no
terms can be too harsh for the Germans including annihila-
tion. I don't think that anything or anyone can change the
Germans or redeem them and I don't see why we get squea-
mish about killing some more people. We have started it and
we might as well follow through until they are stamped out.
There are difficulties in any course that we follow but I think
that we should turn a deaf ear to any plea from anyone about
any softening of peace terms to the Germans. They have
taken a beating but not enough. Our men have torn down
with artillery every German town that we have gotten to and I
hope that the process is continued. They can live in caves
like the Nordic forbears from whom they claim to be sprung.
The Russian ideas on the subject will probably be the deter-
mining factor, and since they have made the greatest contribution to the winning of the war I suppose they are more or
less entitled to call the turn.

I think that I'm getting politics mixed with my military
when I really will be glad no matter who settles it just so that
it is settled. I want to go home and so does everyone else. I
love you and miss you and want you very much. Take care
and hope that the war will be a short one from here on.
(5 February 1945, Luxembourg)

*During the next week, VIII Corps crosses the Our River,
breaches the West Wall along an eleven-mile front, and takes
Pruem; XII Corps crosses the Sauer River and extends and
strengthens bridgeheads west of Bitburg.*

Darling,

The sun was out this afternoon for the first time in a long
while. We came through the City of Luxembourg which is re-

ally a lovely place. The whole city is divided right in the center by a deep gorge in which there is only a tiny stream. The sides of the gorge are clifflike but there are houses down the side of it and in the bottom. Most of the city sits on the high ground on both sides of the ravine. It is a pleasant city, solid and substantial looking with fine houses and many massive buildings that were the homes of the many industries of the country. The people don't have the charm or the flair of the French but the city is clean and there is a definite air of substance and wealth. It looks like a place in which everyone is bourgeois.

We went out to the north on the road to Diekirch and Mersch but made a little turn off en route. It is fairy tale country with hidden chapels in corners of the valleys, great rugged wooded hills, fine castles and little farms, and all in all one of the most charming places in the world. The sun was out and except in the depths of the valleys the roads were fairly dry. The air was mild with a definite touch of spring. We moved along pretty well and there wasn't too much traffic. Some of the traffic was the weary and dreary plodding of the refugees' carts going back to the towns that the Germans have left again. I feel sorrier for them than when I saw them leaving seven weeks ago because most of the towns are a shambles now and they are going home to nothing.

We stopped off at a CP and got some information on what we wanted and then pushed on to Diekirch which also must have been a fine city once upon a time but which is battered and torn now. We had to cross the river to it and the river is very high. From the tree line we could see that it normally is only a little stream (the Sure River) but it is on the rampage now and is a couple of hundred feet wide in spots. Most pathetic sight, I think, was a green park bench just showing above the water where the old banks must be. I am sure it was a pleasant place before the war.

We went on down the river headed east and the war was all around us now. The Germans were over the ridge from us so we were in perfect defilade and could ignore the artillery going both ways over our heads. (13 February 1945, Luxembourg)

Darling,

Spent practically all day up there today. It was a really fine day, light clouds in a clear blue sky, the sun shining and the weather much like a good March day at home. The country is so lovely and we were up there for hours.

I covered the whole east bank of the Sure and the Our and the Sauer as far south as Echternach in Germany. About half of the trip is in Luxembourg and the rest is across the border in Germany. The river Sauer is the boundary between the two countries down there. The river is in a lovely setting in a deep valley with great craggy hills on both sides and with the towns huddled along the riverbank. It's impossible to savor scenery in the middle of a war because of the things that are all around you, especially the constant hammering of the artillery across the river both ways. We passed through all of the towns that have been in the news these past few days, Diekirch, Dillingen, Wallendorf, Bollendorf, and Echternach and some others. They are all lovely little towns but they have been completely liberated; that means that there isn't a whole building in the town and not a single person.

The engineers are the busiest people here putting in bridges of every kind. There is a sort of pattern to the thing that is progressive and marvelous. They started out crossing in little wooden engineer assault boats that hold six men. Then they put in an infantry assault bridge which is just a footpath laid over the top of assault boats that are moored so that they can't float downstream. That sounds simple but is quite a job. After that is finished so that infantry can get across, the next job is a treadway bridge. That is built afloat on large rubber pontoons on which are laid two large strips of heavy steel mesh as tracks for vehicles, and the lighter transport can begin to move across. After that comes the Bailey bridge which is one of the real marvels of the war. I can't

describe the thing except to say that it is assembled on one
bank and pushed across the river like a giant antenna and it
will carry almost anything. After that the engineers put in
timber trestle bridges that will last forever practically. The
fact that they can do the job at all is really miraculous. They
work away with the enemy firing artillery at them and sometimes bombing and strafing them. Their only protection in
many cases is smoke. We saw some of that today.

In one of the places, there were three treadway bridges in
operation and jammed with traffic while—almost alongside—more engineers were pushing their Bailey across. The
area is eerie and strange because the whole thing is covered
with white smoke which shifts and lifts as the wind changes.
The sun is dull through the smoke and in one spot I had to
get out and walk ahead of the jeep because it was impossible
to see two feet ahead. The men who run the smoke generators are a nonchalant lot who feed them and keep them running and sit in the middle of the smoke paying no attention
to anything but their generators while the shells go wham-
ming away over head. We saw some Nebelwerfer (Screaming
Meemies) hitting around but they paid no attention at all.

We turned off the river road and started to climb the hill
along a narrow road that wound up the long hill and into the
deep woods. A battalion was moving up along the same road
in two files, one on either side of the road and strung out so
that there was about ten to fifteen feet between each man.
The column seemed to wind on endlessly, moving at the slow
doughboy's pace. The riflemen had their M-1s slung over
their shoulders. Some of them were singing softly and an
amazing number of them smoked pipes. It's a stiff climb and
the men were sweating a little in spite of the fact that they
wore no overcoats. Each small serial was followed by the aid
man in a white helmet bearing Red Crosses on all four sides
and armed with four blankets and his musette bag. We
passed the weapons platoons bent a little under their loads
of mortar barrel or baseplate or slings full of mortar shells.
Each time the column stopped the men either sat or knelt

down in place and then stood up and slogged off again as the column moved. They looked young and competent and unhurried. They had fought before and would be at it again in a couple of hours. The lieutenants led off each platoon and set the slow easy pace and the platoon sergeant brought up the rear keeping an eye on his men.

The war was very real here. The shells were flying over our heads constantly in both directions—our guns firing at troops on the other side of the crest that we were approaching, and the enemy firing at our artillery on the hills across the river and at the bridge sites on the river itself. The side of the hill was scarred with foxholes and trenches and with the holes that our shells had made on the attack. Halfway up we could turn back and look down on the riverbanks and we wondered how our men had ever fought their way up here. There were several sections marked off with white tape where the mines had not been cleared and we could see knocked out and burned out pillboxes. We met jeeps jolting down the road each carrying three stretchers of the men who had been hit up ahead. It was a long climb and the woods getting thicker all the time broken by rugged rock formations and swift little mountain streams. It was a lovely setting but not for war and death.

We finally reached the end of the lane and picked up the route along the narrow footpath that the troops were following. Off to our left we could hear the crack of rifles and the chatter of automatic weapons where the next battalion had a fight on its hands. We stopped and talked for a few minutes with the battalion commander, a 25 year old captain, and he passed the time of day as he disposed of his battalion as they came along. His instructions were simple and the lieutenants just nodded in acknowledgment as they passed: "Baker Company take the second path to the left. George Company go right at that first pillbox. Fox Company turn off where the tree is blazed." The men began to disappear off the path into the woods quietly and quickly. We went on ahead up the path.

Trees were torn and scarred where the shells had ripped through. Items of military equipment were flung in the brush. Along the path were huddled bundles of green that were dead Germans lying where they had fallen—most of them looking singularly peaceful. They were of all ages from boys to old men and they had travelled a long way to die on a bed of pine needles on top of a rocky mountain.

We struck off through the woods following the twisted strand of field wire that we had been told led to the OP. We had been warned not to go over the cliff and it's good that we were because the wood ended abruptly in a sheer cliff that went straight down for two hundred feet. Poised on the edge were some huge rocks that formed a kind of pulpit on the face of the cliff. We struggled around the edge and stumbled into the narrow slit of rock that formed the OP. It was well-shielded with evergreens and peopled by two young soldiers with an artillery scope and a telephone.

We had come to the end of the mountains and ahead of us were the rolling fields that lead to the Rhine. The observers slid over to make room for us and asked the inevitable question that the front line soldier always asks, "How are the Russians doing?" We were looking up a long narrow valley with a road winding up the center toward two small peaceful looking towns at the head of it. Beyond the towns the wooded mountains were replaced by long rolling fields stretching off to the horizon. The ridge on our left gave off occasional bursts of smoke as the mortar shells hit and we could hear the crack and rattle of small arms fire. At the foot of the cliff to the right was a small stream and we could see one of our patrols making a quick dash across the open space, slow down as they waded the stream and then disappear into the woods on the far side. On the ridge to our right was another small town, half on top of the hill and partly disappearing on the reverse slope so that we couldn't see all of it. The artillery was intense now and the town was slowly being torn down by the heavy guns. We watched it through the glasses and each time a gust of wind cleared the smoke for a moment we could see the gaping roofs and the holes in the walls of the houses.

The observer was trying to locate four tanks that he had seen going up the road but which he had lost around one of the bends. He kept searching with his scope and suddenly all of us saw the flash as the sun glinted on some bright object ahead. Our observer was almost disgusted as he called back to the batteries for fire. "The dumb sonovabitch gave away his position," he said. It was a professional criticism from a soldier who couldn't have been more than twenty. In about two minutes the shells went screaming over and the observer began to correct the fire. He finally called for fire for effect and the batteries whammed away. We saw the church steeple just behind the position disappear and then two tanks came lumbering out of the deep shadow and off down the road. I don't know whether we got the other two but they didn't come out and we probably did. The batteries then began to work on the peaceful looking town ahead and the smoke soon enveloped it. We started back through the woods the way we had come.

It was mid-afternoon and the sun was still bright in the sky although the dimness was heavy in the woods. We got back down the path a couple of hundred yards where machine guns and mortars were dug in now. The cooks had just come up with hot food in cans that keep the food warm. We stopped and had a cup of hot tea and a piece of bread and butter. We chatted for a couple of minutes with two lieutenants, the only two lieutenants who had started with the battalion last October and are still in action. They are both company commanders now. We made our way on back down the hill to our jeep and then twisted and turned back down to the river. We crossed one of the treadway bridges and made our way home. (14 February 1945, Luxembourg)

At midmonth, VIII Corps attacks through the West Wall west of the Pruem and overruns German pillboxes; XX Corps opens an attack to clear the Saar-Moselle triangle southwest of Trier; and

XII Corps envelops and destroys the Germans in West Wall positions between the Our and Gay Rivers.

Darling,

Yesterday I went down to the Fourth Armored Division CP where the General pinned a Medal of Honor on a little lieutenant. It is the first one in the Third Army and only the sixth in the theater. There was a band and a color guard and a little parade and it all added up to a fine ceremony. General Gaffey who commands the Fourth is a good soldier and a pleasant guy, and we rather enjoyed the whole thing. For the first time, the General told me that he could be quoted and we passed a couple of little quotes. They won't make any history and I am very glad of that.

Today is real spring in Luxembourg. The roads are dry and the news has been telling you that our armor has been able to move. We cleaned out the Saar-Moselle triangle in less than three days. It has been a touchy spot for a long time but we completely outmaneuvered them. We had a press conference with the General late this afternoon and he seemed quite pleased about it. He didn't have too much to say but he is always interesting and a lot of fun. The correspondents love it. For the first time since I came here General Gay told me today that the camp is going very well and that he has heard only good reports. Coming from him that's something because he is not a bouquet thrower normally. He had just seen General Allen, the PRO of SHAEF, and had gotten a good report from him. I'm glad that someone is happy about it. (23 February 1945, Luxembourg)

Darling,

Late afternoon about four thirty and taking time to write now because I shan't have time later. Coming down to spend the night with me are [FDR press secretary] Steve Early and Captain Harry Butcher, General Ike's naval aide. I don't know that they want anything. They are most probably just bucketing around the front. The General is busy tonight and won't be able to see them until morning. I am a little tired of visiting firemen but they are part of the job.

The General is going to get a little tired of me. This morning he had Jimmy (Vincent) Sheehan for almost an hour, giving him a lot of stuff on a piece that he is doing on generalship and what it takes to make a leader. He is always interesting and they had quite a chat. Not too long afterward I took over Mauldin, the Stars and Stripes cartoonist, for a little session that didn't take too long but which did tie him up a little. [3] A general in the field always has a tough time because all the floating visitors want to see him just so that they can tell people about it back home. It makes a wonderful thing to stick into a conversation— "Now when I was talking to General Patton, he told me etc." I try to steer them away but it is hard to do and he doesn't seem to mind. He handles them all very well and they all come to scoff and remain to pray.

He is a most impressive guy. I think that they expect some sort of circus performance and are always a little surprised to find out that he knows more about more things than they do. He is the complete soldier and I am sure that he is one of the happiest people in the world right where he is. I am sure that he has no post-war ambitions and for that reason he has none of the hokum that marks MacArthur. (27 February 1945, Luxembourg)

At month's end, XII Corps takes Bitburg, Third Army prepares to cross the Moselle at Trier, and Patton leaves behind the shambles of the West Wall.

March 1945: Across the Rhine

A gaping hole has been torn in the West Wall. First and Third Armies are poised to clear the Rhineland. Elements of Third Army take Trier, fifty miles from the Rhine. Cologne, Germany's third largest city, falls to First Army, which crosses the Rhine at Remagen. Rundstedt is relieved of command by Hitler.

Darling,

Another busy day with the army moving rapidly. We are really on the Rhine now and the disaster to the Germans in this area has been a major blow. We captured one small town today and took 3200 prisoners. The Germans seem to have had it and I don't think that they have the recuperative power to strike another major blow. For practical purposes the war is over and this is a large scale mopping up operation. That mopping up may take a little time but the end is certain now and it is only a question of how long it will take.

The weather has not been so good but we have not had rain and that's something. The days have been cold and gray. The spring that I was writing you about a week ago seems to have deserted us now but it isn't really winter anymore.

If you read the story about Patton's swimming the Sauer, it ain't so. Some GI in Baltimore has a great imagination. (9 March 1945, Luxembourg)

By the third week of March, all corps of Third Army have reached the Rhine. Third Army has inflicted 45,000 casualties and taken 68,000 prisoners in the Saar-Palatinate campaign. The surviving German forces in the Saar-Palatinate are in flight east of the river. On March 24, Patton crosses the Rhine.

Darling,

Got back home yesterday from Paris and ran into a lot of things mostly concerned with our crossing of the Rhine River. It has been a most difficult situation and I do feel that I can handle it even though I am very much under the gun at the moment.

Things can't be too bad because this morning at formation at headquarters I was presented by the General with another Bronze Star Medal. There aren't many people around with two and I am rather pleased. If things keep going badly for the rest of the day, they will probably make me give it back tomorrow and decide it was all a ghastly mistake.

When I got back yesterday there was a nice package from

the Jameses in Bristol probably intended as a Christmas present. I shall write and acknowledge as soon as I have time.

Spring has arrived with a vengeance. Luxembourg, Little
Switzerland, is magnificent with clear blue sky, bright sunlight and soft warm breezes. The fields are green and the
first buds are beginning to swell on the trees. Ironically, it is
fine weather for waging war. When I think back to the bitter
days of the Ardennes and the way that the men suffered in
the cold, I appreciate this weather more and more. It seemed
that the winter would never pass and that the war would
never end. Now spring has come and the end of the war is
near. (24 March 1945, Luxembourg)

March 25—All German resistance ends west of the Rhine.

Darling,

These are wild days with the army across the Rhine and
away as your papers have been telling you, I hope. I have
been working about twenty hours a day, and there isn't much
of a prospect of an immediate letup. This is a rat race now
and we are seeing the dying days of a nation and the death
struggles of the Nazis. The end of the month will certainly
see the end of the war. (25 March 1945, Luxembourg)

Darling,

Nighttime in Germany and a busy night it is for all of us.

Today I came into Germany from the city of Luxembourg
by way of Trier and I retraced some of the ground that I
passed over with the Tenth Armored a couple of weeks ago
when we first entered the town. The roads are simply choked
with convoys as the supply services struggle bitterly to keep
the stuff rolling up to the fast-moving front. It is a stupen-
dous task but it is thrilling to see the huge vehicles rolling in
an endless stream with everything that an army needs to
keep moving. The roads are bad and narrow but the columns
never seem to halt for long. The Germans stand in their
doorways grim faced and unsmiling but there must be a ter-

ror in their hearts when they see the never ending parade sweeping on apparently without break or end.

The first part of the trip is through the miles and miles of vineyards that lie on the sides of the steep hills that hem in the road that picks its way carefully through the valleys. Some of the hills are almost sheer cliffs and they have been terraced with native rocks long years ago so that the vines grow on the level parts of giant steps. Bill Drake and I wondered how people could work on such a slant for long hours every day. There is no sign of green in the vineyards, only the careful geometrical pattern of the sticks that support the vines running along the side of the hills as far as the eye can see. The people are working among them cutting and pruning, and the crop will be made this year and the soft pleasant Moselle will be ready to be drunk some two or three years from now as it has been for countless decades. Some of the fields in the valley are ominously smooth but a great part of them are plowed and the peasantry go on with the work of spring oblivious to this war as they have been to every war that has swept across this land. The empty fields are the bad omen for the future because they are a measure of the people who will starve to death this winter in Germany.

The roads are choked with refugees of every nationality. There are French, Russians, Czechs and some Germans and they all seem to be headed for France, expecting God knows what there. They are on foot carrying great sacks or towing a wide variety of ramshackle carts. Some are driving German army wagons pulled by gaunt German cavalry horses plodding steadily on to get anywhere away from Germany. There are men and women and children. Some of them seem unmistakably Slavic and we saw many who are Mongols from some of the eastern Soviets. They are happy and smiling and long suffering and patient all at the same time.

The Germans of the towns are a different story. The thing that I noticed in every one of the ruined towns is the almost complete absence of men. There are a few old gaffers and some small boys but there is absolutely nothing in between.

The stooping gaunt figures in the field are all women and the plow horses are followed by women in high black boots and short full skirts. The women are cleaning up the rubble in the streets and trying to patch together the remains of their homes. They watch us pass with dull faces and there is no exchange of greetings. Some of the people smile tentatively at us but I never saw any American soldier smile back. The children are wide eyed and curious but they don't move as we pass and there is no waving of hands. God knows what the children think. The only signs of normality in this shattered and stricken land are that the plows are tracing their pattern across some of the fields and that the children play as they do everywhere else in the world. I had the same sudden feeling of recognition when I saw a boy walking a fence that I had when I saw a little Indian in Karachi sailing a boat in the gutter in the rain.

The destruction has been great but not so bad as it is farther back and not really as bad as it is in Normandy. The country itself is some of the most beautiful anywhere with long sweeping valleys and great hills. Much of the land is wooded and there are forests of trees like the trees on the streets at home and lovely evergreen forests where the bushes seem to be bright and green even in late March. The land is littered with the debris of an army in full retreat. There are burnt out vehicles and tanks along the road and many in the woods looking foolish under the fronds of camouflage that protected them from nothing at all. The roads are broken and rutted where the tanks passed and the towns are shabby and dreary where they are not gutted and broken.

Here in our little town we are more than comfortable in spite of the fact that our billet has a shellhole in it. We sit in a small valley with high hills all around us and a narrow stream winding through the center of the village. The streets are narrow and twisting but the columns of trucks and tanks and vehicles roll along in a steadily flowing stream while the natives watch with impassive faces. We pass them on the street and our eyes don't meet as we just look past each other.

Tonight I had a crew of seven men from the local electric company in to fix the lights and they were down in a cave under the street working on them until after the six o'clock curfew. They were sure that they would be shot if they came out but finally elected one emissary to come to me to get a pass for all of them. I wrote it out for them and they went off greatly relieved. All Europeans have a tremendous faith in any piece of paper with a signature on it—except possibly a treaty.

This is only a quick picture and probably not a very complete one but it may help you a little to understand what war means here. The relationship will change as time goes on but the men are not very pleasant now and the Germans know it and give them a wide berth. There are already hints of the change. The standard GI comment on the subject of fraternization with the Germans is that all the ugly women are Germans but that all the pretty women are Czechs or Russians. Leave it to soldiers to find an out some way. (27 March 1945, Germany)

Darling,

The army is moving very fast and since we always move with the advance elements we have to move frequently, too. The Germans are terribly docile and obedient and we get fast service on anything we want mostly because they are scared to death. They all have guilty consciences and aren't convinced yet that we aren't going to shoot all of them. We ask a lot from them and we get it. Our men are unsmiling and grim and the Germans feel a certain terror in their hearts for that reason.

Today there is a steady drizzle but it is a spring rain not a cold winter rain. This is country that looks like the illustrations from Grimm's fairy tales. The town itself is stretched along a single road which lies at the bottom of a narrow valley which nowhere is more than five hundred yards wide. On both sides are steep rocky cliffs that shield the sun from us most of the day. Down the center of the valley is a narrow stream, very shallow and crystal clear, and we can hear the burbling of the river when we are in our sleeping bags at night. The town itself is not very startling with square drab buildings strung along the main street but the surroundings are magnificent.

On top of the point of one of the long ridges, tottering on the brink of one of the deep cliffs, is an ancient schloss that must have been built centuries ago. It is largely in ruins now but the walls still stand and the architecture, similar to the Norman in England, brings back pictures of the Teutonic knights and the Crusades, although it is probably not that old. The most dramatic thing here is the church which seems to cling right to the very face of the cliff some three hundred feet above the town. Actually the church consists of only one wall leaning on the face of the cliff and the church itself is a deep grotto out into the very face of the mountain. There is a narrow twisting trail that leads up to the entrance of it and we hope to get up there before we leave here. It is one of the unique things of the world.

The people of the town are largely women with a sprinkling of old men and children and the usual village idiot. They stand on the sidewalks and watch the convoys roll by, bumper to bumper, and we can see that sometimes they just shake their heads. This is an army the likes of which they have never seen before and they know that all is lost. Coming the other way are countless truckloads of prisoners jammed tight in the long column of vehicles. Some of the prisoners wave to the Germans and some of the children wave back but there is little sign of recognition on either side.

Last night for the first time I assembled all our troops and gave them a talk on non-fraternization. I spoke very briefly and very much to the point in my best military manner but have no idea how successful the pep talk will be. Soldiers always look completely blank on such occasions and you don't know whether they are thrilled, interested, bored or completely disapproving.

I am busy with a lot of things. General Patton's picture will be on the cover of *Time* for next week and Sid Olson of *Time* was here for the story to go with it. I took him over to see the General this morning. The General was as interesting as usual and Olson was duly impressed. We were chatting about one thing or another when Olson said, "The major said this morning that the Germans will probably quit when they have lost the last piece of high ground." The General looked at me with a somewhat surprised expression and said, "That's a very intelligent remark. Very intelligent—and quite true." He seemed surprised that such a statement could come from a PRO and then went on to enlarge on that thesis. A little later when he was talking about Alexander he said, "Now when Alexander crossed, not the Euphrates, that river in India—" I picked up on it and said, "The Indus." He peered at me again and said, "Yes, the Indus." I better shut my big mouth or he will decide that I am too smart and put me in an infantry platoon. It was an interesting session and I hope that the piece will be a good one.

The war is going to its inevitable end and we are seeing it close up. Why the Germans keep fighting, only God knows. Their men and their country are being steadily destroyed and it is incomprehensible that they can hope to stem the tide now.

We are watching the end of the Nazi era—thirteen years of power and five years of war are over. All of the great gains and the huge military machine are crumbling away to nothing. Two armored divisions alone today took 13,000 prisoners between them and the returns are not all in. The war is moving so fast and the complexion is changing so rapidly that there is more news and fresh news every minute. The tempo at a press camp is always fairly fast but the atmosphere now is almost like election night. It is a dizzy pace to maintain. These are great moments and we are all a little thrilled that we are here to see it. An era is ending but God help the era that is beginning. (29 March 1945, Germany)

As the month ends, the Allies have closed to the Rhine from Arnhem in the north to the Swiss border. American field forces number 1.6 million; the overall European theater of operations

(ETO) strength is 3 million. A shattered German army is on its last legs.

April 1945: Overrunning Germany

American forces prepare for the final offensive across the Rhine, a drive to the Elbe, destruction of the last-ditch German National Redoubt rumored to be under construction in the Alps, and a linkup with the Russians. Hitler issues a proclamation calling on Germans to become "werewolves" and prey on Allied troops, Jews, and collaborators.

Darling,

Easter is a gala day in this small town and the Krauts were out in their finery, which is not bad, and which includes silk or nylon stockings for everyone. They apparently all went to church and so did I.

This morning I went over to see the General but got very short shrift because he was going to church. I was amazed to learn that he is a Catholic and was headed for Father O'Leary's mass taking along the Chief of Staff and his aides. After mass I went back and introduced Ernest Lindley to him and the General was his usual brilliant self. Ernie had the common American desire to meet General Patton. They all want to see Patton but I have to sort them out carefully and only bother him with the cream of the crop. The General is always interesting and all of them get something from him that they want.

At 1630 a whole flock of us went off to late Easter mass. The mass was in an enlisted men's mess hall not too far away and was well attended. The chaplain was a big, tough looking guy, but he spoke briefly and gave an excellent sermon. They followed the mass with a brief prayer for the dead and there is something moving about the manner in which the men here answer the responses. Their voices are low with a deep masculine rumble but the responses are given slowly and with great sincerity. These men have a great respect for death even though they have seen a lot of it.

Our trucks and tanks roll by endlessly and the Krauts stand goggle eyed at the show. They were in their Sunday best today but there was no hiding the consternation on their faces. They'll know better than to fool with us again. I suppose that some of them are counting the tanks and then running up to the attic to tap out the number of them on their little radios. I don't know what good that information will do Jerry now. We are still on the move and Patton is happy and content. (1 April 1945, Easter Sunday night, Germany)

Darling,

A drizzly spring day with a little more chill in the air than there should be. The rain is gentle but soaks the ground thoroughly and is probably good for the farmers. At the moment I am much more concerned with the progress of our armor than I am with the fate of German farmers.

We are still very optimistic but there is a general feeling that the war will not have a definite ending but that it will just peter out. It may be that we shall never be able to say that the war ended at any given time on any particular day. There are little pockets of Germans holding out here and there, and there probably will be after the main body of the German army is destroyed. They are unable now to put up any effective resistance and our troops seem to be able to move in any direction at will. The last reports have us 160 miles from Berlin and that distance will be cut down by nightfall. Everyone wonders whether we shall be going to Berlin but that is in the high level planning department and we don't know. As second choice we should like to link up with the Russians somewhere or other. That would be a great story, too.

I should like to see it end right away and let us sweep over the rest of Germany without a struggle. Most of it has been beaten up anyway. Hitler's great gift to us are the autobahns which are like good two lane Jersey roads. They were fine for moving his army but they are just as fine for moving ours. The tanks get on them and really roll.

Although there is no reason to suppose that I shall be released from the army when this European show is over, my
thoughts are turning more and more to the days after the
war. I do think that I shall be able to enhance my prospects
by the fact that I have been General Patton's PRO. All of our
visitors from the States say that he is the biggest name there
and that his stature is growing in the public mind every day.
I can't honestly claim that I did it but I was here while it was
being done. I do think that anyone who knows anything
about public relations will feel that a good job has been
done and that should be some asset to me. God knows we
won't have any cash assets. At my rank I don't even get mus-
tering out pay to get started with. I don't know that I am terribly anxious to get back into the radio–advertising–public
relations–show business atmosphere but I shall probably be
forced to, just because it is the only thing I know.

The war hasn't been just a long gap in my life filled in with
nothing. This experience has been very valuable and I shall
probably get a lot more before I get out of this thing.

I am really torn. I miss you and Rory so much and want to
be with you so much that I should be happy if the army just
decided that it doesn't need me anymore. On the other
hand I don't want to look as though I would quit in the middle and I don't want to do any sort of wangle to get myself
out. About all that I can do is let nature take its course and
hope that I shall be lucky. I have been before.

I hope that you have a lovely spring and that you can feel
that spring is bringing the end of war and winter. I have so
many ideas and thoughts and dreams for after the war with
you that I should like to come home and get them started. In
spite of many things, we always had a good life and a full one
and I have no desire to undo any of that. I just feel that separation will make home and our being together seem so much
finer that we shall be wonderfully happy. Know that I love
you always. (2 April 1945, Germany)

Darling,
Tuesday (3 April) was a lovely day, sunny but chilly, and

the country was beautiful. All this section of Germany on both sides of the Rhine and in the valleys of the Nahe and the Moselle is some of the most beautiful country in the world. Why Hitler should be so covetous of other people's land, I just can't imagine. The Nahe River would be little more than a creek at home, but it must be an old river and the hills that contain it are quite steep. The valley is narrow but it widens out and the hills begin to flatten out as you get nearer to the Rhine from the west.

We passed through Bad Kreuznach, one of the minor spas of Germany, and it is badly beaten up although not razed like so many German cities. The roads were jammed with traffic rolling to the front and we skirted in and out of it as we went. There are roadblocks that have been torn down and huge quantities of German equipment litter the roadsides and are scattered in the fields. There is every indication here of the rapidity of the German retreat. In every town the men are patiently tearing down the roadblocks, apparently at the direction of someone, and the women are in the fields with shovels patiently filling in slit trenches and foxholes and gun positions so that the land can be plowed. The war has swept through leaving its wake of destruction but the peasants are patiently building again.

We finally came to Mainz and the Rhine River which lies in one of the loveliest valleys in the world. Mainz is a scene of absolute desolation with scarcely a stone on a stone. The main roads have been cleared of rubble by the dozers making paths wide enough for the trucks to get through. We tried to take a shortcut to pass a column but the streets are so choked with rubble that they are impassable. Everything— homes, stores, great buildings, the opera house, churches, museums—all are gone. There seem to be only a few hundred people in the town and they are in queues for either bread or water. The desolation is incredible and it is punctuated by the fallen spans of the bridges across the Rhine. We made our way along the west bank and then crossed the Rhine on the longest tactical bridge in the world—1875 feet of pontoon bridge floating in the swift-running water and carrying the heaviest vehicles in an endless stream. On the far shore we stopped to perform the standard American soldier's ritual when he first comes to the Rhine.

On the far shore we made our way along a fine road that parallels the river headed in the direction of Frankfurt upstream from Mainz. The most fantastic sight in the world is seen along the roads, the refugees of every nation making their way somewhere. These are "displaced persons" and they are slowly rounding them up but thousands are making their way on foot and in the craziest kinds of transportation. There are few lone travelers and they seem to split themselves readily into national groups varying from four or five to twenty or thirty. They cry at us along the road, "Me Russhky," "Me Pookki" and so on. Many of them are French soldiers wearing the uniform that they must have treasured for many years in prison camps and at forced labor. Some fortunate few have a battered truck and some have farm wagons or army wagons drawn by horses. They are the exception though because most of them are on foot pulling or pushing everything under the sun. Many have high piled bicycles which two or three men push along awkwardly trying to keep it balanced. There are all sorts of two-wheeled carts being pushed or pulled or both. There are baby carriages and push carts and wheelbarrows by the hundreds, all heavily laden. There are even big military wagons heavily laden and towed by ten or fifteen men or women leaning into heavy ropes and chains like land borne Volga boatmen. They are apparently prepared to walk hundreds of miles and the way is long because the MPs try to keep them off the main roads so that military traffic can pass. Most of the bundles seem to contain food but that can't last more than a few days. What happens then, I don't know. It is perhaps the most terrible problem in Europe but even the heroic efforts that are being made will never be able to cope with it. They will starve by the hundreds of thousands before next year's harvest. I don't want to be here to see it. I don't want to have to watch children, even German children, with bloated bellies and twisted bones.

We finally came to Frankfurt and another scene of incredible desolation. This is second only to Cologne of the Rhineland cities but it is only a hollow shell. It has been beaten and burned to the ground and is a sight that is absolutely indescribable. It is almost impossible to believe that so huge a city could be so completely gutted. There are people here but only a handful compared with its pre-war population. It was the biggest Jewish city in Germany and there are now only 500 Jews there. The rest are mostly dead. We turned north out of Frankfurt along the great eight lane autobahn headed for one of the hundreds of spas with which Germany is dotted. They must try to cleanse their souls with mineral baths. Along the road is a strange thing. The Germans blew a bridge but didn't do their usual good job of demolition. They just cracked the bridge so that the center collapsed forming a sort of V with the sides at about a forty-five degree angle. We haven't bothered to repair it. Our vehicles, even the biggest ones, slide down one leg of the V and then pull right up the other side. No vehicles in the world except American military transport could do it. We left the destroyed area behind and finally came to our new spot.

We are in a small town, completely untouched by the war. The camp settled down quickly amid great enthusiasm but we had the town all to ourselves with no town mayor and no military government, so James became Judge Bean the Law West of the Pecos. I had a lot of problems—and a lot of fun.

Our immediate neighbors are a German military hospital filled with German wounded and staffed by nurses and medics running around in Wehrmacht uniforms and blouses with Red Crosses on their arms. The first thing I did was order them off the street, and they got off fast. We told the burgermeister our requirements in personnel and he produced them quickly. The owner of the Hotel showed me a gold cigarette lighter given to him by Edward VIII but that cut no ice with me and he went out, too. A group of about sixty Poles had been working in a place here and the manager had thrown them out and kept all their food. I got a

jeep, took one of the Poles along, found the manager and
made him whack up the food. The people here have no
food, but until Civil Affairs comes along there is nothing I
can do about that. Our cellar was full of food that belonged
to the hospital and I sent a sergeant to bring the medic in
and told him to get the food out right away and get it into
the hospital. I told him that if one ounce was diverted from
the wounded soldiers, he would be arrested. (I don't know by
whom. I don't want him.) A woman came and said that her
husband, a soldier in the SS, had just come home bringing
another woman with him and had ordered her out of the
house. I told her to tell the husband to get out of the house
in two hours. She was very pleased with that decision and
went off to tell him. I haven't heard from her since. Two
women came to say that they lived four kilometers away but
couldn't go home because of the "Don't Move" order. They
were told to go home and tell anyone that stopped them that
I said it was all right. They seemed pleased and took off. I
don't know what would have happened if they had been
stopped. A cavalry outfit moved in one night and I tried to
give the commander the town but he wouldn't take it on a
bet. Fortunately another outfit with a colonel in command
has moved in today and I told him that he is the boss of the
town and I have been referring everyone to him. He'll find
out. (5 April 1945, Germany)

*In early April, Patton advances toward Ohrdruf and discovers
the death camp there. The following day, XII Corps discovers the
German gold reserve in a salt mine at Merkers.*

Darling,
    We have our regular meeting this afternoon but I am not
sure that General Patton will be here. I hope so because the
show is so much better when he is the star. I met General
Bradley the other day and he spoke to me quite cordially. I
had a long chat with his aide, Lew Bridge. I am still very fond
of General Bradley although my first loyalty is to General Pat-

ton. We hear rumors that MacArthur has been made the Supreme Commander in the Pacific. I don't know how that will affect General Patton's future plans but I do think that he wants very much to fight the Japs. (6 April 1945, Germany)

On April 11, XX Corps advances into Weimar and overruns the extermination camp at Buchenwald. On April 12, Franklin Delano Roosevelt dies and is succeeded by Harry Truman.

Darling,

My new home is in a very nice German town that is not too badly shot up. We are in the general area of the Hessian Hills and the country here is beautiful as is all of Germany that I have seen so far. The Germans are silent and grim faced and we have no contact with them.

The weather is magnificent and spring has really come to central Germany. The hills and fields are green now and the orchids are in full bloom. It is very warm, the sun is pleasant and the skies are a brilliant blue. We seem to lie on the main air route from somewhere to somewhere and the skies are full of our planes all day long. Our men simply can't get over the beauty of Germany. Someone is always asking why the Germans want any other country when they have such a beautiful one of their own. The people are well dressed and well fed and their homes are full of the loot of every country in Europe. There is no transport, of course, but here in the country there is food and they all have well-stocked larders.

We are just beginning to understand the German slave system. I don't know how many nationals of other countries were brought to Germany but the figure is more than several million. Their condition here varied as did that of our own slaves in the South except that here they were not considered to have great value, more were always available, and there was no great effort to take care of them. When they became sick or pregnant or old they were just exterminated ruthlessly and new slaves were brought in. We are overrunning more

and more concentration camps and the sights there are beyond comprehension. You have been reading about them, I
know, and the truth is worse than the stories. The general
story though is of whips and filthy quarters and bad food until they became too ill to work and were exterminated and
their bodies cremated. This by the hundreds of thousands.
The Germans are going to have to do their own work again
and they don't like it very much. (12 April 1945, Germany)

*In mid-April, Third Army is redirected southeast down the val-
ley of the Danube River into Austria and Czechoslovakia for
linkup with the Russians. To the north, 325,000 German troops
encircled in the Ruhr surrender.*

Darling,
    We have yet to meet our first Nazi. All the Germans claim
that they were not in the party and that they hated Hitler.
The Germans are changing though. For a while they were
sure that we were going to butcher all of them and they went
around in fear and trembling. Now that they know they are
going to live, they are looking a little bit more cocky and go
about their affairs with a little bit less of a worried look. The
next step, I suppose, will be when they start to complain
about the service. One man told one of our officers the other
day that the Americans must get the slave workers out of Germany as soon as possible because they are a menace.
    You have probably read about Buchenwald and Ohrdruf
and how the Germans treated those people. Now they are
afraid of reprisal. The stories are so horrible and revolting
that the whole thing can't be told, but the correspondents
have tried to tell as much as they figure the reading public's
stomachs can stand. Most of us have strong stomachs now
and death and blood don't mean much but those places are
incredibly revolting. We are just afraid that after the war the
people at home will forget.
    Bill Drake and I have been kicking around post-war plan-
ning and getting nowhere at all. We are restless and hope

that big things will happen to us when this is all over but we are so cut off from normal contacts that we don't have much to base any plans on. The rest of the world seems too far away and too utterly different from anything here for us to be able to approach the problem with any feeling of reality.

It is now after nine o'clock and has just gotten dark. About three quarters of an hour ago Bill Drake and I went around the hills that enclose the valley. The country is lovely in the dusk with a crescent moon just coming up. We stopped by an ack-ack battery and chatted and watched while they fired a few rounds to settle the guns. We passed one little bivouac in a field and stopped by the hedge to listen to the sweet plaintive music of an accordion. It was a peaceful little interlude because we could see only the silhouette of the men sitting around the player. We came back over the quiet roads intercepted a couple of times by the shadowy figures of the guards at the bridges and at the key points. They spoke softly, too, because it is that kind of a night. It looks so lovely and peaceful except for the armed guards and the RAF [Royal Air Force] passing over and the TDs with their bristling guns placed near the crossroads. The war is hushed and still tonight.

Keep loving me, darling. Good night. (17 April 1945, Germany)

Darling,

Good news for a change—two pieces of it which I shall give you in the order of their importance.

Yesterday I was having a big fight with the administrative guy back at [Twelfth Army] Group. In the course of the conversation he told me that my transfer had been approved. I was too busy yelling at him to pay any attention to that remark but I began to wonder about it after I had hung up. I finally called Colonel Redding and got the whole story. As you know I have been down here on DS [detached service] from Group and could always be recalled there. Yesterday our Chief of Staff here, General Gay, called the G-1 at Group and told him he wanted me to be transferred to Third Army immediately. He stated that he had a lieutenant colonelcy he wanted to promote me into. No one in this headquarters has said a word to me and it is probably supposed to come as a surprise. In view of the fact that I was about to get fired less than two weeks ago[4] this certainly represents a complete change of heart.

Late last night I got a message from the AP in New York saying that President Truman had nominated General Patton to be a four star general. I called headquarters and told them and they were all quite thrilled about it. The word spread all over very quickly and we were glad to be heralds of joy. This morning I went over to the staff briefing and was asked whether public opinion had forced them to promote the General. I stated, naturally and promptly, that there was no question about it. What the hell, we're the contact with public opinion in this headquarters and we might as well claim everything including Maine and Vermont. My own opinion is that public clamor did force the promotion of the General. Anahooo, we are glad that the General has been promoted and we like to think that we played some part in it.

Much later now

I was over to headquarters this afternoon and Colonel Harkins, the Deputy Chief of Staff, greeted me by telling me that I had been transferred to Third Army. He said that General Gay had called Group and told them they should promote me or transfer me here so that he could promote me. I told him that I thought they had asked for the transfer so that they would have court martial jurisdiction, but he just laughed at that.

The big junketeers are here, Lowell Thomas, John W. Vandercook, Howard Barnes, and a couple of others that you probably never heard of. I made a date to take them to see the General tomorrow morning. They visited Buchenwald today and found it so bad that they only stayed about three minutes and got right out again. I'll admit that it is the most horrible spectacle ever seen by men but they are supposed to be reporters. (18 April 1945, Germany)

On April 20, XX Corps attacks toward the Danube in the area of Regensburg. Hitler celebrates his fifty-sixth birthday in the bunker at the Reich Chancellery in Berlin.

Darling,

If there is an ugly part of Germany it is probably in the coastal plains of the north and we haven't seen that. The Moselle and Rhine Valleys, the Saar, Saxony, Hesse and Thuringia are all semi-mountainous, very green and with small clear streams in almost every valley. It could be lovely except that in some of those woods are places like Ohrdruf and Buchenwald to mar all the beauty of it.

I have some pictures of those places that I have made but I hesitate to send them to you because they are the most horrible things I have ever seen. I am very anxious to have them after the war so that I can show them to people who try to tell us that the Germans really aren't bad people at all. I'd show them to the first person that says a good word for the Germans.

I think that we are all sharing the feeling that the war is really over and that this is just a mopping up operation. There was a time when we were flushed with a new victory or hot in some new pursuit but those days are past. We feel that we can go anywhere we please and that there will just be a slow process of tracking each little pool of soldiers and killing them or using them to swell the prisoner total still more. The excitement is gone because the uncertainty is gone. The men feel that they are hanging between a difficult past and a dreary future. Everyone seems to have accepted the fact that there are only two alternatives—the Army of Occupation or CBI [China-Burma-India theater]. There is no one optimistic enough to think that he will get home.

Much later

Just past midnight and I am about to turn in. We had a press conference with the General today and he was his usual brilliant self. He talked very well and was gay and amusing. Someone asked him whether there was any truth to the rumor that our patrols had met the Russians east of Dresden.

"Not unless they're deserters," he told them. Their enthusiasm for him is unabated.

Tonight I got into one of the usual press camp bull sessions swapping experiences and lies until just a little while ago. They are always interesting but never produce anything of educative value. Ernie Pyle's death reminded Jack Hansen and me that we both have Zippo lighters which Ernie gave us. Ernie just became an unsuccessful fugitive from the law of averages.[5] (20 April 1945, Germany)

On April 23, Himmler tries unsuccessfully to surrender the German armies to the western Allies during a conference with Count Bernadotte of the Swedish Red Cross in Lubeck. Hitler arrests number-two Nazi, Goering, for treason and personally takes over the defense of Berlin.

Darling,

Our problems seem to run in cycles and some of them are difficult. The whole business is a constant effort to strike a balance between military security and the giving of full information to everyone who is interested. We have always been sticklers for accuracy and have never had to take anything back yet. The war is so short that I hope to avoid it now. Our problem comes when some correspondent wants to stretch the truth a little because it will make a better story and we have to hold him back against his bitter protests.

America may have been the melting pot of the world but Germany is now. There is every nationality here. The major difference is that there would never have been assimilation because of the slave status of the foreigners.

The feeling about Germany and the Germans is a peculiar thing and the people seem to fall into two categories. The first are those who just plain hate all of them and would rather shoot them than argue about it. I am afraid that I belong to that class because it requires too complicated a mental process for me to attempt to sort them out and I lump them together into collective loathing. The main topic of conversation today is the Nazi atrocities which we run across every day and they are the subject of some difference of opinion. Many people feel that most of the Germans didn't know what was going on in the camps but I feel that they couldn't have been ignorant of it.

One officer said that you could find enough so-and-sos in the United States to run such places and to carry out the same atrocities. The big answer is, though, that such things could never be the policy of the men in our government. Most of these murders were not arbitrary or capricious things but were carried out in accordance with a long range and deliberate plan. There was always a cold and calculated cruelty in the starvation and the beatings and the murders. It is an incredible story and the atrocities become greater and greater as time goes on. Nothing that you read about any of the places can be an exaggeration. (24 April 1945, Germany)

On April 25, First Army and the Russians link up at the Elbe. XX Corps prepares for an assault crossing of the Danube into Austria.

Darling,

It was a beautiful day with bright sunshine. I approached Nuremberg from the north and it is an incredible sight. The road coming in is fine and flat through neat looking pine forests and broad open fields. We came into a little suburb and there the destruction started. Even these little homes are scarred and smashed and burnt and damaged, and the people are either digging in the rubble or trying to put on roofs or put back doors and windows. We finally came into the city itself and the scene of the greatest desolation that I have ever seen.

Nuremberg was one of the show places of Europe and one of the great tourist meccas before the war. It was a medieval city with a great wall surrounding it dominated by huge round towers and broken by lovely arched gateways that led into the city. This was the ancient city of three- and four-story

stone buildings with the spires of public buildings and the
great cathedral standing over all of it. Outside the walls surrounding the old city stands the new one that has been built
since the last war. There are fine blocks of flats built in the
late twenties for the workers and the huge buildings that the
Nazis built in the thirties for their principal Nazi city. The
buildings are fine and modern with the stylized modern art
that marks all the Nazi architecture. This is really an archeo-
logical report because I have had to piece this together from
the ruins that are the city now. There were a half million people here before the war.

Now the whole city is one vast rubble heap that appears to
be the result of some cataclysm that happened yesterday. The
rubble is all lying there and no one has made an effort to
touch it. There are other cities that are probably as bad but
there the ruins have aged a little and all of these look as
though they were the result of last night's bombing. We
drove down the main through street with the walls of the old
city on our left. On our right was the wreckage of the modern buildings that Hitler had built for the party—the huge
post office, the great railroad station, the blocks on blocks of
party office buildings, modern cinemas, hotels. Every one
smashed to bits. On our left we could see the gaunt figures of
chimneys, the skeleton spire of the cathedral, and an occasional tottering wall. Through the gates and the holes that
the guns had torn in the walls we could see endless vistas of
destruction.

We went through the town to the south and out to the
great stadium where Hitler had held his rallies on Party Day
and which we have seen so often in the newsreels. On the
way I passed a gushing fireplug that had apparently been
flowing for days and had already formed a small lake—but in
the town there is no water. We drove into the stadium and
stopped. The place is just about square and is just a huge
grass-covered field. Along the eastern end, about five hundred feet long, is a very simple structure which consists of
about thirty steps surmounted by huge columns all of white

stone. In the center is a stone platform fronted by a white stone podium from which the speeches were made. Those are the steps on which the flags were massed by the thousands so that the searchlights could play on them to whip up the frenzy. At each end of this facade are two pylons on which the great flaming fire burned at the nighttime ceremonies.

I climbed up and stood out on Hitler's podium to look over the place. Down at my feet were a couple of truck companies stopped for lunch and they munched their K rations quite unimpressed with their surroundings. At the far end is a huge entrance through which Hitler used to make his entrance and make the long march down the field through his massed troops. The sides are grassy banks that have been terraced to form rows of seats, and the entire field is surrounded with great square pylons at intervals of about 75 feet. On top of each pylon are tall poles surmounted by the swastika encircled by a laurel wreath. We have seen the picture so often that I could easily visualize the stiff ranks of men and the flags and the band and the carefully disciplined "Sieg Heils" and the speeches and the magnificent show that it must have been. The Nazis were on top then and they must have had a great thrill of Teutonic happiness during those happy days of the thirties.

We left, passing by the walls of the great new stadium that will probably never be finished. The walls are surrounded with the steel scaffolding of the builders of another monument to Nazi invincibility. I finally came back through the town again and swung through one of the holes in the wall into the old town. The Germans looked at us with complete indifference and some even smiled as they got out of the way of our jeep picking its way through the piles of rubble.

The thing is hard to describe. It is as though all of Philadelphia from Erie Avenue to Market Street, between the rivers, had been knocked down and dumped into the streets. Only gigantic machinery and thousands of men could cart the rubble of huge stones and whole sides of buildings away.

In some of the narrow streets we saw people beginning to put together one-room shacks of scrap lumber in front of where their homes used to be. Everywhere people are carrying buckets for water that comes from I don't know where. These are no peasants. This was a proud and wealthy city and it has had war in its most terrible form.

I am filled up with this awful sight. Thank God we live in America. (25 April 1945, Germany)

Darling,

Two letters from you today that contain a further account of the death of the President. We all feel some concern about the [Potsdam] conference with the President now out of the picture but we do feel that the work there may be largely a staff job and that the principal decisions will have been made long since. The big job that Mr. Truman has will be to sell the decisions of the conference and I hope that he will be able to do that. He seems to have started well and it may be that he will prove himself big enough for the job. He is President now. He can have no further ambitions or aspirations and he can be objective and filled only with concern for the good of the country and its future.

As far as I am concerned Rory can miss his generation's war. I hope that we can be proud of our son forever onward but I would like to have a look at him so that I shall know what I am being proud of.

The war still goes apace but it doesn't have much meaning anymore. We are sort of carrying on by the numbers and are going deeper into Bavaria and are almost to the Austrian border. There is little resistance, but the towns that want to argue have a sad fate. Our men are in no mood to stand any nonsense. They call on them to surrender and then lay it on if they don't. We aren't taking a flock of casualties in order to clean out a town house by house. If they refuse to quit we just put the fighter bombers and the tanks and the TDs on them and knock them down and the white phosphorous shells burn up what's left. I think that one of these minutes some

German is going to stand up and tell everyone to quit. You have probably heard a great deal about the National Redoubt but we feel that it is malarkey and that we shall blitz that, too. Patton is out to get them all and he will.

Tonight after dinner Bill Drake and I went for a walk through the town and it is an eerie experience. We didn't get started until almost dusk and we walked in slow step down the deserted streets. There is a strict curfew for civilians and most of the traffic seems to stop in the evening. We saw an occasional vehicle, a jeep or a greyhound, of the cavalry on their ceaseless patrols. Out of the windows of some of the houses there were people hanging and they follow our progress with hostile eyes. It is a strange thing to walk through a fair-sized town and see only one lone MP directing what little traffic there is at the main crossroad. In one window we saw a youngster standing with his mother holding him and he waved at us as we passed. In another was a fine Irish setter and we stopped to talk to him. He was quite glad to see us and made no distinctions because of ideology. His mistress sat back in the room and seemed anxious to snatch him away but they are all frightened and feel that we might shoot them.

It was lovely in the dusk and there was a full moon rising. The trees are in blossom and there are spring flowers in some of the gardens but mostly there is the turned earth that will be green in another two weeks. In the towns every little patch of dirt has been cultivated because the people know that hunger will stalk them and they shall try to beat every last ounce of food out of the earth. It was a lovely walk in spite of the sinister atmosphere that hung over all of it. After all, this is the heart of Nazism and we have no friends here in spite of their protestations.

I came back and met two British officers who had been brought back by one of the correspondents. They had both been captured in Crete five years ago and were liberated only today. They are as thin as rails and pale as ghosts but are very much the quiet, sorry-to-be-of-bother British officer. They had dinner with us and ate very little but got violently ill on the food. They are just not used to it and their stomachs can't handle it. The Germans are bastards and they told just a couple of little stories to prove it.

One American is going to have a wonderful time tomorrow. He bailed out of a plane over Augsburg and landed in the center of the town. The chief of police stripped him naked and then booted him into unconsciousness in the main street. He was liberated today and the infantry has agreed to take him into the town tomorrow and find the chief of police for him. He is going on a special patrol and will probably beat the guy to death. At least one man will get personal revenge on one of his persecutors. (26 April 1945, Germany)

Dear Aunt Kate and Uncle Tom,

I have had adequate opportunity to see so much of the country that the war is fought over, and the destruction is everywhere. It will take the Germans generations to rebuild the place, if they ever can rebuild it at all.

General Patton is our great hero here at Third Army and we are all very proud to be serving with him. I see him every day and have some business with him three or four times a week so I feel that I have gotten to know him rather well. He is always very pleasant and easy to work for so that I enjoy all of my contacts with him. He is a great scholar and his conversation is always larded with classical allusions and historical analogies. He has a wry sense of humor too and he manages to put a sly little twist to so many things that he says.

I hope that you have had an occasion to look in on my son and that you approve of his conduct. You have so many nieces and nephews on all sides of the families that you probably find it impossible to remember which child belongs to whom. I am beginning to get a little confused myself. They will all have changed so much by the time I see them again. (30 April 1945, Germany)

During the last week of the month, the Allies demand the unconditional surrender of the German armies on all fronts, XII Corps rolls to the Czech border, XX Corps gains the surrender of Regensburg, Mussolini is captured by Italian partisans and executed, and Hitler orders the continuation of the war from the illusory "alpine fortress." A day later (April 30), he commits suicide.

May 1945: The End of the Thousand-Year Reich

Effective resistance in Germany is melting away. Piecemeal surrenders are commonplace. The new head of the Third Reich, Admiral Doenitz, is exploring the possibility of overall surrender while trying to buy time so troops facing the Russians in the East can flee west and surrender to the western Allies. Third Army commences final operations in Austria and Czechoslovakia near the German frontier. XX Corps crosses the Austrian frontier at the Inn River near Braunau, Hitler's birthplace. XII Corps moves into Czechoslovakia and takes Pilsen, then advances down the Danube to its final objective, Linz, which surrenders. Berlin falls to the Red Army.

On May 7 (D+335), Germany surrenders unconditionally on all fronts effective 0001 on May 9. Eisenhower closes out the Thousand-Year Reich: "The mission of this Allied force was fulfilled at 0241 local time, May 7, 1945."

Darling,

This is the sort of special letter that I shall carry over for two or three days because it is the story of the end of the war. It may be of interest with some of the others. I think that after the war we might edit the letters and have them printed and bound for Rory to read when he is old enough.

The end of the war has been visible to all of us for days but there was no knowing of the date and the hour. Yesterday the most immediate signs became more apparent. The German

Eleventh Panzer Division surrendered to our 90th Division
and they are the best looking German troops that we have
seen and they still had some tanks and self propelled guns.
Yesterday also negotiations were continuing with the White
Russians and the Hungarians in Czechoslovakia. Army Group
G had surrendered the day before and we thought it might
include the troops facing us but it didn't. It included only
the troops in front of the Seventh Army and it meant that the
Third was to carry on.

It is ironic that the Third Army, which, except for the period of the Ardennes battle, has always been the smallest
army, became quite suddenly the largest. We had four Corps
and eighteen divisions to fight the estimated 400,000 to
500,000 Germans in front of us. Of this number, it was estimated that about 125,000 were combat effective. We had
added a whole Corps, the Vth, and had picked up the 9th
and 16th Armored Divisions.

The White Russians, who numbered about 100,000 plus
their wives and children, had been fighting primarily against
the Russian armies but wanted to quit now. They were willing
to surrender but they wanted to make the proviso that they
would not be turned over to the Russians. We were in no
state of mind to make any provisos and they were told again
that they would have to surrender unconditionally or be destroyed.

The Hungarians had been recruited by the Germans and
some of them had fought fairly well on the eastern front.
They also had their wives and families with them in the field.
They wanted to surrender on condition that they not be returned to Hungary which is now under Russian control.
There were about 125,000 of them. They were given the
same answer and individual units began to surrender in large
numbers.

Yesterday we teed off into Czechoslovakia and moved very
fast, with the 16th Armored taking Pilsen yesterday morning.
During the afternoon we listened to the Prague radio calling
for the Allies to come to their rescue and saying that they

could hold against the SS there. I felt bad because I knew that our 4th Armored had a phase line that would stop them short of Prague. That was tough on the Czechs. The Prague uprising was a little premature and was probably started by the BBC's announcing that we were in Pilsen two days before we had even crossed the Czech frontier.

This morning I had suspicions that something might be breaking. A friend in one of the top jobs told me the war was over. I went to the staff briefing attended by the Under Secretary of War as well as the General and the briefing went off with no mention of surrender at all. That was a bit of a blow.

I went over to the Chief of Staff's office and I found out that early this morning higher headquarters had called and said that the Germans had surrendered completely and that the surrender would be effective at 0001 on 9 May. The "Cease Fire and Stand Fast" order had been given to Third Army troops at 0800 this morning. No announcement could be made until it was first released by the governments in Washington, London and Moscow.

While I was in the Chief's office General Blakeley, CG [commanding general] of the 4th Infantry Division, came in. He is a fine looking soldier and a very pleasant person. He said, "This is very embarrassing. Here we are with a big army and no war. I suspect in the next couple of months we will wish that we were back in a nice clean fight." On that note, I left.

I came back to the press camp and made the announcement as simply as I could. There was no cheering and only the feeling of a bit of a letdown everywhere. I told them all I knew, told them that I didn't know the answers to most of their questions, and then gave them the operational story for yesterday. They all wrote that halfheartedly and then began to write the hold for releases on the surrender. The radio men are out getting reactions. I called Group for some guidance and they didn't even know it yet. That's the situation at roughly 1400. More later.

About two o'clock I was listening to the radio coming back from the States and I heard the announcement of the surrender giving fairly complete details and crediting the whole story to AP. Since AP got the only credit, I knew that only they had it out. I heard the same thing on three or four stations giving AP credit and I knew that trouble had begun. At 1400 our time, the German radio announced the surrender. I called higher headquarters and tried to get a release of the story on the basis of prior release but they said absolutely not. I told the correspondents that AP had the story out some way but that there was nothing we could do but wait for the official announcement.

The men began to write a lot of stories about GI reaction and that sort of thing and pointed out that the Third Army was the last army engaged and the copy just piled up. About six o'clock I was informed that SHAEF had ruled that no AP correspondent in Europe could file any copy at all. I knew the ruling couldn't stand up when AP got to the White House and other places. It was a stupid ruling anyway because there are too many papers who subscribe only to AP and their readers couldn't be deprived of the news because someone had done wrong. I turned out to be right because just before midnight I was informed that the ruling was rescinded and that only Ed Kennedy was barred. I knew then that he had broken the embargo.

We had a briefing in the evening with the reports of the day's activity but no one was really interested. (7 May 1945, Germany)

On May 8 (V-E Day), Third Army is halted at Pilsen with orders not to advance to the relief of partisans in Prague. Patton holds his final press conference of the war. In an address to the German people, Doenitz declares that the foundation on which the Reich was built—unity of state and party—no longer exists; all power in Germany has passed to the Allies.

Darling,

I was awakened by the telephone at 0745. It was the General's aide, Charlie Codman, to tell me that [*New York Times* correspondent] Martha Gellhorn, who is Hemingway's wife, had called the General the night before at 2330 to announce that she wished to spend the night at the General's house but was politely turned down. I was asked to locate her, take her in hand and tell her that no correspondent can see the General without clearing through me. I never did locate Martha so that turned out to be no problem.

I went over to briefing and it was a rather sad affair. It followed the normal formula but there was not much to say. After the briefing was over, the General stood up and spoke briefly to the staff. He said in essence, "This is our last briefing in Europe. The war is over for us here. I think that I have had to do less work than any army commander in history just because each one of you on the staff has performed so well. I thank you very much and I congratulate you on what you have accomplished." He put on his helmet and walked out alone and we all stood stiffly at attention and were for a moment very proud.

I went over to his office after the briefing and asked the General if he would see the press and he agreed and set 1130 as the hour. I went in to see the Chief and he was most cordial. After some chitchat he agreed to put through Bill Drake's promotion.

I called the camp and told them to deliver the correspondents at 1130 and then sat to listen to the radio and the announcements that the prime minister would speak at 1500 and the king at 2100. I went back over to the war room for the General's last meeting with the correspondents. He was in very good humor, very witty and very good and they all enjoyed their last meeting with him. He had little to add to what I had already told them but they always enjoy listening to him. After that was over, we made the class picture with the General on the steps and he was very patient. I also got him to pose for a picture with the officers of the section and I shall send you a print.

We came back to camp and some of the correspondents left on the afternoon plane for Paris. We listened to the

prime minister at 1500 and the minute that he announced
the surrender I told them to start rolling out the thousands
of words of copy that we had already punched. That was the
end. Since then we have just put in time. There is no jubila-
tion, no celebration. The men's reaction is just "So what."
    I can only wonder what I shall get up for tomorrow.
(8 May 1945, Germany)

*May 9—The end of the war in Europe for the 3 million Ameri-
cans under Eisenhower's command.*

Darling,
    There is a clear blue sky and the weather is warm and
mild. Yesterday the banks of the Danube were full of people
and many of them were swimming in the swift current.
    We call the street outside our window Catfish Row because
it reminds people of Porgy and Bess. The street is narrow
and we see a lot of our neighbors across the way because they
spend most of the day and early evening hanging out the
windows just like Thirteenth Street around Master. The children are very nice and they have gotten to know me well because I toss chocolate bars across to them and they give me
big smiles. The Bavarians tend to be friendly anyway but we
are still prohibited from fraternizing. They are not a handsome people but they are healthy and strong looking.
    Last night we took a little walk along the river bank and
came up to a spot where one of our ack-ack guns had been
dug in and sandbagged. Sitting around the empty position
were boys and girls about twelve to fourteen singing those
sentimental German songs. The engineers working on the
bridge stopped to listen and some few soldiers gathered at a
distance because their voices sounded clear and lovely in the
half light with only the swift-running water for background.
It was a nice moment in the day and we came home rather
quietly. It seems a great tragedy that children sing songs in a
place that was a gun position only a few days ago and when
the backdrop for it are the skeletons of wrecked buildings.

This is the place about which was written "You know
we French stormed Ratisbon" because Ratisbon is the
French name for Regensburg. I have been unable to find
the little hill where Napoleon stood but there is a plaque
on one of the houses just down the street that says that it was
Napoleon's headquarters. They are right opposite the Cathedral but I imagine that the Emperor never crossed the street.
(9 May 1945, Bavaria)

*May 11—Americans and Russians link up at Linz (Austria) and
Pilsen (Czechoslovakia).*

Darling,

Just about five o'clock on a quiet peaceful Sunday afternoon and Sergeant Tyner has just given me your letter of
May 5 which is very good service from Philadelphia to the
middle of Bavaria.

By this time you have the answer to some of the questions
that you have asked. The crisis that I did tell you about did
start with the bullion story and I felt that my handling of it
was right and I stuck to my guns. The net result was that
someone here finally found out that I was not a complete idiot and the transfer and promotion followed. I hope that I
have learned a lesson about sticking to an opinion through
hell and high water. This one paid off.

I couldn't send you a cable about my promotion because
they have to go to Paris for transmission and take as long or
longer than a letter. To top it all off, G-1 now tells me that I
am to get a French decoration but the orders aren't cut.[6]

By this time you have our view of the end of the war and
you know that we were fighting around Linz in Austria and
that we pushed into Czechoslovakia and that we did finally
meet the Czechs and the Russians.

The major topic of conversation over here is the adjusted
service rating; that is, how many points have you got? It is estimated that 85 points will be sufficient to make you eligible
for discharge but there is no guarantee. In any event the

point system does not apply to officers although the average is being computed for all of us. My score is in excess of 90 points. I don't know whether that has any significance but it may be a hopeful sign. We are not too pessimistic now that the war is over. I am shooting at Christmas and really hope that I will make it. Don't give up the ship.

I had a wonderful trip yesterday down into the Bavarian Alps. It is a land of lakes and beautiful green valleys broken by great forests of tall pine trees. The scent of the pines is everywhere. On the south shore of the lakes the Alps spring rather suddenly out of the earth. They are not bare and barren like the Rockies but are green and tree-covered as far as the eye can see and are dominated by the magnificent snow-capped peaks.

The farm houses and the summer houses on the lakes are one story of natural stone and a second story of light pine wood with a balcony all the way around the second floor. The woodwork of the balcony is beautifully carved and the houses are topped with broad slanting roofs of pinkish red tile. It is dairy country and there are fine Bavarian cattle in the fields but the herds are not large now. Most of Germany is filthy but this is a spotless and shining country. On the wall of every house are the bleached skulls, surmounted by great horns, of the chamois that have been shot in the mountains over many years.

The people are very charming and attractive. The men and women in the fields wear bright colors and make a fine picture against the green of the rich grass and the brilliant yellow of the flowers of some forage crop that is in full bloom now. The women wear what they used to call "dirndls" or something in the States and they are all made in bright patterns and are most attractive. They are made with a tight bodice that has a low-cut yoke neck, with a tightly gathered waist line and a flared short skirt that comes just below the knees. (I hate to confess that I noticed all this but I did.) They nearly all wear either colorful bandannas of red or blue or wide brimmed straw hats. The little girls seem to wear dresses made of the same material and the same pattern as their mothers and the whole effect is very nice. They are friendly and smiling and attractive.

The whole area has been the great hospital area for German soldiers of the SS, the Wehrmacht and the Luftwaffe, and the hotels are all bedecked with Red Crosses and the streets are full of the lame, the halt and the blind. There is a lot of medical personnel in the uniform of the Wehrmacht and many white gowned nurses. The soldiers look at us blankly as they sit out on balconies, lie in the sun on the green grass, or hobble down the streets on crutches or with their arms or their heads heavily bandaged. The American medics supervise the whole area and there are patrols on the road.

In one area I saw what is left of the 17th Panzer Grenadier Division. They had already surrendered and were gathered in the fields under guard. They are only a remnant now but some of them look good. I remember them from Normandy when they were considered a hot outfit and I remember the day that they mortared the aid station of the 2nd Battalion of the 116th Infantry of the 29th way back when. Most of them are dead now but the rest of them seem not too displeased to be prisoners. They are the elements of so many divisions that are coming in and filling up the cages. This whole country now is almost entirely a country of women.

Catfish Row has been quiet today. I have fed my children across the way their daily candy and they are most appreciative. Their mothers are beginning to say good morning to me across the court, and the whole other side of the alley is hanging out the window watching me as I type this. One little boy stopped me on the street and took my hand today and I discovered that he is from the floor just lower than mine and a little to the left. He is very nice.

The other day I sent you a couple of pictures. One is of the General and some of the correspondents and the other is of the officers of the section. Don't let them frighten you, and I know that my helmet is crooked. (13 May 1945, Bavaria)

Darling,

Your letter is full of the aftermath of your Washington weekend and I am sorry that the whole thing left you with something of a letdown. I am afraid that our social life has not been much these past two years but I have no fears we can pick up the threads rapidly when I get home or, at least, pick up as many of the threads as we want. I know that your life has been dull and burdensome but there are many interesting things to do and we shall sample them after the war. One thing that we must do is go to Europe even if we have to starve the rest of the year. I've got a lot of other ideas, too.

Last night we had dinner with three officers of the Fourth Division that I know in a nice house with a fine view of both the Regen and the Danube Rivers and just a glimpse of the spires of the cathedral over the trees. One of the officers, Bill Gude, is only 23 years old but he has the Silver Star with two Oak Leaf Clusters and the Purple Heart with two. He made the last attack in the Huertgen Forest with only 27 men left in his company. He said that he already had his mattress cover all picked out because he wanted to be buried in one that fit. We came home early and I found a little work to do.

Tonight our section played G-3 softball and I went over to the game which we won 17–5. The men are always pleased when the CO turns out for the show. They are playing the Signal Section tomorrow night but my interest in softball is limited. Ten days ago the war was going full blast and now we are worried about who wins the softball game.

The food problem is going to become acute before winter ever gets here. Hitler held on just about six weeks too long and the crops just aren't in the ground and there is absolutely no transport of any kind. I don't know what the solution is. There probably isn't any until some sort of normal economy is restored here and that will take a couple of years. I have four little clients across the alley that I throw life savers but those kids are the exception. The people are living on what food they have on hand and that can't be much. The trouble is that the prisoners will eat and the women and children will starve. Right now we are sorting over all the prisoners as fast as we can and are sending the farmers home. They check the list and unless they are members of the SS or have some specific offense, they lead them to the gate, point them toward home and give them a boot to start them off. That will help a little. (15 May 1945, Bavaria)

Darling,

The Pacific situation could be very interesting. MacArthur has been in control and has successfully played down all his subordinate commanders who have done all the fighting. Patton would be rather hard to play down. We have never built up Patton at the expense of anyone and our divisions have gotten more credit for what they have done than those of any other army. That's the Old Man's policy. He is a great man for passing the credit around and always has been. The passing around of the credit is one of the reasons for the high morale of our troops.

Today I got a wire from SHAEF requesting that I come there on temporary duty pending the formal request for my permanent services. I went to see Colonel Harkins, the Deputy, and told him that I want to stay with Third Army. He suggested that I talk to General Gay, the Chief of Staff, and I did. He said that he would tell SHAEF that they did not wish to release me but he seemed pleased at the request. He pointed out that they could force my transfer but that the General would resist it. I thought that was mildly flattering. The wire asked that I come to Paris on a few days' TD [temporary duty] and the general said he would approve that if I want to go. (20 May 1945, Bavaria)

June–December: Aftermath

Darling,

Sunday morning in Paris and somehow it is like Sunday morning almost anywhere else in the world. There is lovely golden sunshine and a soft breeze and the whole pace of life seems slow and pleasant. For a moment I can forget all the problems that are everywhere here and just enjoy the day. The people on the streets are the churchgoers and the few people who have to keep the world's work going on, and there seems to be a plentiful sprinkling of little girls in long white dresses and veils headed for their first communion. The flower vendors are watering their stocks. Paris has the most wonderful flowers that I have ever seen. Already there are a few people comfortably seated at the tables of the sidewalk cafes sipping the watery beer or the dubious white wine. It is a good day and like all good days a homesick day.

I am really going back to Third Army tomorrow after having been delayed for two days here. It has been very pleasant here but life with an army seems much less complicated and much more productive. I have lost my taste for high level policy and long meetings. We have always been concerned with getting things done right away and I can't stomach this careful weighing of a lot of tenuous factors and the ensuing hesitancy about going ahead even after the decisions have been made. We have been taught that any decision is better than no decision and that it is more profitable to embark on a bad program than to sit still.

These years may have taught me some things but I can't be sure of their practical value until I get home to see. It may be that these are the years that the locusts have eaten but I don't think so. We used to joke about psychic income but the phrase has a certain merit. I know that I have learned many things about places and people so that a lot of my life after this should make more sense to me. I have absorbed by exposure some of the feelings and the attitudes of other peoples and think that that will make changes in our way of life. All of these people have learned leisure and that is an important thing. They all too seem to have learned that there is pleasure to be found in the simple good things of life and that we can well learn, too. They select the cheapest wine with great care, they lavish attention on the simplest meal and no one is too poor to have flowers in his home. This paragraph seems to be made up of a little off the elbow philosophy but it contains some element of truth.

There is another side, too. The French have carried all this to such an extreme that there seems to be no spiritual quality left. Theirs on the surface is a pleasant and gracious materialism but there is no soul underneath the glitter to sustain them.

The situation here is acute and everyone makes dire predictions of some sort of revolution. There are occasional small outbreaks of trouble by some group or other but there is probably some general outburst in the wind. I think that de Gaulle has been so concerned with making certain that France will have its undeserved place at the tables of the mighty that he has neglected the fact that the internal situation is impossible and can't last. The men who attended his press conference yesterday say that he was very sarcastic and bitter and that the text of his remarks can't properly reflect the tone in which he made them. I am just a little tired of the French and Mr. de Gaulle.

I am still inclined to think that I shall get home faster out of Third Army than out of a big headquarters like this. The balancing factor is that here one does come in contact with a lot of people travelling to and from the States who might be able to use a bright young man in their business. The answer really is that I don't know the answer.

Best love and stuff, darling. (3 June 1945, Paris)

June 5—Representatives of the United States, the Soviet Union, Great Britain, and France meet in Berlin to assume joint authority in Germany.

Darling,

Back home in my Bavarian hideout and I find this very peaceful and most attractive after Paris.

Jackson continues to amaze me and I love your accounts of him. The fact that he is so healthy and so good just means that you have lavished so much time and care on him. I am afraid that he will have another birthday before I get to see him but there should be some of his cute years left. I am glad that he knows that somewhere he has something that is known as a father but I don't suppose that it can mean very much to him. I always have a lurking fear that when I first get to see him he will just turn his head away and yell and break my heart completely. Do you think that he will be pleased with his father home from the wars? Even a fellow as little as he should have a father around and even a fellow as big as I should get a chance to see his son. I hate war.

The Old Man made a trip to London and then came back here to make faces at Marshal Tito on the Yugoslav border. Tito went home and that worked very well. Now he is on his way to Los Angeles for an appearance and many of us, especially I, are scared to death. He will be all right on the set speeches but I am just frightened that he will come up with one or two of his Pattonisms and they won't be understood by people who don't know him. Here we had a lot of safeguards and controls and he got to know we were always backstopping and that he could speak freely and he did. All he has to do in the States is come up with a crack line like "The SS are just like the Democrats in America." I am not sure that my being there would help matters but it might.

I have no special feeling about the people that we knew before the war and no special desire to get back to any pattern of life that I have had. I want things to be a little different and they will be. The people who haven't bothered to see you can disappear from my book without concerning me in the slightest. I shall be glad to see the people that you know and like and that will be that. We shall have to adjust to some reduced income when I come home but I am sure that we can do that. Before the war I made about $400 per month and that is the scale that I reached again after more than two years in the army. London was moderately expensive but since I have been in the field I have spent very little. When I get home I should like to have enough to get a complete set of civilian clothes and then I shall go to work and try to make some money again. For a while I shall probably be a rather expensive luxury.

Paris gave me a special concern.

I spent my time with a whole different set of people, the great bulk of whom came directly from London to Paris. While we have been constantly moving, they have been static, making some acquaintances and building a pattern of life that is far from unpleasant. In Paris, and perhaps more so in London, they have met a great many people and at least one woman. There have been movies and dinners and nightclubs and dances and Class A uniforms. Life has been rather pleasant and there has been a great freedom from responsibility and from the normal taboos of society. They have been away two or three years, and home and the women they had there are rather distant because their thoughts have turned homeward less often. The war is over and the return home is not so vitally important to them. They have fleeting fears of the boredom that they may find with the little country girl from Iowa now that they are sophisticated men of the world. They don't really want to go home.

They are the real tragedies of the war. They will go home someday and life will be dull. The girl they went to high school with will be a dull little creature and they will be bored with her. They will have memories of the aperitif on the corner of the Cafe de la Paix and won't be able to find a counterpart in Schenectady. The line soldier will have none of this but the rear echelon officers will. I met a lieutenant colonel that I knew slightly in Paris and he is the principal of a high school in Gary, Indiana. He introduced me to a splashy girl, French and very charming, and he invited me to have a drink. He told me that he has a flat in Paris and that life is very good. I don't think that he will be thrilled to go back to his 45 year old wife and two children in Gary. The young lieutenants and captains are even more tragic because they have been married to girls for only a short period and never got to know them very well. Now the whole picture has dimmed and their nostalgia is for London instead of Waycross, Georgia. It really is a mess and there is no solution.

You have probably heard the story of the finale of Ed Kennedy. It really is a wonderful story. He was to go home by boat and reported into one of the staging areas. His boat was scheduled to sail in about four days. He found the second lieutenant who was PRO and gave him the business. He explained that he was the European manager of Associated Press and that it was important that he get home as quickly as possible. The PRO was the only man in the theater that never heard of Kennedy and was impressed. He made a special effort and told Kennedy that he had gotten him on a boat leaving that night. Kennedy climbed aboard and took off. The next day the poor PRO in a panic found out that the boat was going to Trinidad and wouldn't arrive for more than two weeks and that it would have a ten day layover there. Everyone just laughs and laughs and likes to suspect that SHAEF did it on purpose. It's too bad that they didn't.

Okinawa is the beginning of trouble in the Pacific. The Army philosophy is to make maximum use of all the supporting weapons and be as economical as you can with your personnel. To the Navy the most important thing is a ship. The Army is moving slowly and their losses in killed are low while the Navy is losing ships offshore. It is a difficult decision militarily, but I have seen a lot of dead Americans and a lot of ruined ships and the ruined ships leave me cold. (5 June 1945, Bavaria)

Darling,

I got a phone call from Captain Harry Butcher, General Ike's naval aide, who said that he was coming to spend the night with me so I got set for him since he is an old friend.

He arrived for dinner and had with him Frank Page, the president of IT&T, who is a special consultant to the Secretary of War on public relations. I know him because I worked with him a little when I was at SHAEF. We took a walk to the lake shore after dinner and then came back and sat on the

balcony and I found out the purpose of the visit. They
wanted to tell me that they want me to head up public relations for General Clay and the American Control Commission, which is a job for a brigadier general. As nicely as I
could, I said no thanks. We shall talk more about it tomorrow. They gave me the "Your country needs you" routine but
I wasn't having any. I just kept saying over and over, "I wanna
go home." We settled by admiring the sunset on the lake and
the mountains.

Tomorrow I am leaving to take them to Italy. Know that I
love you and miss you and that someday I am coming home
to you. (7 June 1945, Bavaria)

Darling,

It started as a fine, clear, hot day and we headed south
from here on the way to Innsbruck and the Brenner. It was a
magnificent trip through lovely farm and dairy country with
sudden valleys between the mountain ridges, swift streams of
an indescribable blue color, and gleaming wide lakes in the
bottom of every valley.

As we got farther south the peaks got higher and were
snow streaked across the bare rock faces above the timber-
line. We finally got over the last ridge of hills and made the
long descent into the valley of the Inn River and Innsbruck.

The valley here is a couple of miles wide and Innsbruck
sits astride the river with the great mass of the mountains
hemming it in. Life looks deceptively good. The trolleys are
running but the shops are still closed and the streets are full
of people with nothing to do. The paralysis is almost complete and these communities of old men and women and
children have bitter days ahead.

We crossed the Inn River on a timber trestle bridge that
the Engineers had labelled "THE LAST ONE???" and had
dedicated to one of their dead, as they always do. On the very
outskirts of the town the road begins to wind up into the
Brenner and we followed that all the way into Italy. This is
one of the real breaks in the mountain mass. The road winds

across the face of the cliffs and we could watch the stream and the little villages hundreds of feet below us. There is some little damage in the pass where the railroads were bombed but the place is apparently much as it always was.

We finally came to Brenner and the railroad station where Hitler and Mussolini had their meetings. We noticed rather apathetically that the station and the tracks had been bombed but it wasn't important anymore. Hitler is a charred corpse in a Berlin cellar and Mussolini will always be remembered as the man who hung upside down in a square in Milan so that his followers might spit on him—because he lost.

We finished our lunch and retraced our route back to Innsbruck and back across the river to the road along the north bank of the Inn headed for Salzburg. The valley here is narrow and fertile and the hay was being gathered. It was very hot and we commented on the cold days of winter when we longed for a warm sun that would really beat down on us. The people in the fields are bright spots of color in their native costumes and there are almost no marks of war here at all. There is snow everywhere in the high peaks and we could see the long plumes of the streams that plunge down the sheer cliffs for thousands of feet. It is one of the fine sights of the Alps and every turn of the road brought a new view. The only reminders of war are the now empty barracks that the Germans built for the slave workers and little pools of enemy vehicles and guns gathered in the fields.

We finally turned off the main road toward the south and headed out of the valley into Berchtesgaden. There is an excellent road here provided by a grateful government to the Fuehrer. We came into the town itself. On the side stands the private train of Hermann Goering and the wreckage that the French gave the town after they came. We made some inquiries and then crossed the river and started up the mountain to Hitler's home. It is quite a climb in a car and we came across the torn and twisted trees that the RAF gave them as a present when they got the place. The typically German touch to the whole place is the profusion of birdhouses that the SS have tenderly placed in the trees along the mountain road.

We finally came up to the little plateau partway up the mountain where there are Hitler's home and Goering's home, the barracks for the SS troops, the hothouses for Hitler's flowers, and a fine view of Germany and Austria. The place is a complete shambles. The RAF hit almost everything there and the French came in and set fire to the rubble. Three thousand yards above us, perched on the bare top of the mountain, was the "Adlerhorst," the Eagle's Nest that Hitler loved so well. We started up the steepest road that I have ever driven, with sharp turns, sheer cliffs and sentry boxes at every turn for the SS Palace Guard. The road goes through tunnels in the side of the mountain and finally winds up on a flat piece of ground where the vehicles have to stop because the road builders could go no further. Here are the doors to the elevator but the French have wrecked that, too.

We parked the car and started up the footpath that leads to the hideout on the peak where Hitler could look out over his domain and could see the Austria from which he came. It is a bitter climb that makes the heart pound and the breath begin to rasp and the sweat begin to pour out even in the cool air of the mountain heights. We finally made it and came out on the peak and to the building which clings there against the sky. It is a rather severe, oblong building, of gray stone with huge windows and little of architectural distinction.

There is a small entrance hall with the bronze doors of the elevator on the right but the French smashed them, too. Straight ahead is the dining room and we went in. There is a long rectangular table with armchairs and seats thirty people. Sitting at the huge table was one lone American soldier, a part of the guard detail, and he was writing a letter home. Our driver gave a typical GI greeting, "Got enough room, bud?" The room is stripped except for the chairs and tables. Off to the left is another dining room which would seat about six people and is a little more intimate. We went back through the dining room and into the great oval room of which you have seen so many pictures. It is about forty feet in

diameter, furnished with comfortable chairs and lounges,
and its sole occupants were two GIs stretched out on garden
chairs before the fire in the huge stone fireplace. The room
has windows on all sides looking across the mountain peaks.
Here sat Hitler and his gang so often whiling away Sunday afternoons while another country fell. He used to always pre-
cipitate a crisis on weekends and this must have been the
place that he paced and ate the carpet.

While we were there one of the sudden mountain storms
came up and the peaks were shut out abruptly by the clouds.
We could see the lightning leap away in the distance and
hear the roll of the thunder echoing against the peaks. It
made me think of the sudden storm that we ran into on our
honeymoon in the Poconos. These things could be so much
more wonderful if we were only together to see them. We
came back down the path in the rain, then began the long
slow roll down the tortuous road with the car in low gear all
the way. We rolled out onto the lower plateau and stopped
off to see Hitler's home.

It is not a huge place and it is little more than a shell now.
There are only ladders to get from floor to floor and there
are gaping holes in the walls and floors. We went first into
the living room of which we have seen so many pictures. It is
about fifty feet square with a slight rise at one end and that
famous huge window at the other. The window is only an
opening now and the room has been burned completely.
Over in the corner is the metal framework of the grand piano with the wires twisted and blackened. I thought of the solace that Adolf found in Wagner and Beethoven. The destruction was complete. I picked up one wire from the piano
frame and I shall send it along as a little memento of what
happens to dictators and their pianos, too. There are the
fragments of pieces of furniture, twisted strips of metal that
must have been lamps, and iron grillwork that must have
been the legs of tables. It was a fine room but is no more.

We climbed a ladder to the next floor and went into
Hitler's bedroom, about thirty by twenty, with two large win-

dows. There is a fireplace and against the opposite wall the remnants of Hitler's bed. Adjoining is the guest room, also a wreck, with its own bathroom. In the bathroom is a bidet. This must have been the room of the fair Eva Braun that we have only just heard about. We went through the rest of the place quickly and then started home in the rain.

I think that nothing made me more conscious of the ignominy of defeat than the shambles of his own home that still had the marks of his presence among the debris. The casual way in which we take our victories, though, is in the GI writing a letter on the great dining table where the clan gathered. He and the men who were stretched before the fire were dry and reasonably content that there is no more fighting to do, but they have no bombastic thoughts of victory and no special consciousness of history. (9 June 1945, Berchtesgaden)

Darling,

I decided to take the job [as executive officer, Public Relations Division] at SHAEF since they have put in a second request for me. I went to see the Chief of Staff and told him that I should like to go. He concurred and was very nice about it. I started to mumble my thanks but he cut me rather short. He told me that I must come in and say good-bye before I leave. Considering the fact that he is considered the hardest-hearted man in the headquarters, that is the most sentimental thing that could ever have happened to me.

Yesterday I took off in the morning to go to the ceremony giving the Presidential Citation to the Fourth Armored Division, only the second division in American history to get one.

The sun was bright but the day was cool and the wind across the parade ground whipped the colors and standards. They had representatives of every outfit in line and they formed up across the field from us in approximately 13 companies in field uniforms but shining and strong and tough looking. Back on our side were gathered the rest of the division and they all were just a little proud of the whole show.

The troop commander gave the commands across the parade ground and the standards and colors of each of the companies with their guards started across toward the reviewing stand while the band played. The color bearers held the flags high and the standard bearers dipped their battalion flags and then the band played the National Anthem. When the anthem finished, the adjutant stepped forward and read the citation over a public address system to the assembled men. When it was finished the band played while the general stepped forward to the red and white standard of the division with its red "4" in the middle. It was dipped to him and he fastened the blue and white of the Presidential Citation to the top of it. The band stepped off, and the review started to pass around the field.

First in line were the tankers and they looked strong and fresh and young and bore little resemblance to the haggard, pale and old men who were at Bastogne. These weeks of rest have done wonders. The whole outfit marched amazingly well and no one expects tankers to be able to march. They had their folding stock machine guns slung across their shoulders at precisely the right angle and they gave the eyes right smartly. They were followed by the armored infantry with their M-1s and every bayonet in a perfect line. Then came the artillery with slung carbines followed by the Engineers again with M-1s. Next the Ordnance with slung carbines and then the proudest men of all, the Negro 444th QM truck company who have been with the division since the beginning. Their heads were high and they had every hand smartly on the right spot on the carbine. Then came another company of the men of the headquarters and finally the medics with their Red Cross brassards.

They finished the march past and then formed in perfect ranks into a hollow square around the stand and General Devers spoke very briefly and very well. I think that all of us suddenly knew one of those frequent moments of pride that come from being an American and a soldier.

The weather is good today. I went out and played a little

softball with the men. While I was at it the men from my motor pool came and told me that they had the power boat repaired and running. We explored all of the lake in it. I don't know why I am leaving this place to wind up in the ruins of Frankfurt. (15 June 1945, Bavaria)

Darling,

Just before I left [Third Army], the General sent a message, which they showed to me, saying he was in trouble and was coming back here. I don't know how much of what has happened could have been prevented but I am sure that I could have helped if he had taken me along.[7] I do know him and understand him and feel that a lot of it could have been headed off. He promised not to make any statements without writing them out and having Charlie Codman check them out but he and Codman never could seem to understand that his lightest reference would make print. It is really too bad that it worked out as it did but I suspected it and other people did, too.

The trouble is that he can't be quiet. People here in Paris, officers and correspondents, say that I have misrepresented Patton to the public and there is a lot of truth in that. The General is the ideal soldier. He is militarily one of the best educated men in the world. He understands war and strategy and tactics and his reactions are so immediate and so certain that they are no longer opinions. The factors involved in any given situation are so apparent to him that he appears to have no need for consideration. Militarily he is incomparable. He has never made a mistake and has never made a bad decision. He has won every fight that he ever had and he can inspire troops to great heights of combat. There is no general in the army comparable to him as a troop commander and as a leader for the men who actually have to meet the enemy face to face.

They are his assets and the country needs those assets right now. He has said that he feels he will be killed in battle and I think that the wish is father to the thought. He is a me-

dieval knight in OD [olive drab] armor and could probably
sign the code of Bushido with no mental reservations. He has
said, "I love war. I like to fight." We insist in our era on thinking that such a man is an anachronism, a throwback to an
earlier and less intelligent era. The fact is that the basic mission of an army is the destruction of the enemy's armed
forces, that is to kill the soldiers of the other army. He knows
that and he has done that and that is what we have soldiers
for. He is a pure soldier. He thinks like a soldier, he acts like
a soldier and his reactions are those of a soldier.

The trouble is that America doesn't like soldiers and
doesn't trust them. It feels that militarism is a dirty word and
is the peculiar affliction of some country other than our own.
There have been stories pointing out that he is scholarly and
they have neglected to mention that the scholarship is purely
in things military. That I did with malice aforethought because I do know how people react. We can't accept in America that greatness may have only one dimension. General Patton is only a soldier but a very great one. His opinions on
anything military are invaluable and probably right. His
opinions on anything else are valueless and shouldn't be
given the slightest credence. We have always insisted on asking Henry Ford for his opinions on education and Thomas
Edison for his opinions on the hoop skirt or smoking cigarettes. We can't believe that any genius has a peculiar talent.
We have to think that he is the fully rounded man, an oracle,
an authority on every subject.

General Patton is neither philosopher, politician nor saint.
He is a soldier and we are fortunate that he is on our side.

He wept as he thought of the men who died but that is
only a surface emotion and there are no tears in his heart.
He would have killed a million of us if it were necessary to
win. We made much of the fact that our losses in the Third
Army were the lowest of any army. That is true. General Patton spared his men because he needed men to win, and replacements might be hard to get. A soldier, a man, is part of

an army and must be conserved just as you conserve a truck or a tank. There is no room for sentimentality and he knew that. He was a soldier—he wanted to win, to kill the enemy—and he always did. That is his proper place and the thing for which he is great. Patton's political or moral opinions do not vitiate his military greatness any more than Jeanne Eagels' cocaine detracted from her art on the stage.

I knew these things but I knew, too, that the true picture could not be given to people because they could not understand. In spite of policies and great statements about freedom from censorship, I had always one basic control. They could write nothing about General Patton and could not quote him at all unless I approved—and I seldom approved. What would happen at home when people read a statement like, "The SS are just like the Democrats in America" or "The guards at the concentration camps are pretty bad but we could find enough bastards in America to run the same kind of places" or "Don't say we are winning the war or those sons of bitches in America will all quit work"? They are not good statements and their publication would have produced a terrible storm. The net result would have been that the people would have insisted on the removal of our greatest soldier because they did not approve of his opinions on other subjects. We are not yet ready to accept men for what they are but someday we will learn the lesson. He is a great soldier and a great leader of men in war, and the service that he has rendered to us all can never be disputed.

The army and this war have made a soldier of me and I am proud of that. I miss you more than mere letters can ever say but you know that because we have lived together heart to heart. Don't ever feel that separation has dimmed the memory or made life without you possible. Never stop loving me and never stop knowing that I live only to come back to you. (22 June 1945, Paris)

June 26—United Nations charter signed in San Francisco.

Darling,

I made the trip to Berlin on Sunday. We landed at Tempel-
hof Airdrome, which is a huge installation and not very
much damaged.

I don't believe that Berlin is damaged as much as many
other cities. It is such a huge place that it is hard to evaluate
properly but the damage is certainly not as complete as in
such places as Cologne or Nuremberg. The center of the city
is completely gone. All the government buildings are badly
damaged by Russian artillery and great areas have been lev-
eled or burnt out by bombs. Steps are being taken to clear
up the rubble, the streetcars are running in some areas and
so is the underground, and the electricity was on in some of
the streetlights. The people must be few because there are
none of the crowds that should fill so great a city. The people
are in two categories: the Berliners who look well dressed
and with no signs of starvation; and the refugees streaming
back and looking like refugees always look. They are the
same as elsewhere in Europe—ragged, dirty, tired and always
towing or pushing all sorts of improvised carts containing a
few pitiful household possessions.

In spite of the tripartite occupation there are not a great
many troops of any nationality in evidence. The city is big
enough to swallow the few thousand troops that are there.
The American soldiers are in Class A uniform, always armed
and are models of military appearance, courtesy and deco-
rum. The British look good, too. The Russians are a con-
glomerate mass and they wear all sorts of uniforms. Most typical are the long blouse, baggy trousers and high boots that
are so familiar in pictures. They don't look very soldierly but
there is apparently no questioning of their fighting ability.

The marks of the Russians are everywhere. There are direction signs in Russian and the street marking system is very
good apparently. I never observed much Russian writing before but the strange thing is that occasional Russian words in
Russian characters look much like the same word in Arabic
characters. They have done a very good propaganda job and

there is a big sign on almost every corner containing a message in German signed by Stalin. The gist of most of them is that the city's destruction was caused by the Nazis, and the Red Army is not responsible. The Russian soldiers seem to be quite friendly with the Germans and you can see them making wild gestures at each other on street corners. The center of Berlin is dead but there is life in the surrounding areas although it is hard to describe what it is like. We have seen so many wrecked cities and the aftermath that we have no clear power of observation anymore.

In the American and British areas the traffic police are all Germans in their green military looking uniforms, with the stiff peaked Graustarkian-looking cardboard helmets. The great sight of Berlin are the female MPs in the Russian area. They are an integral part of the army and can fight as well as direct traffic. They are generally short and stocky, wear skirts and boots and a blouse and cap that look much like ours. They work on little platforms about a foot high and do their traffic directions with a yellow "Go" flag in their right hand and a red "Stop" flag in their left. They carry a rifle slung across their backs and a bandolier of ammunition around the waist. They are extremely military and their motions are stiff and mechanical.

The Russians have a great many American trucks and jeeps and they do a fine maintenance job on them. We took time out to look over a couple that had gone about 25,000 miles and they are in excellent condition. They have a variety of civilian transports and they drive in the French fashion—they lean on the horn and go like hell. The thing is further complicated by the fact that many of them have never driven cars before and they are always wrecking the cars and killing themselves. The military vehicles move slowly and in orderly fashion. The Russians are great saluters and they throw high balls from miles away when they see you coming.

We went from the Unter den Linden through the Brandenburg Gate, which is not very damaged, and along the Tiergartenstrasse. The Tiergarten looks like pictures of the

Argonne from the last war. This was one of the last German holdouts in Berlin and the beautiful park is filled with twisted and torn stumps of trees, knocked out guns and deep pockmarks of shells. This was a real battleground. Along the street the Russians have arranged two sets of pictures. One is individual portraits of Stalin, Churchill and Truman. Facing it across the way is a group picture taken at Yalta of Stalin, Roosevelt and Churchill that you have seen so often. The streets are lined with Russian graves, and many little nooks of Berlin have the grave markers of the Russian dead. They bury their dead where they fall and make some effort to mark them but I noticed that many markers contained no names.

Across the street is the Reichstag and we went over and in. It was hit by a bomb and has been pumped full of Russian artillery shells. The walls are still standing but the inside is a complete wreck. The floor is a foot deep in rubble, papers and junk of all kinds. The bare walls are filled with the names of Russian soldiers up to a height of twenty feet and we wondered how they got them up there. There are headless statues lying on the floors, pockmarked gilt work, and chopped off Doric columns. The war here came back where it started.

We left there and went over to the Reich Chancellery and started down in the air raid shelter where Hitler and Eva Braun are supposed to have died. There is little to add except that the Russian major in charge says that Hitler's body has not been found or identified. We came back above ground and into the Chancellery itself. We went into the room where Hitler signed all his treaties and found it deep in rubble. The great crystal chandeliers have been lowered so that people could take the bulbs. So many of these rooms look familiar because we have seen so many pictures.

We went into Hitler's own office and found it a wreck, too. The leather has been cut out of chairs, the tables and desks were smashed, and even the wooden panelling had been stripped from the walls. There was nothing left to suggest that the Fuehrer had once been here. We went upstairs and rummaged through the offices and found some of the Fuehrer's personal stationery. Across an open space we saw a room that seemed to be filled with medals. The only way was across some iron beams and we started to walk across. Charley Madary came across a brick and kicked it off out of his way. There was a brief pause and then there came up from below a long Slavic wail. It had conked one of the Russian sentries on the head and knocked him cold and his partner didn't like it. We ducked expecting a rifle shot but all we got were what must have been some very dirty Russian words. We found the medals and I have a hatful.

That about did it and we came back to Paris. (10 July 1945, Berlin)

On July 26, the Allies meet at Potsdam and issue an ultimatum: Japan is to surrender unconditionally or face "utter destruction." Four days later, Japan rejects the Potsdam ultimatum.

Darling,

Wiesbaden is one of those unfortunate places. It is a Rhineland town, best known as a spa, and contained some nice hotels and some lovely homes. One night last winter the air force came down the Rhine looking for Mainz and got the wrong town. As a result they bombed it for forty-five minutes and put a lot of holes in some very nice houses.

Just north of the town is a small hotel situated in a lovely wood. The place is being run by Polish DPs [displaced persons] and we had a lovely meal prepared by an Italian chef and included a big chocolate cake on which was written "WELCOME TO GERMANY."

I was in Berlin last week and in the consultation on the issuance of the ultimatum to Japan. As a matter of fact, I wrote part of it. In the eighth paragraph where it mentions something about Democratic principles I got them to change the large D to a small d. Therefore, I am really a co-author. Afterward I had dinner with Charlie Ross, who is the President's press secretary. He is a very high-priced American newspaperman but he has had little experience with the international press. He was rather timid about facing them and kept asking me afterward whether I thought he had handled them properly. He checked me as to whether I thought his answers to some of their questions were acceptable. I felt very old and wise and my vanity was tickled.

Berlin is a most depressing place. They are making amazing strides in getting the place organized but the problems are so gigantic that there would appear to be no escaping famine and disease there. We are worried about the health of our troops if there should be large-scale disease among the Germans. The MG [military government] has thousands of Germans at work and they have plenty of applicants. The pay is only five cents a day but they don't care about the money because that amount wouldn't buy a newspaper. They work primarily because they are given one meal a day if they work eight hours and two meals if they work twelve hours. If they work less than eight hours, they get no food. The food is C ration made into soup and poured over some dehydrated potatoes but it looks good to the Germans, many of whom live by stealing the contents of our garbage cans. The Germans have to bring their own utensils and they line up in long queues for the food. They also get one slice of white bread which they think is cake. These queuing crowds are interesting because many of them are very well dressed and obviously never did manual work before.

In addition to the huge crowds on all sorts of jobs, the women bucket brigades are lined up everywhere clearing away rubble and piling it up. It is a primitive system but it does work—slowly. It is a painfully simple affair. If rubble is to be moved from the street into a vacant space they just put a solid line of women from one area to the other. They have all sorts of buckets which they pass from hand to hand. At one end is a woman who fills the bucket with a shovel and at the other end a few more women who dump them on top of the pile or who neatly stack the stones and bricks. Then the empty buckets pass back by hand to the starting point. Many of these women wear dust-covered clothes that must have looked very fine a few days ago but they work anyway. No work, no food.

Berlin, more than any other city, is a city of women. There are old men and children but the normal male population seems to have disappeared. The queue has been carried to the utmost point here and there are queues for everything that stretch on for blocks. Because there are no real news media, every little neighborhood has a rough bulletin board at a street corner on which the people place their handwritten advertisements for rooms, for furniture, for clothing and for information about families. One of the hard jobs is to make the people sit still. They jump from one national zone to another as they hear rumors that there will be more food here or there or somewhere else. All in all the place is terrible and I don't want to be stationed there. (2 August 1945, Wiesbaden)

August 6—Atomic bomb detonated over Hiroshima.

Darling,

I borrowed a beaten up German car and Andy and I got off about ten o'clock on Saturday morning.

We went through Versailles and Dreux and wound up about lunch time at Verneuil, which is a not very splashy French provincial town. We went across the flat earthen "place" that is the center of every French town, out around the ancient cathedral with the shattered tower, and found a little French restaurant. The few people in the restaurant looked curiously at Americans and I thought back to the thousands of troops that had streamed through this town almost a year ago.

The war seems a long ago thing here in Orne and in Manche and all of Normandy that we saw. It is harvest time for the hay and wheat, and the fields seem full but the drought here has taken a heavy toll. We never saw an American soldier or an American vehicle after we left Versailles and we almost had to strain to find signs of war in the countryside. There were no visible bomb holes or foxholes and even the shattered woods had concealing foliage. Occasionally we ran across forgotten but familiar signs tacked to trees and posts but they were few and far between. I looked at them closely and tried to realize that I had seen thousands of them when they were part of the normal army life—"MINES CLEARED TO HEDGES," "MAIN SUPPLY ROUTE," "2D BN CP," "KEEP 60 YARD INTERVAL." They are little ghosts from an ancient past.

All the little flotsam of war has disappeared and the main remnants are the twisted frames of vehicles lying in the ditches where the dozers had pushed them, and the countless burned out tanks sitting where they had been disabled and marking the places where their crews had died. I was shocked to see the great number of Shermans, covered with rust instead of drab gray paint and looking deceptively strong. It was hard to notice the inevitable hole as we whizzed by. I was a little impressed with the skill that both armies had. Their eye for terrain and concealment was good, and most of the tanks were in very good cover and usually on the commanding ground when they got it. The army, even in those ancient days of last summer, was better than we thought and the Germans were still tough and strong. We skirted the area of the famous gap where the German Seventh was wiped out and we passed through Argentan which was the southern jaw of the pincers. We also went through Mortain where the Germans threw their counterattack and where one battalion of the 35th was cut off for three days and only 80 men survived. The last time I had passed this way it was impossible for a vehicle to get through the town and the engineers had simply cut a path around it with their dozers.

The towns bear all the evidence of the war but surprising things have been done in a year. If anything, the destruction looks more shocking now than it did then. Where there were burnt houses and gaping walls, there are now flat spaces with brick and stone laid in neat piles. In some of the towns the areas of destruction are proportionately vast and I realized just how much of these towns had been destroyed. They have done a good job of cleaning them up but there has not been much reconstruction. The work goes on with a great number of German prisoners but the bulk of the workers are French. Many of the houses have been patched up and are lived in but it will take years to rebuild the towns to their pre-war size. Some of the towns are ghost towns and will never be rebuilt. I thought of the towns we saw in the South on our way to Miami that had had big populations before the Civil War destroyed them. Some of these places will never be rebuilt.

We came finally into the area near Mont St. Michel and discovered that we had run into the great fete of all time. There was to be celebrated everywhere the Feast of Saint Michel (for the first time in six years) and also the anniversary of the liberation of this area by General Patton. The work that had been done is incredible. For miles along the road they had either planted small trees or stakes, and strung along them were vines with real or artificial flowers. Every little town had four or five arches over the road with a patriotic or religious motto. The peasants were everywhere putting on the finishing touches and the sight was beautiful to behold. Nothing that I have ever seen for a celebration could touch the work that had gone into this simple but elaborate outpouring. Everyone in the country was working on the decorations and no town or home was too humble to be colorful and gay.

We went through Pontorson and then hit the sea with its clean fresh smell and there lay Mont St. Michel. I shan't attempt to describe it. I think that it and the Taj Mahal are the two most beautiful things that man has ever made.

We rolled over the causeway and onto the beach and pulled our car up by the great wall. All of Mont St. Michel was out finishing the arrangements for the next day's festivities. We walked up through the arched postern gate and along the cobblestones of the Mont. After dinner we wandered down along the beach on the bay side and watched a beautiful sunset over the water. We were tired and wandered back to bed just after dark.

[Sunday morning] we went down to see the town en fete. There is only one street in Mont St. Michel and that is only about 250 yards long. The rest of the town is steps, up to the Mont, up to the houses, up to the old ramparts, and up to the terraces. The little boys of the town were dressed in the ancient page boy costumes of a few centuries ago and the young girls were in colorful medieval gowns that must be very old and they wore veils around their heads bound by highly polished circlets of brass studded with artificial gems. We were the only foreigners in the town and people stared and smiled at us.

We followed the crowd up the hill for the great high mass in the magnificent abbey church on the top of the mount. There was a band in the church heavy with bugles and drums and with some instruments that I had never seen before. When the mass was over, the whole procession moved out to the highest of the stone terraces and the bishop blessed the sea and the fishermen, with the sea breezes whipping the gold vestments and the people answering the responses into the wind.

It was after noon now and we would have to leave for Paris to get back that night. We talked it over and for the first time in the army for me I decided to go AWOL and not return that day. We wanted to see the finish of the horse race that started at Pontorson, twelve kilometers away. When the race was over and they led the horses back to the plows we looked over the five or six tents that had been set up just like a carnival back home.

We tried the wheel that spins and got nowhere but we had better luck with the hoops. You toss them at bottles of wine and I managed to lasso a bottle amid lusty cheers from the French. We opened it and passed it around and the peasants were so pleased that they gave us a ride on the railroad. The engine was a farm tractor with a cardboard stack and attachments to look like a locomotive and it towed little wooden cars down the beach and back. Very thrilling at a five mile an hour clip. We came back and took a crack at the French equivalent of our knock down the milk bottles. I stepped up and gave them my Carl Hubbell sidearm whip. That drew an admiring throng and brought out all the ham in me. I began to heave the balls at a tremendous clip amid the enthusiasm of the spectators and my arm is still stiff. Always a wise guy.

We wandered down to the beach just as darkness was coming on, watching the rich pinks and the dark clouds in the west where the sun was sinking into the flat waveless sea. We came down to a little chapel which sits on the beach at one of the points and started up the winding stone steps. We were almost to the top when we noticed a little gathering there and stopped. Before the grilled door of the chapel standing in a little group were about twenty bare-kneed boy scouts with bowed heads listening to the soft words of the scoutmaster. The figures were dim in the half-light but their standards were very straight against the sky, and their conical hats were at their feet and they stood with their hands clasped behind them. The scoutmaster was giving them an inspirational talk in a rapid Norman French that I found almost impossible to follow and they prayed briefly for the dead soldiers of France. It was solemn and impressive to me and must have been doubly so to the youngsters who were a part of it. We pressed back into the shadows so as not to interfere but my thoughts kept turning to the days that also must have been solemn and impressive when Nazi boys gathered around campfires and dreamed of "morgen die ganze welt." I hope that the scoutmaster was telling them good things and not preaching of the glory of war and the revenge of la Patrie.

They finished and he announced that there were ten minutes until ten o' clock and that they should meditate tout seul. They broke up very quickly and streamed down the steps past us leaving four of their brothers before the chapel door. We walked slowly up the steps and looked at the four

youngsters kneeling very straight with their bare knees on
the cold and moss-covered rock, their eyes closed and their
hands clasped in prayer. We stayed only a moment and tip-
toed away down the steps feeling suddenly terribly old and
unduly wise and somehow vaguely embarrassed.

We came to the turn in the steps and looked on a scene
that might have been lifted from Mont St. Michel ten centuries ago. Along the edge of the beach at irregular intervals
were the whole troop. Some stood straight by the water's
edge, some were sitting on the rocks with their chins in their
hands and their elbows on their knees, and some sat on the
beach with their arms around their drawn-up knees. They
were only silhouettes against the failing light of the western
sky. The spell was broken by a high shrill whistle from down
the beach and they all rose and started in that direction on
the double. We strolled after them but they had disappeared.
I am glad that we didn't find them and I am just as pleased
that I am not certain what it all meant.

It was a good trip and we shall make it together someday
although I am afraid that Rory will have to climb the heights
alone. His father is too old already. (7 August 1945, Normandy)

*On August 9, a second atomic bomb is detonated over Nagasaki.
On August 10, Japan sues for peace. On August 14, Japan surrenders unconditionally (V-J Day). The next day, the rationing
of gasoline and canned goods ends in the United States.*

Darling,

The evening (almost nine) of what is our official celebration of V-J day. The whole theater was supposed to have the
day off and I almost did. We went to look at some houses for
a mess that will be nearer our broken-down billets and I began to feel sorry for the Germans. We pulled up on the
porch of a house and knocked at the door and the old gent
that opened the door looked scared to death. I told him that

we wanted to inspect the place and he took us through. We decided that we wanted it but we didn't tell him. I told him that the place was too small for us and he was pathetically grateful and shook my hand. It was a lie, of course, and he will be bounced out tomorrow but the fact that I feel sorry for him probably proves that the Germans will win the ultimate victory. I still remember enough of the war not to keep myself awake at night worrying about their being cold or homeless or hungry.

The admin officer here made up a list of our section and my name was fourth on it with 104 points. The name was carefully scratched out. I raised hell again and tried to pin the exec down to a date when they will let me out. He says now that I can get out when I have gotten the Nuremberg trials all organized. That is the first of October or a little later.

Things in Germany are bad for the Germans and are getting worse. There is no food and the small amount to come into the country from England and the U.S. won't make much of a dent. There will be little coal because there are not enough miners and those that are working are on a slowdown strike so that they are producing very little. Beside every army kitchen here there are lines of kids with pails waiting to get first crack at the garbage. The only food shops are bread shops and the bread is a dark ersatz. They are urging people to lay in wood for the winter and there is some activity in that direction. There are no young men around to do the work and every youngster and old person is lugging something down the streets. The men that should be doing the work are either dead in Russia and Poland or in prison camps. We have released a couple of million prisoners but they are a drop in the bucket. The people that looked sleek and well fed when we first came into Germany are beginning to look thinner and paler.

The Germans probably have drawn no lesson about the evil of starting a war but they have certainly learned not to lose one. (17 August 1945, Wiesbaden)

September 2—Formal surrender of Japan; the end of World War II.

Darling,

    Another chilly gray day for which the Rhineland is famous and there are very definite signs of fall everywhere. The season is much farther advanced here than it is back in France and the winter will be long and cold. The degree of suffering of the Germans is beyond all conception and the winter will be a time of horror. I fear there is no conception in most of the world of the completeness of German disintegration and there is no immediate salvation in sight for them. The British will do some things to ameliorate conditions. The Russians will do nothing and the French are aggravating the situation by their completely reckless stripping of their portion of the occupied zone. The mood of America is scarcely ready to extend the necessary help, and the scars and the bitterness of this occupation will simply bring another war of revenge some of these years. The Germans are getting into the complete hopelessness in which Hitler found them and the net result will be either communism or chaos or both. (11 September 1945, Wiesbaden)

Darling,

    Saturday afternoon of a rather busy day with the usual gray skies of the Rhineland doing as little as possible to add to the joy of the day. We seem to get very little good weather any more. There is occasional sunshine but there is a slight chill in the air always and the leaves are falling from the trees. Autumn is almost on us and the prospect is not good. You can almost see the increase in the activity of the Germans trying to prepare for the winter but it is too late now.

    Aside from any other consideration there is no estimating the toll that has been taken of basic human dignity. Every German here, many of them well dressed and of some former wealth and position, staggers along with huge bundles on their back. A German never seems to move unless he is bowed under a rucksack. The fortunate few have hand carts or baby carriages or carts made from odds and ends for which there can be no name. These contrivances are loaded with scraps of lumber, great logs, odds and ends of household equipment, and the little things that people have salvaged from the war. Yesterday in Nuremberg I saw an American coal truck slither around a corner and some of the briquettes slithered off into the street in a fairly nice section that is only partially destroyed. People came out of the houses and scrambled to gather up a few small lumps to add to their hoards. It is not a pretty picture anywhere and it is depressing to be immersed in it. We fare very well and are that much more conscious of the horrible contrast. None of us can escape the terrible sense of foreboding about the coming winter. People will do any kind of work for any number of hours just to get one meal. They beg for work and there are no holds barred. A GI gives a candy bar or three or four cigarettes for a woman. Things are bad here but even worse in the larger cities.

The day before yesterday I went down to Nuremberg. I was met at the airport by Charley Madary who took me out to Faber Castle at Stein where the press camp for the trials will be. It is owned by Baron Faber of Eberhard Faber that makes all the pencils in America.

There were five of us at dinner. The finale came with the coffee. We had just started when the head opened the double doors and from the corridor outside came the harmony of female voices singing "Lili Marlene." They finished and went into a local folk song which they sang very well. We insisted that the singers be brought in and they came sliding in from the corridor bashful and giggling, the serving maids of the castle. They slid along the wall and took up places under the tall candlestick by the musicians. They wore colorful kerchiefs, the typical bright print dresses of the country and crisp white aprons. Their harmony was excellent with good rich sopranos and altos supported by deep voiced contraltos. We applauded vigorously and enjoyed it very much. I couldn't be unconscious of the fact that they sang with no less good will because the present lord of the manor was a country boy from Philadelphia named Quirk.

I was very busy yesterday running around the camp and the courthouse and trying to cover every angle in one visit. There is a lot to be done but the work is going ahead very well by the German prisoners ramrodded by American soldiers with rifles. Prisoners never work very enthusiastically but a hundred of them can do the work of about twenty-five men, and there are a lot of prisoners. We use only the best, all from the Waffen SS. (15 September 1945, Wiesbaden)

Darling,

Monday night and the sirens have just let forth their unearthly howl to tell the good Germans that curfew is only ten minutes away. The all clear will sound in a few minutes, curdling our flesh anew, and all the good Germans will be in their homes. Some of the bad Germans will not be in their homes and we shall hear the shots banging back and forth across the town as the sentries and security guards shoot at each other. This is just the beginning of another tasteless week and the best that I can say for tomorrow is that it will probably be no worse than today.

I was busy today with several things. I issued the orders to stop all facilities for correspondents in the United Kingdom effective November 1 and you will hear the repercussions in the American papers in a couple of days. The press has gotten to like the subsidy and they hate to see it stop. I sent a cable off to the War Department recommending that we make deep cuts in France and you will hear even more about that. I can't say that I have any special feeling of regret about the thing because I feel they have been riding the gravy train long enough. The French contingent are largely the hams and the phonies anyway, and we shall be glad to be rid of them and let them start working for a living again and spend their expense accounts instead of banking them. I am still busy with Nuremberg but there will probably be another postponement there. Mr. Jackson's circus may not be working out as he planned it. He will probably get the expected publicity but I am not sure that it will be good for him. Cross him off as a presidential candidate.[8] I also have some consolidation to do in Berlin where we have to cut down. That will take some working out but I have started on it. The old hatchet man, that's me.

Steps are being taken to make me the Press Attache of the American Embassy in Paris. The whole thing is in the very preliminary stage so don't start to pack. I was a little shy of the project. We can dream about it, anyway. (17 September 1945, Wiesbaden)

On September 28, Patton is relieved as commander of Third Army for intemperate remarks about denazification. He will be paralyzed in an automobile accident in December and die. (Rundstedt's assessment: "Patton was your best.") In October, the demobilization of 15 million American veterans begins. (The draft will expire on March 31, 1946; 12.8 million veterans will be returned to civilian life by June.)

Darling,

I have been terribly busy these past few days winding up the preparations for Nuremberg. Yesterday afternoon I left for Nuremberg with Dick Merrick and we made it after some minor misadventures. We got to the Faber Schloss about eight and the place looked magnificent and mysterious and medieval in the light of the full moon. Charley Madary had an excellent dinner for us and the serving maids sang for us again. Madary has fulfilled an ambition because they finish up their German folk songs and hymns and then add Mairzy Doats, etc. It's a terrible touch and I told him to eliminate it. The choir will sing in the castle chapel on Christmas Eve—but not to me.

I had a long session with Dean and Mims of Jackson's staff and we settled quite a few problems that still were facing us. The plans for the coverage are quite elaborate and we have done a good job on them. We were up fairly early this morning and went down to the courthouse and looked over the place and then took a quick turn through the old town. It is possible to get through more streets, and more people have burrowed holes to live in but there are no real improvements. The only signs of rehabilitation that I saw were that many people have built themselves one room wooden shacks in the suburbs near Furth and the whole family will spend the winter there. The Jackson crowd have managed to make the courthouse look like Washington and the people do, too. For the Germans no hope.

I was tempted to stay and see the First Division play the 45th football with General Ike in attendance. I made the air reservation for five o'clock and then decided that the day was so lovely we should come back by car. It was a magnificent day and we rode through the wooded hills. The trees are in full color and the countryside is beautiful. It is a shock to leave it to wind your way through the ruins of Wurzburg and Aschaffenburg and the little towns that are gone.

Barring some unforeseen circumstance I shall get away from here November 8. We are beginning to feel sorry for those that are staying behind and they are beginning to feel sorry for themselves. The mess is smaller all the time and there is a farewell to say to someone almost every night. It is like the last day of school long protracted.

I am purposely refraining from making a lot of plans about home until after I have gotten there. I have been away a long time and all of the ideas that I have are probably silly. I have no set plan as to what I should like to do. I shall have about three months terminal leave due me and that will give us a little time before we start over the hill to the poorhouse. I have made some excellent contacts here but their post-war value is questionable. The bug of returning to Europe is still with me but that can stand exploration later on. We have always wrestled with the devil on these things and I am still of the opinion that we don't have to have a lot of money to be happy even though it helps. We have the happiness of our future to secure and we shall do that in whatever way seems best after we are together again. I have missed you these years. It will be a great reunion. (21 October 1945, Wiesbaden)

Darling,

I feel that I am leaving the whole world in the lurch but the real fact is that I am tired and washed out and my particular contribution is becoming smaller and less valuable each day. The army and Europe will struggle along without my efforts but the cumulative subtraction of so many men will hurt badly. I have thought about all these things but nothing can overbalance the simple fact that I want to come home.

There are a couple of things that may open up for me. One of my officers had been the personal assistant to Walter Annenberg before the war, handling his magazine publishing. He is going home for discharge and is most anxious that I join the Annenberg operation. He says that they are planning a big expansion in radio, with WFIL a mere beginning. It's a huge organization and there should be a job for me there. How good a job is another story. I shall be very happy if we are able to maintain our wartime income but I am not sure that we can. My being home will be much more expensive than my being here.

These days are busy. I am cleaning up Nuremberg and tonight I plan to pack some stuff in wooden crates to be mailed home. Anyway I'm coming home at long last.

Count the sleeps and kill the fatted calf. Best love, darling. (30 October 1945, Wiesbaden)

November 20—The war crimes trial of the German leadership opens in Nuremberg.

28 November 1945
Antwerp

WESTERN UNION
ELIZABETH QUIRK
4022 CHESTNUT ST.
PHILA

SAILING TOMORROW SS ARCHBISHOP LAMEY HOME
ABOUT FIFTEENTH
= JIM

Chapter Three: Between Wars
1945–51

Lieutenant Colonel James Quirk returned to Philadelphia on Christmas night 1945, arriving at 30th Street Station late in the evening. It had been two years and four days since his departure for England. Except for his stateside stint at Fort Leavenworth in the fall of 1943, he had been overseas, in North Africa and Europe, for more than two and a half years.

In that time Elizabeth had lived in a small walk-up apartment in a converted row house on Chestnut Street in West Philadelphia, taken a job as a welfare caseworker with the Philadelphia Department of Public Assistance, and raised her young son with the help of a sixty-seven-year-old live-in housekeeper, Miss Mattie. The housekeeper's frequent outings with her young charge included the placing of an occasional bet with Jules, who ran the corner newsstand and kept a little book on the side. Elizabeth's relations with her neighbors were cordial but somewhat strained because, in their view, she had exercised decidedly unpatriotic judgment in permitting her son to play with the little Japanese American boy who lived downstairs.

The Chestnut Street walk-up to which James came on that Christmas night would be home for the next year. With his three months of accumulated leave, James and Elizabeth had an opportunity to figure out their next step. One possibility was that James would return to college on the GI Bill, finish his degree, and go to law school. They discussed it seriously. Had he gone back, James would not have been alone; more than 2 million veterans attended colleges and universities on the GI Bill in the

*postwar period. But few of them were thirty-four-year-old lieu-
tenant colonels who had left school fifteen years before. Although finances were a consideration in the decision, the bottom line was that James was impatient; he wanted to get on with
his life and make a few dollars. A return to school, although offering possible long-term benefits, was a detour.*

*James spent the next months looking for work and reac-
quainting himself with his young son. He found the latter the
greater challenge. "I always have a lurking fear that when I
first get to see him he will just turn his head away," James had
written Elizabeth. A father-son reunion photograph taken in the
backyard shortly after James's return captured snowsuited son
fixing the photographer with a skeptical who-is-this-guy? gaze
while simultaneously trying to slither out of the paternal grasp.*

*"I don't know that I am terribly anxious to get back into the
radio–advertising–public relations atmosphere," he had written
Elizabeth, "but I shall probably be forced to just because it is
the only thing I know." The lead-in to the Annenberg organization that he had mentioned in his final letter home panned
out. Walter Annenberg's Triangle Publications, best known for
its racing publications (the* Morning Telegraph *and the* Daily
Racing Form*) along with the hometown* Philadelphia Inquirer*,
had decided to move aggressively into broadcasting, both radio and the infant medium of television. Among the radio stations that Triangle had purchased was WFIL in Philadelphia.
And it was there that James landed in the spring of 1946 as promotion director for WFIL and the new WFIL-TV (the nation's
thirteenth television station).*

*In January 1947, James and Elizabeth moved to a house in
what had been prewar farmland west of Philadelphia. The community of modest detached brick houses with neatly manicured
small lawns in front was called Havertown. The neighborhood
of young marrieds, many of them veterans, with lots of children,
was a short commute in the family Packard to WFIL.*

*As James began to rebuild his prewar career, Elizabeth and
Miss Mattie reconstructed a home for a little boy whose life until that time had been a world of walk-ups and city streets. There*

were quiet times, together times. A big night out was going down to the abandoned quarry and watching the older kids and their dads fly their noisy, gasoline-powered model airplanes, then coming home covered with a misting of the spent fuel, the odor of which took days to dissipate.

It was during that period that a mysterious box materialized in our living room. Many an hour was spent watching the television test pattern, which seemed to be the major programming staple. Neighbors would stop in to gawk, and our family acquired our Warholian fifteen minutes until the novelty wore off.

On the Fourth of July 1947, James and Elizabeth hosted a small neighborhood cookout in the backyard. In addition to sparklers and the usual fare, someone had brought a plastic rocket with a detachable nose cone. The idea was to remove the cone, insert an explosive cap from a cap pistol strip, screw shut the cone, and hurl the rocket into the sky. It would come hurtling back and strike the ground, at which point the metal detonator in the cone would set off a dramatic explosion. Right around dusk, one of the older boys threw the rocket high into the darkening sky. Children and adults craned their necks to watch the reentry. But the trajectory was off course. The rocket struck my father in his upturned face, shattering a lens in his eyeglasses and driving shards into his eye. The rocket was summarily consigned to a trash can while Elizabeth took a sterile solution and tried to wash the glass out of my father's eye. I reflected on that incident in later years, wondering what would have happened if he'd lost the eye, what two-eyed officer would have gone to Korea a few years later in my father's stead, and how dramatically different his life—and ours—would have been.

That summer, I took a walk with Miss Mattie to a nearby farm to look at the animals. The last thing I recalled was reaching out to touch a thoroughly bored-looking cow and saying to Miss Mattie that I felt funny. I woke up in a hospital. The next four months were a succession of raging fevers, pinballing in and out of hospitals, and being poked and probed by mystified specialists, who when in doubt (which seemed to be perpetually) prescribed penicillin shots. Finally, the last in a line of specialists told James and *Elizabeth with uncommon candor: "I have no idea what's wrong with the boy, but I'm quite certain he'll outgrow it." Which I did.*

Around this time, James made his television debut on WFIL-TV as host and jack-of-all-trades of a weekly quiz show titled You Tell Me. James and the other cast members would reenact events from history as the audience at home presumably tried to guess the events being beamed into their homes. The budget for the show hovered perilously close to nonexistent. The show's "regulars" performed in their day-job suits and skirts, which must have made coming up with the right answer a challenge for the befuddled viewer. Scripts and rehearsals were extravagances, as were props. In a pinch, if a scene called for a child, James would dragoon his son out of the wings and plop him down on a chair or a desk while the cast improvised its way through the signing of the Magna Carta or Edison creating the first electric light (it was tough to tell the difference). Unlike WFIL-TV's 1950s local programming sensation Bandstand, the quiz show graciously moseyed off to broadcasting Valhalla after a season, much to the relief of the cast—and the host, who had wisely kept his day job.

In the winter of 1948–49, we moved to Charleston, West Virginia, where my father hooked up with his World War II colleague Joe Smith (the tongue-in-cheek mops-for-chars proponent mentioned in one of my father's first letters home). Smith had been owner and general manager of a radio station in his hometown of Beckley, West Virginia, before the war and was seeking to expand operations into television. He intended to open the first television station in Charleston.

Television had yet to fulfill the optimistic pronouncement of the chairman of the Federal Communications Commission that "an entirely new world of entertainment and culture will open for the American home with the coming of television." By mid-1948, television remained a novelty. There were 28 stations (as opposed to more than 16,000 radio stations), and they all had one thing in common—losing money. There were only 325,000 sets in operation in the entire country (of which half were in the New York metropolitan area). Nine out of ten Americans had never even seen a TV program.

Still, for those with an entrepreneurial bent, the timing seemed right. Two figures going in markedly different directions portended a bright future. The cost of a TV, once prohibitive, was in decline: A no-frills Admiral ten-inch television cost $249.50, putting it within reach of the middle class. And TV advertising revenue, which hadn't come close to covering operating costs in the early years, had ballooned to $25 million by 1949. (It would quadruple the following year.)

James and Elizabeth, Miss Mattie, and I moved to Charleston, to a small brick house on a cul-de-sac off Virginia Street in the shadow of the capitol building and adjacent to the Kanawha River. The pace in Charleston ran the gamut from languid to tranquil. For a five year old, it was perfect. Warm days were spent on a neighbor's sliding board (a "slicky-slide" in the local patois) or with James on the bank of the Kanawha sailing a decidedly unseaworthy model boat attached to a fishing line. For hours, my father would play out the line and I would reel it in. The boat usually had the waters to itself except when one of the local factories belched something unspeakable into the river. The resultant fish kill would surround the sailboat, the armada of wide-eyed fish bobbing sightlessly in the murky water.

Elizabeth would take me to the glassblowing factories in the hills where we would watch vessels of various sizes magically take shape on the end of the glassblower's pipe. For a pittance, Elizabeth would pick out wonderful pieces, with flaws perceptible only to the craftsman, and display them around the house. Winters were spent in the gym of Sacred Heart High School watching our neighbor, a strapping Gulliver among Lilliputian opponents, score baskets effortlessly (albeit at short range, a limitation that became apparent the following year at the University in Morgantown, where his career went into immediate and irreversible eclipse).

If things had worked out, we probably would have stayed in Charleston. The television venture progressed in fits and starts.

Mountainous terrain, lagging TV sales, and start-up costs caused frustrations. Complicating matters was a Federal Communications Commission freeze on television licenses, leading some observers to conclude that TV was nothing more than a fad and creating what one broadcasting historian has called a "strange twilight period" in the evolution of television. One station actually made it onto the air in nearby Huntington, signing on in late 1949 (although live network programming didn't occur for another year). It was the first station in the state, and the only one.

For the most part, the West Virginia broadcasting forty-niners, unlike the California forty-niners of the previous century, were panning dross.

That point was brought home one evening in the summer of 1949. James summoned me to the car to assist him with some items in the backseat. We took them out and lined them up by the front door. The matched set of fine luggage fit for a transatlantic cruise was Elizabeth's gift for their wedding anniversary, my father told me. We rang the doorbell and backed off into the shadows. When she opened the door, my mother was visibly surprised. Each piece of luggage was brought into the sparsely furnished dining room and was gone over with great attention. When all of the pieces were in place, James surveyed the incongruous scene, the thoroughly exquisite luggage in the unexquisite room, and said semiconvincingly: "Someday you'll get to use them, I promise." Elizabeth smiled and mustered a semiconvincing hug. It was a six year old's first inkling that things were not going so well.

The second inkling hit closer to home. We had spoken all winter of returning to the New Jersey seashore for a few weeks in summer, as we had every year since my father had gotten home. By spring, the discussion was wreathed in mumbled uncertainties. By midsummer, even the mumbling ceased. Labor Day came, then went, and the issue was moot.

In January 1950, the Charleston experiment ended. Television would prosper in West Virginia in the mid-1950s, long after we were gone. We went back to Philadelphia, and my father returned to Triangle. We moved into a two-bedroom apartment just across the city line in Bala Cynwyd, having come, it seemed, full circle in the housing market—from apartment to house to apartment.

My father's new duties brought him into the publishing side of the organization, as deputy promotion manager for the Philadelphia Inquirer, the morning paper locked in a losing circulation battle with the afternoon Evening Bulletin. (It was a spirited rivalry, perhaps best encapsulated in the Inquirer's ingeniously cropped photograph accompanying a story about a traffic accident outside their competitor's building. The photograph lopped off a portion of the large logo emblazoned across the front of the Bulletin building, so it read, "THE EVENING BULL.")

Switching first grade at midyear proved problematic. The Charleston school didn't introduce cursive writing until second grade; my new first-grade classmates had been writing since September and were seemingly light years ahead of me. The first grade into which I was transferring, already demarcated into adjectival learning groups (nothing so harsh as "fast group" and "slow group" but something not much better) now added an additional track for their new block-letter laggard. Evenings were spent with a rubber eraser balanced on the back of my writing hand as I tried to trace the graceful loops that the Palmer Method demanded. The theory was that if my hand were aligned properly, the eraser would remain in place. I spent most of the evening picking it up off the floor. Things did not get off to an auspicious start on the social side, either. A reflexive reference to the sliding board as a "slicky-slide" branded me for a short time with an embarrassing scarlet R, for rube.

As the year progressed, things picked up for the family. By the midpoint of second grade, the slicky-slide faux pas mercifully forgotten, I had moved into the academic and social mainstream—no budding Rhodes scholar but no longer the academic anchor. My sole barometer for measuring our family's financial well-being was also on the rise: We returned to the seashore that summer after the year's hiatus. Life was good.

We had fallen into a comfortable familial pattern in which even the surprises were steeped in reassuring familiarity. Saturday mornings were spent with my father at the paper; he went in half days most Saturdays. He would prop me on a stool in the art department, and I (and a lucky classmate or two) would spend the morning watching the artists draw the comic strips for the Sunday paper. Afterward, he would take us to the Horn & Hardart automat, where we would select lunch from the offerings arrayed in the small enclosures behind the glass doors, deposit our coins, take our food, then watch a seemingly disembodied hand pop a replacement onto the vacant shelf.

My mother was the best-known person in our small apartment complex by virtue of her volunteer role as civil defense warden. She executed her duties with a customary seriousness of purpose. Every entranceway boasted a placard (preserved against the elements in a clear plastic cover) containing information on what to do in the event of nuclear attack; we were to proceed to the basement, as I recall. In the space at the bottom of the placard identifying the key contact person in an emergency, my mother had entered in her neat hand her name and our apartment number. Not that anyone stopped by, but she had extremely high name recognition nonetheless. Every few months, I would accompany her as she made the rounds of the stairwells, damp sponge in hand, wiping the fingerprints and smudges off the protective plastic. The residents of 4 Bala Avenue were thoroughly prepared for Armageddon. The nuclear slackers in the other buildings couldn't hold a candle to her.

For Christmas, I got a two-wheeled bike. The street in front of the apartment house was too heavily trafficked for a novice biker, so James and I spent the rest of the Christmas vacation in the narrow alley beside the building trying to keep me upright. To no avail. Although the narrowness of the alley prevented any serious swerves, I spent many an afternoon careening off the brick wall of the building, across the alley, and into a chain-link fence.

My snowsuit provided a protective cocoon when I fell, which I did—repeatedly. Exasperated, James would gently suggest that perhaps the dead of winter wasn't the best time to take up bike riding; we'd reattack the problem in the spring.

As 1950 gave way to 1951, I was only dimly aware of the telegrams from Washington, the closed-door discussions between my parents, or my father's trips to the basement storage locker to take some forgotten clothing out of mothballs—until the January evening when my parents sat me down on the couch between them, a pair of grim-faced bookends. While my mother tried to look composed, my father told me that he had to go away for a while and that until he got back I would have to be responsible for helping my mother with some of the things he had always taken care of, such as taking the trash downstairs and putting my bike in the basement. (No problem there; it wouldn't move for the entire time he was away.)

Confused, I asked him where he was going. He named a place I had never heard of. The next afternoon when I got home from school, he was gone—recalled to active duty. We were a family again at war.

Elizabeth in Canada, August 1940, my parents' last summer vacation before the war. During the trip, they stopped off at the home of the Dionne quintuplets, and plucked a good-luck "stork stone" out of a bin.

James (far left), in his lieutenant's uniform, at a defense plant in Denver, August 1942. The coveted Army-Navy E for Excellence pennant was awarded to plants that met wartime production quotas. (Mile High Photo Co.)

James, now a major, with 12th Army Group in France, October 1944. After landing in Normandy on D+5, he had risen rapidly to become General Omar Bradley's public relations officer. (Army Signal Corps)

James (second from right) at a memorial ceremony at Verdun, October 1944. "It was quite a historic occasion," he wrote Elizabeth, "because the Germans allowed no memorials during the Occupation." (Army Signal Corps)

With my mother, 1944. My father carried this photograph with him throughout the war—"in my shirt pocket," he wrote Elizabeth, "and I sometimes just get sick for the sight of both of you."

General George S. Patton awards my father the Bronze Star Medal, March 1945. "He is a most impressive guy," James wrote. "People expect some kind of circus performance and are always a little surprised to find out he knows more about more things than they do." (Army Signal Corps)

V-E Day, May 8, 1945. Patton (center) with my father (to Patton's right) and the officers of the section. "I can only wonder what I shall get up for tomorrow," James wrote Elizabeth. (Army Signal Corps)

Home from war. My parents in the backyard on Chestnut Street shortly after my father's arrival on Christmas night, 1945. "I shall be happy if we are able to maintain our wartime income," he wrote Elizabeth, "but I am not sure that we can."

With my parents on an outing to Darby Creek, Spring 1946. Still trying to get adjusted to this strange man who had appeared unexpectedly into my life on Christmas night.

War again. Korea 1951. My father with General Douglas MacArthur as he issues his poisonous "stalemate" pronouncement. "He is sort of fascinating and detestable," James wrote. "He tried to ignore the national policy of his own country." (U.S. Army)

In the field with Matthew Ridgway, Korea 1951. "The difference is General Ridgway and nobody else," James wrote of the man he had come to respect deeply. "The men here think that he is the greatest ever and he probably is." (*Saturday Evening Post*)

Ridgway's staff (my father, second from left) headed for Tokyo to relieve MacArthur, April 1951. "I was being precipitated into the big leagues," James wrote, "and was afraid of messing something up right off the bat." He didn't.

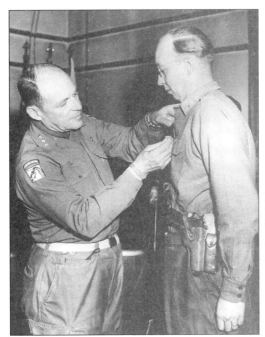

Receiving the Legion of Merit from Ridgway in Tokyo for "exceptionally meritorious service" with Eighth Army in Korea—"the first order he ever published in the new job," James wrote Elizabeth. (U.S. Army)

Ridgway and his staff—dubbed the "Korean Carpetbaggers" by my father (at left)—after taking over in Tokyo. The name stuck. "We are afraid to give the word any currency," James wrote, "because it has a certain aptness." (*Life* magazine)

Ridgway and my father greet John Foster Dulles upon his arrival in Tokyo for discussions on the Japanese peace treaty. "This is a remarkable time in our history," James wrote," and I have been standing in the middle of it." (Acme)

Back in Korea in the wake of the major Chinese offensive to take Seoul, April 1951. The plane in the background bears the three stars of Ridgway's successor at Eighth Army in Korea, General James Van Fleet.

With my mother at Rockefeller Center, 1952, to celebrate my (finally) making the honor roll. My first trip to New York was nearly marred when a cabbie tried to short-change us outlanders. Bad idea; Elizabeth nailed him. (Rockefeller Center)

My parents on *TV Guide* business (James with the omnipresent cigarette), at the Pump Room in Chicago, 1954. The publishing "Titanic" was on its way to becoming a publishing phenomenon. (Shiro)

James (left) and Walter Annenberg (with shovel) at ground-breaking for the new *TV Guide* headquarters in Radnor, 1956. The employee who'd asked in 1953 if he could go back to his old job when *TV Guide* cratered, had fretted unnecessarily.

With my parents at my high school graduation, 1961. My diploma put me one up on my father, who had never graduated from anywhere. It was the *only* thing I ever bested him at.

My father introducing the All-America football team to President Kennedy at halftime of the Army-Navy game, 1962. Moments earlier, a tipsy spectator had rushed at Kennedy and been belatedly intercepted. "If the guy had had a gun," James noted of the security lapse, "the president could have been shot."

Our last picture together, taken shortly after I'd received my commission as an infantry lieutenant, 1966. My father, just 55, had begun to age noticeably: at 6-foot-3, he had always towered over me; now, he was the shorter one.

With my platoon sergeant, Wiley Clark, along Highway 4 north of My Tho in the Mekong Delta, 1968. Vietnam, our family's third war, would be one too many for my father.

With my family—Clare, Chris, Elizabeth—in the peace of the Bishop's Garden at the Washington National Cathedral, Spring 1999. (Llewellyn Bensfield)

Chapter Four: A Family at War
1951

With Ridgway

Matthew B. Ridgway was born in 1895. He graduated from West Point (Class of 1917) near the top third of his class and was assigned to the infantry. Like Omar Bradley, he missed the fighting in France during World War I despite repeated efforts to participate.

In the peacetime army, Ridgway served on several occasions with George C. Marshall, who was favorably impressed. When the 82d Division was activated after Pearl Harbor, Ridgway was named assistant division commander under Bradley and succeeded him in 1942.

In August 1942, the 82d was redesignated the 82d Airborne Division. Ridgway's paratroopers saw some of the hardest fighting of World War II in Sicily, Normandy, and the Ardennes. As commander of the 82d Airborne (and later of the XVIII Airborne Corps), Ridgway distinguished himself as one of the elite American combat generals ("a 12th Century knight with a 20th Century brain," in the words of one colleague).

In December 1950, following the death of Gen. Walton Walker, Ridgway was sent to Korea to succeed him as commander of the Eighth Army, which was then in disorganized retreat before the Chinese Communist Forces. MacArthur's unfettered charge was: "The Eighth Army is yours, Matt. Do what you think best."

Ridgway would serve as the commander of Eighth Army for four months. "It is not often in wartime," Omar Bradley wrote years later, "that a single battlefield commander can make a decisive difference. But in Korea, Ridgway would prove to be the exception. His brilliant, driving, uncompromising leadership would turn the tide of battle like no other general's in our military history."

December 1950–January 1951: Rebuilding Eighth Army

The Eighth Army that Matthew Ridgway inherited the day after Christmas 1950 was a disheartened, demoralized, and defeated lot. From the North Korean invasion of the South in late June (when the war seemed surely lost) through the disintegration of Douglas MacArthur's "Home by Christmas" offensive in December (just when the war seemed all but won), Eighth Army had yo-yoed down and up (and down) the Korean peninsula.

Things had gone badly at the outset. With the South Korean capital of Seoul in Communist hands and the South Korean army imploding, President Truman had ordered U.S. forces to South Korea. Thrown into the breach in early July, Eighth Army, nominally combat ready but softened by years of garrison duty in Japan, could do no more than fight a delaying action, withdrawing southeastward into the Pusan Perimeter in early August.

The tide turned dramatically in mid-September with the amphibious landing of X Corps (1st Marine Division and 7th Infantry Division) at Inchon, on the west coast of South Korea in the Communist rear. That action, coupled with the breakout of Eighth Army from the Pusan Perimeter, sent North Korean forces reeling northward, as though the film of the first few months of the war were being played in reverse. Seoul was recaptured in short order, and United Nations forces were rolling to the North Korea–South Korea border at the thirty-eighth parallel.

In early October, the United States, notwithstanding strong United Nations misgivings, upped the geopolitical ante. The original defensive goal (expulsion of the North Koreans from South Korea and the preservation of that country) gave way to defeat of the North Korean forces and reunification of the Koreas under a democratic government. United Nations forces crossed the thirty-eighth parallel and swept forward against weakening North Korean opposition. *The war appeared all but over.*

All but. In late October, U.N. forces encountered Chinese troops on the Korean battlefront for the first time, portending a much different war. Their presence was discounted. MacArthur ("like Custer at the Little Big Horn," Ridgway would observe later) ordered his troops farther north. With Eighth Army in the west and X Corps in the east racing on a slapdash line toward the Yalu River at the border between North Korea and China, MacArthur announced the "final offensive" of the war, declaring that some troops might be home by Christmas. The only troops home by Christmas were South Koreans, in circumstances little to their liking.

In late November, after repeated warnings that they would not sit idly by, Chinese Communist forces, 300,000 strong, mounted massive attacks south of the Yalu, driving the stunned U.N. forces southward in a month-long retreat that at times approached a rout (a "humiliating defeat," in Omar Bradley's assessment). On December 23—with North Korea once more in Communist hands, Eighth Army back below the thirty-eighth parallel, and the future of the South again imperiled—Eighth Army suffered another blow. Its commander, Gen. Walton Walker, was killed in a jeep accident. Ridgway was sent from Washington to succeed him.

The Chinese attack had shattered the confidence not only of Eighth Army but also of Douglas MacArthur. His Olympian "Home by Christmas" pronouncements turned sharply Dunkirkish and defeatist. Absent reinforcements, MacArthur cabled Washington, his command would be destroyed and Korea lost.

In marked contrast to these dire pronouncements, Ridgway went to work with a decisive, dogged optimism, transforming Eighth Army from "a retreating, ready-for-peace group of men into a responsive military instrument," as one historian described it. Heads of can't-do commanders rolled. Readiness and training were stepped up. Woefully equipped and clothed troops were resupplied. Ridgway was everywhere along the front—questioning, probing, demanding, even handing out gloves to *soldiers who had lost theirs, so they could function in the frozen climate.*

The Communists wasted little time testing Ridgway, mounting a major New Year's Eve offensive across the thirty-eighth parallel. Seoul fell for the second time in six months, forcing Eighth Army into now-familiar withdrawal—except this time Eighth Army withdrew in good order ("as a fighting army, not as a running mob," Ridgway recalled), with its equipment intact, and regrouped. Throughout January, Ridgway hammered home to commanders the changed culture: He didn't want to see their defensive plans, he told them; he wanted to see their attack plans. The troops sensed the change. Morale rose. Eighth Army, in shambles a month earlier, was an army again ("the equal of any army [in Europe] in World War II," in Bradley's view).

One member of Ridgway's new team, a thirty-nine-year-old lieutenant colonel from Philadelphia who had been recalled to active duty at Ridgway's request, was James Quirk.

16 JANUARY 1951
WASHINGTON

DEPARTMENT OF THE ARMY
Office of the Adjutant General
Washington, D.C.

SUBJECT: Active Military Service
TO: Lt. Colonel James T. Quirk

By direction of the President, you are, with your consent, ordered into the active military service, effective 21 January 1951 and assigned to the Far East Command. You will proceed to Travis Air Force Base, Fairfield, California to arrive on 24 January 1951 for travel by aircraft to destination.

Travel of dependents and shipment of household goods at government expense are not authorized.

On January 25, less than a month after Ridgway's arrival, Eighth Army goes over to the offensive, a posture and a mind-set that

*would characterize the entirety of Ridgway's tenure. Turned
around mentally and geographically, Eighth Army moves north.*

Darling,

    This is the end of a long, long trip and I am writing this to
you before I take off to bed at the unprecedented hour of 8
p.m. Since my letter to you at Honolulu, I have done not
much else except fly and I am desperately tired.

    Ten hours out of Honolulu, we stopped at Wake Island. A
bus met us and took us over to a mess hall where we had a
most indifferent meal and I had my first reacquaintance with
canned butter which tasted as foul as ever. The date line lies
somewhere just east of Wake Island so somewhere there in
the Pacific we lost Friday completely. Wake is a grim and mis-
erable place. It is a tiny and entirely treeless tropical atoll surrounding a central lagoon. It consists of a runway and Nissen
huts and would make a wonderful Siberia for any one of the
military services. Even at 3 o'clock in the morning it was
warm and they say that it is frightful in the brilliant and un-
shaded sun of a tropical day.

    It began to get a little grim. It took us thirteen hours from
Wake to Tokyo which meant that I had been flying almost
continuously since late Tuesday. We had a lovely experience.
About four and a half hours out of Tokyo we began to smell
burning rubber, a happy thought in an airplane. While the
crew checked frantically to find the source, the pilot took the
plane down from 8000 feet to 400 feet so that we could ditch
in a hurry if we had to. We checked and found out that we
had two twenty-man rafts aboard and thirty-eight people.
While a few of us sweated that out, the crew finally found the
source of the trouble. There was a defective plug on the steward's coffee urn and the insulation was burning.

    Tokyo is interesting but I am too tired to tell you much
about it. Suffice it to say that I am here in one piece and that
tonight I shall sleep in a bed for the first time since Monday
night. Meanwhile best love to you and Rory a half a world
away. (27 January 1951, Tokyo)

Darling,

   I have been able to give you only fragmentary reports because things moved more rapidly than I could absorb them
and my reactions have been slowed by fatigue. I will soon settle down to the abnormal life of war as though it all hadn't
been more than five years ago.

   This is country that has no parallel anywhere. It consists entirely of rugged, completely eroded mountains and narrow
valleys which are now just dusty but which will be filled with
water for the rice paddies when the rainy season comes.
There is no road net. There are a few roads which are un-
paved, narrow, rocky and rutted so that travelling anywhere is
a very difficult job. I am going to the front tomorrow but have
to travel by plane because it would take all day if I tried to do
it by road even though the distance is not great. It presents a
supply problem that the American army has never had.

   The people lack the life and volatility of the Japanese. They
are a stolid people, in spite of the fact that it is one of the oldest cultures in the world. The country is just too unspeakably
grim to describe until I have been here a little longer but it
makes the Arab countries look wonderful in comparison.

   Today I had my session with General Ridgway. He was wonderfully cordial and I am to be his personal public relations
adviser with access to him regularly and reporting to him
only. He is an overpowering personality but I think that I can
take him in stride. He suggested that I take a trip to the front
to look things over and asked me when I could do it. I said
"Tomorrow" and the answer seemed to please him. As a result I return to the wars tomorrow after a long lapse. There is
a lot to be done and I sink or swim on what happens from
here on out. I have some ideas for him—a whole lot of
them—but I want to absorb some more before I pop off.

   The whole thing is rugged but I feel good and can figure I
am just as tough as the next fellow. I am glad that I did it
once before because it all seems so familiar to me. Even the
food comes out of the same can we used in the last war.
(30 January 1951, Korea)

31 JANUARY 1951
KOREA

COMMANDING GENERAL
EIGHTH UNITED STATES ARMY KOREA

[To: Commanding Generals, All Divisions]

Lieutenant Colonel James Quirk, distinguished American journalist, having recently volunteered for active duty in this theater, has been assigned as my special adviser on public relations. Would appreciate any courtesy shown him when in your areas.

RIDGWAY

February 1951: Eighth Army Advances

Dear Merrill [a *Philadelphia Inquirer* colleague],

This is sort of a portmanteau letter to everyone at *The Inquirer,* so will you please pass on pertinent portions of it to those that might be interested. A lot of it will have significance only to you because this is not exactly the army we knew. The ETO at its lowest never descended to Korea at its best.

I spent the best part of a four day period in an airplane from Washington to Korea with stops in California, Honolulu, Wake Island and Tokyo.

My travel has been expedited all the way and I was shoved through as though I were carrying a vital part of the atom bomb in my lap. I knew the army too well to figure that could go on without some snafu and it came. I landed on a dusty airstrip in Korea and finally persuaded an air force bus driver to let me on his bus with roughly a hundred pounds of luggage. He dropped me about five hundred yards from the gate of my headquarters and I struggled through the Korean mud with my bundles. I finally found the AG [adjutant general], checked in and created quite a stir because a full colonel had been waiting for me at the airstrip since early morning. How he missed me is one of the army's great mysteries, but the army has so many.

General Ridgway was up front and I didn't see him until the following day. I checked in with the PIO [public information] section and found two senior colonels in a high state of timidity. They asked me very delicately just what the General wanted me to do and I said I was damned if I knew. I met quite a few of the correspondents that I knew and they all asked the same question and got the same answer.

The next day the General came back. He told me that he wanted me to be his personal adviser on public relations, reporting only to him and with no administrative responsibility. He was very frank, very friendly, and seems to have a complete grasp of all his problems. He is a big and overpowering man, with a tremendous air of strength and purpose and drive. He is on the move constantly and spends most of his time at the front leaving the C/S [chief of staff] to run the headquarters. He urged that I get the whole picture quickly and especially the front line picture and the setup down at the divisions and corps.

The next day's events worked out peculiarly. When I got down to the strip early in the morning I ran into General Ridgway. He took off and I took off a few minutes later. When I got up to the strip where I was going I met him again. He asked me where I was going and I said one of the corps. When I left the strip I changed my mind and went to one of the division CPs of the major attack division. There I met General Ridgway. I chatted with him and the division commander and was invited to stay for lunch. After lunch the division artillery commander took me with him to see the artillery positions and we finally worked our way down to the CP of the assault battalion. There I met General Ridgway. Said he, "Quirk, I hope you don't think I'm following you."

We spent some time with the Turks, who were attacking, and they were wonderful soldiers. They wear our uniforms and look better in them than we do, and we watched them attack up a hillside with great dash and in wonderful order.

They were on their objective ahead of time and were bitching because they couldn't go on. They like to fight with the bayonet and we counted more than sixty of the results. I don't know whether all the North Koreans were still standing up when they got the holes in them but they were really punctured. When we got back to their CP, we saw some Turkish medics tenderly bandaging up some Korean civilians who had been badly burned by napalm.

I get a good reception everywhere because the General sent a message to all corps and divisions telling them to take care of me. They seem to want to show how rugged it is, and it is. This is a terrible war for troops. The place names which you read in the communiques are merely villages of mud huts with straw roofs. As a result the GIs feel that even when they advance they aren't getting anywhere. They have that feeling especially because they have been over this territory twice before—once going and once bouncing back. There is no feeling that when they get to the next town they might find a drink or a friend or a dry place to sleep. The men have to live like pigs up front and it is tough to see them stretching out in a rice paddy for the night with just a blanket roll and a rifle. It's a stinking, lousy war.

The questions here all concern the international political situation because there is strong hope that will bring a political settlement to this unhappy affair.

Against my better judgment I am enclosing a copy of the memorandum from General Ridgway. For God's sake don't show it around the paper. It sounds silly enough here and I couldn't stand the guffaws that would greet it on the fourth floor.

Sincere regards from the Distinguished American Journalist. (1 February 1951, Korea)

Darling,

I have had an exhausting ten days. I have gotten my second wind, and feel as though I have been in the army for a long time. It has taken me a little longer to get broken in but

I am not as young as I was last time. On the other hand I have some of the security of rank, of knowledge, and of remembering that I shall be home in three and a half months.

Yesterday morning I took off to visit up front. I met the division commander, General Kean, whom I had known in Europe and was invited to stay for lunch. After lunch, I went out with General Barth, the division artillery commander. We saw the American artillery in action and I was most impressed. This is a pretty professional army and in some ways they just look more competent and more confident than the army did in Europe. There was one young soldier, who looked about 17 years old, working the radio to the OP and calling out the corrections. He looked calm and unhurried and unimpressed with the job he was doing. He was sitting on a ration box, over his ankles in mud, with a microphone in his hand, relaying back and forth a lot of technical artillery data. It's amazing what a little bit of soldiering can do to mature high school boys. The artillery was having a busy day and they are always happiest when they are firing.

After we left the artillery we worked our way down to a battalion command post where we could watch the attack. When the enemy has no air and not much artillery, the conditions of warfare are quite different. On each hill crest was sitting a tank, silhouetted against the skyline, pointed at the enemy, so that they could help out with harassing fire in case of counterattack. In Europe such a maneuver would have been the end of one tank and one tank crew. At the battalion CP which was running two American companies in the attack on the flank of the Turks, I got the same feeling of bored competence that is always the mark of the professional. The CP was set up in a mud-walled hut with a thatched roof and consisted of a couple of maps, a telephone and two radios for communication. It seemed so familiar to hear the old army code words like, "Boxer Easy to Boxer Fox, Boxer George says they are getting fire from your flank." The battalion exec was concentrated on the problem at hand like a draftsman over a drawing.

Just beyond the CP, we could see the Turks working up one hill and the Americans up another. The artillery was coming from our rear and we could hear it pass over, then burst on the crest of the ridge ahead. It was a small, unspectacular segment of the war but we were losing a few men and the slow steady attrition of our boys was going on. Their losses are far higher than ours but that is little consolation.

Coming back the men were getting chow and some of them were bedding down for a little sleep so that they would be awake and alert during the night when the Chinese and the Koreans love to attack. It is pretty grim to see the men finishing up field rations and wrapping up in blankets to lie down in a rice paddy for some rest. It is especially bitter when you think that many of them have been doing that for seven months. It is almost entirely a dogfaces' war and they are taking the losses. The tankers and artillery are anxious to help but the little man with the rifle has to do the dirty work.

In the hills where I was yesterday the ground is frightful. It thaws in the afternoon sun so that there is mud everywhere and then freezes into hard ridges in the bitter cold of the nights. (1 February 1951, Korea)

5 FEBRUARY 1951
KOREA

HEADQUARTERS
EIGHTH UNITED STATES ARMY KOREA

MEMO FOR COL QUIRK:

There are two topics I wanted to discuss with you today, and on which I would appreciate your counsel.

First, how do we go about developing in the minds of our splendid men, recognition, of the almost certainty, that America will not in their life-time know again, the quiet, peaceful insulated comforts of other days?

Second, what information can we assemble, and how and to whom transmit, so that our Government can deflate the falsely acquired military reputation of Communist China's Armies, in the minds not only of our people, but above all of the populations of Asia?

Please think these over and let me have your ideas, when convenient.

RIDGWAY

Darling,

With the type of war that General Ridgway is fighting there is a major change from the past. The other fellow started out to bleed us white. As things are going now, our losses are so small and his are so great that we are slowly bleeding him white in spite of his great size. He can't stand this forever but neither can we. The great feeling here is that some diplomatic solution must be found, but our army is very good, very professional, and they shall fight on well forever if that is necessary. There is something heartening about this sort of an army. They don't feel that they are taking a chunk out of their civilian lives. This is their life and they are willing to settle for it, even though it is a lousy life.

I do feel my love for you more and more. Good night, darling. (7 February 1951, Korea)

During the next three days (February 8–10), Eighth Army drives Communist forces northward across the Han River, retakes the port of Inchon and Kimpo airfield, and advances toward the south bank of the Han across from Seoul. For the first time since the Chinese intervention, the Communists have been driven back.

Darling,

The weather turned mild today and the sun was out to take the chill off things. It is felt that we might get some more bad weather but the worst is really over. The days are getting longer and that is a bit of a help.

The amazing thing about the army over here is the complete integration of the Negroes. There is one whole regiment of the 25th division that is Negro and all the rest of the divisions have Negro troops. The whole situation is just beyond comment here and the complete acceptability of the whole arrangement would seem to indicate that the army has no problem anymore. I suppose that it could be done in civilian life if people put their minds down to it. (12 February 1951, Korea)

In the central X Corps sector of the line, the Communists launch a major offensive against Hoengsong, Wonju, and Chipyong. Elements of the U.S. 2d Infantry Division are mauled in "Massacre Valley" near Hoengsong, but the Communists fail to take the road hub farther south at Wonju and sustain heavy casualties. To the west, elements of the encircled 23d Infantry Regiment hold on to the road hub at Chipyong. In the aftermath of these major defeats, the Communists prepare a wholesale withdrawal to the north.

On February 18, Ridgway drafts a plan to continue the Eighth Army attack across the Han. On February 19, he briefs his generals and gives a not-for-publication background briefing to the press. On February 20, the eve of the offensive, MacArthur flies to Korea and tells reporters on the record: "I have just ordered a resumption of the initiative."

Darling,

This is sort of a Hollywood war where the headlines are more important than the action. The Supreme Commander, that's the Supreme MacArthur, arrived today to announce that he had ordered the attack that General R. had already planned. He always makes his appearance for the victories and the start of the offensives but he is conspicuous by his absence during the retreats and the losses. He may have been a great man once but he is a querulous old man with the shakes now and has nothing to sustain him but his supreme ego. (20 February 1951, Korea)

Darling,

More and more it seems to me that the great MacArthur is
a monumental faker supported by a group in America who
are on his side because they suspect that he opposes the Administration. They don't realize that he would be just as trou-
blesome to any administration, because there is nothing political about his Jehovah complex. Can you imagine Senator
Taft and Douglas MacArthur agreeing on global strategy?
Harry Truman was a soldier once, however briefly and long
ago, and he has some glimmerings of what the military problems are. MacArthur has no more to do with the victories in
Korea than I do but he always gets himself into the act when
things go well and then wraps himself in a mantle of silence
when the going is rough. He was the Supreme Commander
when the army was doing badly and it's the same army. The
difference is General Ridgway and nobody else. The British
and the French swear by the General, and the GIs in the line
think he is great.

That's the real test. (21 February 1951, Korea)

Darling,

I had Hugh Moffett of *Time* working on the final phases of
the cover story on the General, which will be on the news
stands on Thursday. On Tuesday I start with two *Life* men on
a *Life* cover and picture story on the General to run in mid-
March. I also have a *Saturday Evening Post* feature practically
set. This is all in addition to the run of the day news.

General MacArthur muscled back into the act to the consternation of everyone concerned. When the war was going
badly GHQ [general headquarters] ceased issuing communiques and stated that all communiques would come from
Eighth Army. Our father who art in Tokyo wanted no part of
association with his famous Home by Christmas offensive
which flopped. In recent times the prestige of General Ridgway and the victories of the Eighth Army have been killing
him and his staff.

On Monday, General Ridgway told the press that we would
attack and gave them all the details. Naturally they wouldn't

write it until it came to pass. On Wednesday, General MacArthur made an unexpected trip to Korea and stayed long enough to hand out a statement saying that he had ordered the Eighth Army to attack. Our security people had a heart attack on that one but no one could stop the Supreme Commander and the story ran everywhere. On Thursday morning we moved over to the attack as planned but we simply based our communique on what had already happened and not on what was going to happen. Our patrols made practically no contact so the enemy didn't yet know that we were really all out after them. With no prior notice at 10 a.m. Thursday, the hour before the attack started, The Great Ego put out a communique in Tokyo saying that the United Nations Forces were attacking on a fifty mile front. At that point, Chinese intelligence could cut down their staff since all their work was done for them. So great was his anxiety to be identified as the architect of victory that he showed not much concern for the men on the line who can now attack forces that will be all set for them. It's shocking.

His last trip here was to have his picture taken when we arrived at the Han River in front of Seoul.

This isn't exactly a love letter, but it gives you some idea of the things with which I am deeply involved. They are important, too, because they undermine the confidence of people everywhere in the competence of the command. (24 February 1951, Korea)

Darling,

Day before yesterday was really busy. At 0720 I got a summons to see the General. He had a Drew Pearson column pointing out that General Ridgway is doing a great job and that MacA is a bum. With it was a little friendly note from the Undersecretary of the Army, Mr. Johnson, mildly suggesting that there was no percentage in making the Supreme Commander unhappy. I agreed with that thinking and am now trying to figure some way to point out that there is complete understanding between Korea and Tokyo. The General and I discussed it frankly and at some length. He agreed with my suggestion but there is the problem of who can discuss it with General MacArthur. Best guess is that it can be taken up with him by General Hickey who is his chief of staff.

We had a very frank and interesting talk. The General reminded me that he had served under General MacA when he was the superintendent of the academy [West Point] and General Ridgway was the manager of athletics there. He pointed out also that MacA has always called him Matt and still does and that their personal relations are cordial. He also told me that he was over here on a mission last summer and that when he was leaving General MacA said to him without reference to any previous conversation "Matt, you are my number one choice." That was while General Walker was still alive and there was no thought of change in command. Therefore, the belief that the Department of the Army sent General R. over here in spite of GHQ just isn't true. In spite of my personal distaste for MacA I am trying to figure a way so that the world can be assured that there is no rift. The results, if any, should show up in the next couple of weeks.

The General was also concerned with a little ceremony at Pusan when General Moore's body[9] left for Tokyo and he invited me to go along. When we arrived at the strip the four motors on the big B-17 were running and we leaped aboard and were headed down the runway before we could get our belts on.

The ceremony there was brief and simple. The casket was on a three-quarter ton truck covered by a flag. There was a band and an honor guard with men from each of the divisions. The General, Ambassador [to Korea John J.] Muccio and some other officials fell in and the procession moved at slow step toward a C-54 while the band played the Dead March. The casket was carried up a ramp to the plane, everybody saluted, and it was all over. The whole thing lasted a little more than five minutes. It was simple, rigidly military, and very touching. The General seemed quite moved.

While we were there we learned that the 5th Cav Regiment had driven the Chinese out of their positions northeast of Hoengsong and that they were out in the open moving north through a valley. The calls for air were out and every fighter and fighter bomber that could be mustered took off to work them over. The General decided that we should go take a look.

We took off to the north and the navigator had the precise spot of the air strikes. The General did a thing that I have often heard about but never have seen. He lay down on his bunk and in about two minutes his breathing was perfectly regular and he was sound asleep. I clocked him and he slept just twelve minutes. He stretched, got up, sat down and picked up the conversation again with his usual vigor.

When we got near the valley the General beckoned me on, so we squeezed through the bomb bay, ducked down under the cockpit and crawled on our hands and knees up into the nose of the plane. It's a spectacular spot, almost entirely surrounded by plexiglas, and with a magnificent view of the mountains and valleys. In spite of the size of our plane the pilot took us down into the valley so that we were looking up at the peaks. There were a lot of planes in the air—Corsairs, F-51s, the jets and the fighter bombers. It was a bird's eye view of the war as we watched them sweeping the valley and hillsides with bombs, napalm and rockets. We stayed over the area and I was grateful I was up here looking down and not down there looking up. (27 February 1951, Korea)

March 1951: South Korea Retaken

On March 7, Eighth Army crosses the Han River east of Seoul and prepares to drive to the thirty-eighth parallel. MacArthur, in a press conference at Suwon, states that there should be "no illusions"—the conflict is approaching a military stalemate unless he is given broader freedom of action and is reinforced.

Darling,

The right hand letters in this letter are being written by the hand that shook the hand of General MacArthur. We

started a new offensive this morning. The Great Man, therefore, came on to the scene so that once again he could pose
as the Architect of Victory. I was asked to set up a press conference for him and I did. In the normal course of events he
brings with him his trained correspondents from Tokyo but
on this occasion he took notice of the Korean members of
the press. That may be because they have all been doing so
well for General Ridgway.

I was also handling a D/A [Department of the Army] beef
about a story on the men that were killed in the 2nd Division
back on the night of 12 February.[10]

At 1230 I herded a motley collection of correspondents together and finally got them to an air strip and on a C-47. The
wind was against us and it snowed so we arrived to see MacA
about forty minutes late. I expected to be summarily executed but General Ridgway was most charming. It may be
that he was glad to see the Old Man wait. He introduced me
to General MacA and we had a fascinating conversation:

QUIRK (with his best Sunday salute): How do you do, sir.

MacA (flipping his right hand like Hitler): How do you
do. (Quirk and MacA shake hands.)

MacA: Is everything ready?

QUIRK: Yessir.

MacA: You seem to be having no trouble with the press.

QUIRK: No sir.

After my thus telling him off we got under way. He had six
pages handwritten on copy book paper and he read it off at
dictation speed. You have already heard and seen the text so
I won't go into that. When he finished, some of the press had
missed some so I boldly borrowed his notes and reread to the
slow group. At this point the Great MacA and I really had a
chat:

MacA: I want those notes back.

QUIRK: Yessir.

I gave him back the notes.

I then asked him for a radio shot and he reread the thing
at normal conversational speed instead of at the dictation

speed. During all of this General Ridgway said nothing. I had been working on the idea of getting MacA and the General to appear to be absolute pals. The General agreed and that was the purpose of the whole thing. Either nobody told MacA or he chose to ignore the whole thing.

He is handsome, looks twenty years short of his seventy years, talks well, and leaves everyone with the feeling that their opinion of him could not possibly be as high as his own opinion of himself. He is sort of fascinating and detestable.

When he took off to go back to Tokyo, the General and I had an anxious chat. MacA said the war was building up to a stalemate. Our troops had just started a major operation. The morale of the troops is certainly helped by knowing that they are fighting in a hopeless stalemate. MacA is thinking of glory in the UN. The General is worried about the battalions in the line. We have to do something about it and that is my problem for tonight. I am to see the General in the morning with the answer. (7 March 1951, Korea)

Military historian Clay Blair summarized MacArthur's extraordinary performance and its aftermath:

Indeed, the statement *was* extraordinary. It was laced with subtle phrases criticizing the Truman Administration: "abnormal military inhibitions," "existing limitations upon our freedom of counter-offensive action," "no major additions to our organized strength" . . . "obscurities which now becloud the unsolved problems." It also ridiculed—and challenged—Peking at a time when the Administration was still doing its utmost to coax Peking to the negotiating table. Beyond that it was an indiscreet and wholly unnecessary public review of military strategy. . . .

Seeking headlines, the media seized upon two phrases: "savage slaughter" and "theoretical military stalemate." In journalese, MacArthur's discourse would be boiled down and known as his "Die for Tie" statement. Thus truncated and interpreted, the statement had an unsettling and, in some quarters, a demoralizing impact on Eighth Army. "Stalemate" connoted defeat, not victory.

Beyond any doubt, MacArthur's broadside was clearly a calculated and premeditated flouting of Truman's December directive to clear such policy statements in Washington—the third violation within a period of about three weeks. To MacArthur watchers, a pattern seemed to be emerging. MacArthur would fly to Korea, visit the battlefront, then issue a communique containing criticism of the administration's war policies.[11]

Darling,

I have framed the counterattack on the stalemate statement and it should be in next Saturday night's or Sunday papers. I have to write it tomorrow but in final form it will be far more Ridgway than Quirk.

Today I went boy scouting, scared myself to death and proved that I have very little sense. I went leaflet dropping over the enemy lines. The General's navigator was navigating the flight, because the drop has to be very accurate. Flying over the snow covered mountains is a magnificent sight but I lost my taste for scenery.

The routine is to drop a half million leaflets in Chinese and Korean to tell them to quit fighting and surrender so that for them, too, life can be beautiful. Because they have to be dropped from low altitude and at low speed so that they will not blow too far from the objective, the drop is made from a C-47 which is slow, fat and unarmed.

The plane flies over the area at from 500 to 800 feet and the leaflets are pitched out a wide-open back door in huge bundles which the wind then whips open. Two men stand inside the open door with straps attached to their parachutes hitching them to the plane so they can't fall out. That's the theory, but what are the parachutes for? In any case a third man slits the string on the bundle, hands it to the drop men and they heave them over the side. At low altitudes in the mountains the plane slips and slides and bounces and the open door looks like an awfully big hole in the side of the plane.

Our first drop went off about three miles behind the enemy lines where our artillery had been working some troops over. It went off well but one of the dropper-outers got sick from the motion of the plane and wound up stretched out on the floor looking green. Who was available as a substitute? You guessed it. I got into the parachute but the straps that hitched me to the plane wouldn't fit so I developed my own technique. I held on with one hand and shoved the bundles out with the other instead of heaving them. You know how I feel about heights.

The second drop—my first—was about 40 miles behind the enemy lines. The pilot lights a red light over our heads at the rear and we stand by to drop the bundles, although I wasn't sure that was all that was going. That parachute on my back seemed awfully inadequate. Then he rings a bell and flies low and slow until we heave the leaflets out. After the drop was over I collapsed on the floor and cursed the day I ever left Philadelphia. I didn't get a chance to worry too much because the light went on for the third drop and then the bell and then the yawning door and then a stop and then a light and then a bell and then the door and then the leaflet bundles again. I was doing it one-handed and was afraid I would let go with the wrong hand.

I should have been used to it by the last drop but I wasn't. When we were all finished, the corporal whom I was assisting gave me a nod of condescending approval and I went up and sat in the co-pilot's seat to warm up from the cold sweat. I munched on a chocolate bar and tried to look as though I had spent half my life hanging out airplane doors by one hand. We pulled up and watched the fighters mussing up the snow on the hillsides. Their job is easy. They keep the doors closed and they use two hands besides.

The flight back was a great relief and getting on the

ground was even greater. I tried to be nonchalant but I probably just looked slightly witless. The pilot explained to the
operations officer, "The Colonel stood up there without any
hitching strap and heaved them right out the door." I didn't
stand there. I got down on one knee so that I could hook
one foot around a stanchion in addition to my weak one-
handed grip. The operations officer looked at me as though
I have holes in my head. Maybe I do.

Tomorrow I'll write a statement for the G. I'll use both
hands, stay on the ground and keep the door closed.
(8 March 1951, Korea)

> 8 MARCH 1951
> KOREA

HEADQUARTERS
EIGHTH UNITED STATES ARMY KOREA

[To] Lt. Col. Walter F. Winton
Aide-de-Camp

The Supreme Commander's [stalemate] statement may
have an adverse effect on the morale of the troops. Recom-
mend that the General hold another press conference within
the next forty-eight to seventy-two hours. The ostensible purpose would be to review the progress of the attack now developing. At that time a prepared statement could be issued giving the General's concept of the Eighth Army's mission and the
importance of the fight against communism. This statement
would not be in conflict with the Supreme Commander's
statement but would give purpose and direction to the soldier
who is called upon to do the fighting.

Such a statement would be well received at home and at the
front. I shall work on such a release, if the General desires.

J. T. QUIRK
Lt. Col. Inf.

[Hand-written response at bottom] Would like this . . . MBR

12 MARCH 1951
KOREA

Excerpt from General Ridgway's Press Conference

We didn't set out to conquer China. We set out to stop Communism. We have demonstrated the superiority on the battlefield of our men. If China fails to throw us into the sea, that is a defeat for her of incalculable proportions. If China fails to drive us from Korea, she will have failed monumentally. . . .

The things for which we are fighting here are of such overwhelming importance I can't conceive of any member of our fighting forces feeling that there lies ahead any field of indefinite or indeterminate action.

This war is positive from beginning to end, and the potentialities are positive.[12]

In the press conference, Ridgway also directly contradicts MacArthur on the stalemate issue, stating that if South Korea were liberated, it would be "a tremendous victory" for U.N. forces.[13] By mid-March, with Seoul outflanked, the Communists abandon the South Korean capital and continue their withdrawal to positions above the thirty-eighth parallel.

17 MARCH 1951
KOREA

HEADQUARTERS
EIGHTH UNITED STATES ARMY KOREA

MEMORANDUM FOR: COMMANDING GENERAL
EIGHTH UNITED STATES ARMY KOREA

The "Massacre Valley" story was a bad one. On February 13 preliminary information indicated that the 2nd Infantry Division had fled and left most of its equipment. Our concern at the time was to protect the 2nd Infantry Division from any censure, direct or implied, that might do severe damage to their morale. Therefore, there was no reference to this incident then.

When the Marines began to uncover the area someone erected a sign reading "MASSACRE VALLEY. SCENE OF HARRY S. TRUMAN'S POLICE ACTION. NICE GOING, HARRY." The original stories pointed out the finding of bodies but gave no figures as to casualties. The AP version in the States carried a figure of 2000. We checked the AP file and no such figure originated here. It was inserted in the U.S.

A long AP story was then filed out of here pointing out the long and hard fight that had taken place and giving the correct figures in so far as they were available. As always, the correction was never given the circulation that the original story was given. The other services and newspapers carried only the correct figures but the gist of their stories was that a lot of American soldiers had been killed.

The coinage of the term "Massacre Valley" by the Marines was unfortunate but we had no basis for stopping its use. Our only offset was to make available the results of the long investigation of the incident pointing out that there had been a major fight extending over 14 hours. In my original anxiety to protect the reputation of the 2nd Division, I made the mistake of giving out no information. However, at the time of the Chinese counterattack, the impact of these losses might have been greater than they were three weeks later [when the story leaked]. Sooner or later we have to admit our losses as well as tell of our successes. We waited too long. If the necessity should arise again, I hope that I shall be able to handle it more intelligently.

JAMES T. QUIRK
Lt. Col. Inf

On March 20, the Joint Chiefs of Staff notify MacArthur that once South Korea is cleared, President Truman will announce that the U.N. is prepared to discuss a cease-fire and settlement. On March 23, a U.N. airborne-armor operation seeks to trap fleeing Communist forces at Munsan south of the Imjin River before they cross the thirty-eighth parallel into North Korea.

Darling,

This is the night before Easter Sunday and I wonder what is going on at home. I suspect the Easter Bunny is a thing of the past but [Rory] has still expected his full quota of loot. I have contributed nothing to it and I hope that he is not disappointed.

Yesterday was quite a day. We had been planning this airborne operation for quite a while.

We got off about 0730 on a beautifully clear, magnificent day with fine visibility. We picked up the flight of the C-119s that were carrying the paratroopers and flew along their course. They were flying in Vs at about 800 to 1000 feet and we were just above them. The protective fighters were buzzing high above us and then roaring down to strafe a hillside or take a look at the ground.

The cargo planes with the troops seemed to be moving slowly and majestically in perfect formation. We kept inching on past the flights and we could plainly see the faces of the crew men in the cockpits and we could see the men in the white helmets who streaked past us in the jets. At four minutes of nine the tension in our plane began to mount and we knew that the paratroopers were standing and hooking up. We saw the figures appear at the huge boxcar doors on the rear of the C-119s and then we saw the drop zone under our nose. Almost on the second the first two figures came hurtling out of the plane and they poured like sand in an hourglass. There was a terrible, tense few seconds until that first chute opened and then they began to bloom in the air in profusion as the planes came over the drop zone and the sticks of men poured out. The chutes are brilliantly colored and they float through the air like flowers settling and swinging to earth.

We saw the first man hit and the chute folded down to the ground slowly into a rough irregular blotch of color like a daub of paint on the dark brown of the rice paddies. We were flying in a circle over the area and the men kept pouring out of each flight of planes. It was in the sixth or seventh flight that we saw the first and only streamer, a parachute that failed to open. We watched transfixed as the blue rag of silk trailed above him and he plummeted to the ground. We were a little white for a minute when he kicked up a small cloud of dust as he struck.

Most of the men landed in the drop zone and we could see them gathering around their commanders. As the commanders hit they set off colored smokes which flare up to indicate the assembly points for the companies and battalions. There was a regiment of paratroopers in the operation and two Ranger companies. There was some fire in the area but not much, and the men started to move out toward their objectives quickly. At five minutes past nine the next wave came in and again the leaping figures, the colorful floating chutes and their collapse after the men hit the ground. Some of the men landed in a small orchard and their chutes lay draped across the trees like something that you would spread on a bush to dry. At 0915 the next wave came in carrying the command group. They landed and we saw them work toward the CP location at the major crossroads there.

In the middle of all this we saw the General in his light plane circling over the area. Mike Lynch, his L-19 pilot, made two passes at the only straight stretch of road to check for obstacles and then he swung around and made his run and landed the General on the road. Some troops began to gather but we saw them break up quickly and we knew that he had told them to get to their objective, which was the high ground north and east of Munsan to keep the enemy from escaping across the Imjin River as they fled north from Seoul.

At 0930 the last battalion came in but were off the drop zone and some men landed on top of the low ridges and some sailed in the breeze across the ridge into the valley beyond. The drop was not as tight and the men were widely dispersed. They drew some fire but we could not see the results from the air. At 0935 two helicopters came egg-beating in and landed and we saw the medics pulling the wounded into the baskets on the side. In two minutes they were off the ground with the first wounded who would be in a hospital in fifteen minutes twenty miles away.

At 1000 the planes carrying the heavy stuff began to stream up from the south. The huge cargo chutes opened carrying 75mm and 105mm guns, jeeps, machine guns, ammunition, mortars and radio equipment. We saw one gun tear loose from the chute and fall free. When it hit the ground it sent up a great column of dust like a bomb or a shell burst. For no accountable reason a jeep in a huge white chute took off cross-country in the breeze, missed the ridge and sailed about 2500 yards before it came to earth. It must have been FOB to the North Koreans.

We took off down the road which was the axis of advance of the link-up force. That force led by a battalion of tanks had started at 0630 to drive north to open a route to the paratroopers. We followed the road at low altitude and could plainly see the square patches where the road had been hastily mined. We finally caught up with the head of the column. They were still eighteen miles away at 1030. They were stalled at a bridge with a span out but the British were coming up with their special bridge-laying tanks and the delay would not be too long. Hannah on the radio told the commander of the column about the mines in the road ahead. Patrols were moving out to investigate the villages along the road and they flashed their identification panels at us as we came over.

We finally came home about 1130. (24 March 1951, Korea)

As Eighth Army closes to the thirty-eighth parallel, MacArthur publicly torpedoes the pending Truman peace initiative, belittles the capabilities of the Chinese Communist Forces (CCF), and threatens China with a wider war.

Darling,

This is Easter Sunday and it has been a dismal day in Korea. It started to rain last night and is still at it. The temperature is mild and the rain is like any spring rain back home but

the results are so different. We are now up to our knees in
mud, our boots weigh a ton, and our trousers are splattered
and damp. The First World War really dramatized the mud of
Flanders but mud is the same in any war. Just a couple of
weeks ago I was complaining about the snow and freezing to
death. I suppose that soon I shall be telling you about the insufferable heat. I hope to get back to the insufferable days of
May in Philadelphia before that problem gets too bad.

This isn't much of a letter but I love you and Rory, too.
(25 March 1951, Korea)

April 1951: The Relief of MacArthur

Darling,
I have been going up and down this peninsula so much
that I feel like a yo-yo.

Peterson, my Texas driver, picked me up at 0630 and we
headed for the air strip. Our usual strip is too deep in mud
to use, so we had to take off from the main strip where we
have to fight the fighter planes off the ground.

It was coming on toward daylight as we bounced over the
rutted dirt road. In spite of all the engineers' efforts, there is
no deep base to the roads and they begin to break up after
the weather is bad even for a little while. There isn't much
military traffic but there are signs of soldiers everywhere,
washing, shaving, stretching, lining up for chow, dipping
their mess kits in the GI cans of boiling water, or pounding
on down the roads to their duties somewhere.

In spite of the Oriental atmosphere, there is something of
the same air of early morning back home so far as the civilians are concerned. People are scurrying along the road to
whatever jobs they have over here. The farmers are out in the
rice paddies scattering their foul treasure on the rice plants.
The women carry almost everything on their heads and a lot
of them are headed to the river banks with the laundry which
they wash in the streams, beating it with a stick. Housewives
come out of the huts and heave pails of water into the road

and the kids are washing their faces in basins or tin cans or
the gutters. They all look a little sleepy, too.

We bounce along, not very fast because of the road, and
the MP at the gate carefully takes a note of the trip ticket
number and the name of the driver and the name of the vehicle. No one, including the MP, has the slightest idea why
he gathers the information, but they are his orders. There
must be millions of sheets of paper around the world on
which the army has entered records of trip tickets. Some day
I may find out what purpose it serves.

I climbed aboard and there was the usual motley crew on
a lot of different missions. General Farrell was off to try to
get some word on a Korean Corps Commander who disappeared in a light plane in bad weather and probably flew into
a mountain. General Burns, the Artillery Officer, was going
to see General Ridgway about something. One GI had a
small puppy that he had brought back from Japan and all the
big, tough soldiers beamed like old ladies looking at a baby.
The puppy got passed from one end of the plane to the
other so everyone could see him, and the soldier tried to
look modest about the whole thing. An Inspector General
from Tokyo was on the plane headed for Tenth Corps. General Almond is still General MacArthur's Chief of Staff in addition to commanding Tenth Corps and he was the one who
helped MacA louse up the Home by Christmas offensive.

In connection with General Almond: Tom Lambert of
Time had a long interview with the Marine Commanders on
how they think that General Ridgway is a great man, which
they do. At the end of the interview he asked General Chesty
Puller, "What is the most important lesson that the Marines
have learned in Korea, so far?" Without batting an eye, General Puller said, "Never serve under Tenth Corps." I persuaded him not to use the quote. (2 April 1951, Korea)

*On April 3, Eighth Army crosses the thirty-eighth parallel. All
of South Korea has been cleared. The Communists mass 475,000
troops in the North.*

Dear Aunt Kate,

This is a belated thank you for the birthday card that you sent me for my fortieth birthday.

General Ridgway, with whom I work closely, is a fine man and it has been a privilege to be with him. He is strong, brilliant and has a wonderful grasp of all situations. The men here think that he is the greatest ever and he probably is. It's sort of a futile war that will have to be decided somewhere other than in Korea but meanwhile it goes. (4 April 1951, Korea)

On April 5, MacArthur, in defiance of a presidential gag order, publicly criticizes U.S. policy in a letter to the House minority leader. On April 9, with the unanimous concurrence of the senior military and civilian leadership, President Truman makes the decision to relieve MacArthur of command. Two days later, MacArthur is relieved, and Ridgway is named Supreme Commander for the Allied Powers (SCAP).

Darling,

I know that you have gotten a message from the War Department initiated by the General telling you that I have switched from Korea to Tokyo. I started to keep notes so that I should be able to tell you the whole story but even that became impossible and I shall have to try to reconstruct (on a typewriter that skips) all the things that have happened since a week ago today. Thus far we feel that we have escaped very well and the wrath of everyone at everyone else has not hit us. I plan to continue with a loud burst of silence until the dust settles a little.

To go back: This is not as complete as it might be but a week ago is another era and I have forgotten an awful lot. I shall try to give you the whole story because it is one of the historic moments and I sat in the middle of the whole thing. I want to get it down as well as I can because the facts may be important later.

Wednesday, April 11, Korea

The Secretary of the Army [Frank Pace] was over and we had received him the night before with some honors. About 1515 I got a call from one of the correspondents telling me that AFRS [Armed Forces Radio Service] had carried a news broadcast which said that President Truman had relieved General MacArthur and had named General Ridgway to the command. It sounded improbable, but I had been a lone voice predicting MacArthur's relief and everyone had told me I was crazy. One of the reasons for their lack of belief was that *Stars & Stripes* carried not a word that anyone disagreed with General MacA on any point. In about fifteen minutes the bulletins came through from the States and I had confirmation that it was true.

The General and Mr. Pace were way up front and were going to be hard to reach. I dashed over and confirmed to a stunned Chief of Staff that General MacA had been fired and that General Ridgway was to succeed. Willie Collier caught up with the General [Ridgway] on a field artillery battalion field phone, no mean feat in itself. The General was then told by General Allen what had happened. The time was just about 1600. It was confirmed from Tokyo about twenty minutes later.

The first word that the General heard on the subject was at the 5th Regimental Combat team where some GIs said they had heard the news on a radio broadcast. The word was passed but the General took little stock in it and carried on with his trip. It was a half hour later before he got the news that I had given General Allen. When the General did get the message from General Allen his first comment was just "Oh, my God." I had butterflies in my stomach but pointed out that the only possible reply to any questions was "No comment."

There was a major surmise that Mr. Pace had brought the news to General Ridgway and there was even speculation that the Secretary had delivered some sort of ultimatum to General MacA the day before and that MacArthur's firmness on the subject had precipitated the dismissal. This is definitely not so. The Secretary was taken completely by surprise. Since he had left Washington on 7 April, it must be presumed that the decision by the President was made sometime between the 7th and the 11th. This is the fact. Pace knew that there was a growing crisis but he did not know that the President was prepared to act so soon or what definite action he was going to take. This may be a subject of dispute in later years but these are the facts and I am sure of my facts.

The staff was urged to say nothing and the General didn't plan to say anything either. The correspondents had to be satisfied with GI reaction. My only reason for silence was that the news was so earth shaking that I wanted to wait for the dust to settle and I wanted to see where the shots were going to come from if they came. None came. There was a lot of anger in America, apparently, but none directed at General Ridgway. That night I called off the press conference for the Secretary and the General the next day because I couldn't think of a single question that could very well be answered.

That night more news kept coming in so that we could piece the thing together and General Van Fleet [appointed as Ridgway's successor at Eighth Army] became an added starter. The official orders [appointing Ridgway] arrived from General Marshall but, strangely enough, no orders covering General Van Fleet. (The next day we checked on those orders but none arrived. We had only press reports.[14])

About ten o'clock at night Walter Winton, the General's aide, called and told me to pack to go to Tokyo. It was after two a.m. before I got to bed, feeling excited and a little forlorn and scared to death. I was being precipitated into the big leagues in a crucial time and I was afraid that I might let the General down by messing something up right off the bat.

Thursday, April 12, Korea

Joe Dale, the General's junior aide, called me early in the morning and told me that I was to be at Pusan by noon. The

General and the Secretary of the Army were going to call on [South Korea president] Syngman Rhee and Ambassador Muccio and then take off for Tokyo.

About 11 we went over to the strip and heaved ourselves on a C-47 for the flight to Pusan. It was afternoon when we got there and we taxied up alongside the Secretary's huge Constellation already standing on the apron. It was chilly and windy on the strip right beside the Sea of Japan. We were afraid to put our baggage on the plane because we had not been told that we were to go positively. The General arrived with entourage. There were a lot of good-byes and the General looked at us and said "Let's go." That was the word. The steward heaved our baggage on the plane. The General and the Secretary climbed aboard and we followed along. We were off just a few minutes before two o'clock, headed for Tokyo and the Lord knew what.

We settled down in our seats with butterflies in our stomachs. Across from us were General Fox, Deputy Chief of Staff of GHQ, and General Beiderlinden, the G-1. They were painfully cordial but kept looking at us out of the corners of their eyes. I told Walter Winton, "There are the rebels looking at the Korean Carpetbaggers." The name stuck and we still refer to ourselves that way. We are afraid to give the word any currency because it has a certain aptness. There wasn't much time for rest. In a few minutes the General came back and handed me 60 mimeographed pages on the subject of the Japanese Peace Treaty. The problems of our little Korean war were now only part of a bigger picture.

Then the General gave me three sentences that he planned to say when we reached Haneda Airport in Tokyo. One phrase was "I hope to carry out my duties to the best of my ability and to the satisfaction of the authorities who have honored me by this assignment." I objected saying that it sounded like a left-handed crack at General MacArthur. The General and the Secretary agreed and I scrawled out a new sentence. The General memorized it and we were set. I warned the General that the reception at Haneda might be pretty rough and I told him to expect the worst. He resolved to make his little statement and say no more. Then in his usual calm, assured fashion he went to sleep. (18 April 1951, Tokyo)

Darling,

I am in Tokyo with the General. You probably heard that I got the Legion of Merit[15] and that was the first order he ever published in the new job. I have sent you some pictures. I look rather sad but it took me by surprise. It is a tough league. The tactical reports are no more and I get involved in difficult policy questions and try to interpret them properly to the press. Thus far, results are good. I don't want the General to get the backlash on the MacArthur thing just because Ridgway is the successor. The correspondents are enthusiastic about the new regime and I am doing everything to keep it that way.

The pressure for me to stay has been great but the General has been true to his word to me. General Marshall cabled that if I should stay on I could become a special consultant at $50 per day plus a per diem. That amounts to about $22,000 per year. I have turned it down. I still could not bring you and Rory out here. I cannot stay if you cannot come. The situation is this: I shall stay one extra month. General Marshall is to get in touch with Walter Annenberg to get his approval. There is the insurance on which you can always borrow if we get short. I hate to spend the extra time but the time is so historic. We can always feel that we did our little bit for our country.

I hope that the extra month is not too much of a blow but I know that you understand I simply could not do this to him at this time. I think he knows now that the Korean job was so important. Because we never ventured into any questions beyond the confines of Korea, there is no one now who can find a stick to beat him with. We were wiser than we knew.

Tonight before dinner we played badminton because the General was yelling about getting no exercise. He beat me 15–9. He's a great General but he wouldn't be any flash at

Cynwyd Badminton and Lager Society sessions. He's the fastest, ruggedest 56 year old I ever saw. (22 April 1951, Tokyo)

On April 22, the Chinese launch a massive offensive with 250,000 troops to retake Seoul. Over the next nine days, Eighth Army will inflict 70,000 casualties in the largest battle of the war.

Dear Win [James's sister],

This has been a remarkable time in our history and I have been standing in the middle of it. Thus far we have stayed out of serious trouble but I have great fears for the future. It is thrilling to ride on the coattails of history but I am liable to fall off at the next turn.

I am not in sympathy with General MacArthur. I have always had a questionable regard for him but every day that I spend among the ruins of the empire that he built, my opinion of him and his works gets lower. General Ridgway has always been meticulous in his relationships with MacA in spite of much provocation and many slights. MacA's trips to Korea were for publicity purposes only. The disasters of last fall came about when he was directing the war from Tokyo. On him must rest the great defeats and the terrible loss of life.

If the congressional investigation is conducted in any normal manner, the facts will bear out that he tried to ignore the national policy of his own country. He is a general, not the President, and he felt himself beyond all control. His position now is the same as the position he took in 1942. He proved to be wrong then and he is wrong now. None of this can I say publicly, but I feel strongly about it. History will tell the true story. (25 April 1951, Tokyo)

Darling,

Your letter says that you had a lousy time at your [Frankford High School twenty-fifth] reunion but there must have been some satisfaction in blitzing in there in full regalia, especially since you didn't have to show your bank balance. I think you were even lovelier than you think you are and I want to come home and be with you. I am anxious to see your new outfit and I hope that the day of my homecoming will be cool enough for you to wear it.

Walter sent a wire to General Marshall saying that it would be "unthinkable and unpatriotic" to expect me to return and that I could stay here so long as "it is agreeable to Quirk and General Ridgway." It was a nice wire that impressed the General. I have no claim on the *Inquirer* for any money after May 20. I don't know what they will do, but we can dream. If they cross me off the payroll, I can't feel too hurt but we shall sweat a little. We've been poor before, but never on such a large scale. (28 April 1951, Tokyo)

Darling,

Sundays are just like any other day because we work the same hours but most of Tokyo is shut down because they have readily adopted the Western custom of taking Sunday off. Today is the Emperor's birthday and there was quite a shuttle around the Imperial Palace as people came to sign the visitor's book, an old Japanese custom. More than the usual number were in Japanese dress and they made a colorful sight from our window. Hank Adams and I have the best view. The General's windows overlook the roof of the city jail and about all he can see is the Japanese lot of prisoners who are taken up there for exercise.

We had a long session about depurging a lot of the Japanese and the General will announce it for Japanese Constitution day. The Japanese will be happy about the liberality of the new SCAP but the big problem is to get enough officers depurged so that we can build up the Japanese police reserve so that there will be some non-communist army somewhere in the East. We have troops here and will after the peace treaty but we can't stay out here forever.

This is really a high level job and I am learning a lot but there is a lot to learn. It is complex. The General is the ruler of Japan without limitation and that power is remarkable. He is probably the only real absolute monarch in the world to-day. (29 April 1951, Tokyo)

The CCF offensive to retake Seoul has failed. As the month ends, the Communists are regrouping to drive Eighth Army from Korea.

May–June 1951: The End Comes Into View

Dear James—
I am glad that you have learned that the *Inquirer* won't cut off the show and you will breathe more easily knowing that we are going to get along without any trouble.

Also today, I received an utterly wonderful letter from the G.

> Dear Mrs. Quirk:
> I have long intended to try to convey to you something of my grateful appreciation for Jim's great help here.
> From the day of his arrival his individual contribution to our combined effort in Korea was great. It has steadily grown in volume, and today you and he can have in your hearts that deep satisfaction which only comes from a consciousness of high-principled selfless service, well performed.
> That this contribution is not Jim's alone, I am well aware. Into it has gone as much of your heart as his, and to perhaps only a slightly lesser extent the heart of your son, Rory.
> While I can express my grateful appreciation of what you have both done, the higher appreciation of the organizations you both so faithfully serve—The United States Army, and now our Military Establishment—may never reach you in the volume it should.
> Please accept my cordial and respectful best wishes.
> Sincerely,
> M. B. Ridgway,
> Lieutenant General, United States Army

I have never been so thrilled and yet humble—that this great man, so burdened with problems and responsibilities, would take the time to write to me! It almost makes me feel guilty that you are leaving him—almost.

Rory got his snapshots and the shoulder patches today and loved them all. When he read the G's letter this afternoon he said tremulously, "Is my daddy dead?" He also told me that he is having trouble making a decision as to what he wants to be when he grows up but first he has to be a soldier.

Try not to worry about us, darling, and just always know that we love you and want you and count the days. (14 May 1951, Bala Cynwyd, PA)

In mid-May, the Chinese resume the offensive with 175,000 troops against Eighth Army's weaker right flank and suffer an estimated 80,000 casualties. Ridgway cables the Joint Chiefs of Staff: "The enemy has suffered a severe major defeat."

Darling,

On Friday I spent about five hours in the nose of a B-17 with the General and a map flying along the northeast coast of Honshu, the main Japanese island on which Tokyo is located. There are a lot of good invasion beaches there and he now knows most of them.[16] He thinks of everything. (27 May 1951, Tokyo)

During the last half of May, Eighth Army clears South Korea of Communist forces and moves above the thirty-eighth parallel for most of its length.

Darling,

Back in Tokyo after the better part of two days in Korea. We saw a lot because we were all over the place and I ran across my first large lot of Chinese prisoners and was not impressed. They have been fairly tough but they are beginning to give it up as a bad job. (30 May 1951, Tokyo)

Darling,

I have been getting all sorts of reactions to the General's press conference of yesterday. Was this conference requested from Washington? Why did the General make a special point of the surrender of soldiers of the CCF? Is that a foreword to a possible announcement of negotiation? Why was the conference called so suddenly and why did he come right to the conference from Korea? Is this directed primarily to the United Nations or to the Communist countries?

I was shooting mostly at the Chinese and the countries of Southeast Asia who are wavering. They aren't concerned with Communism or Democracy because they don't think much of America or the Russians. They are just trying to figure out who is going to win so that they can join the winning side. I was telling them to latch on to us. We are beating the Chinese badly and their own people are deserting them. I think it is a good point and the General thought so, too.

Hugh Moffett of *Time*, who calls me "Ridgway's Evil Genius," said, "The voice was the voice of Ridgway but the words were the words of Quirk." That's about true. (31 May 1951, Tokyo)

On June 1, U.N. Secretary General Trygve Lie, at the urging of the United States, declares that a cease-fire roughly along the thirty-eighth parallel would fulfill U.N. Security Council objectives. United States efforts to open back-channel negotiations with China fail. Despite staggering losses, the Communists have rebuilt their forces in North Korea to 450,000. On June 8, Secretary of Defense Marshall arrives in Korea, confers with Ridgway, and holds a press conference.

Darling,

This is just about the next to the last letter that I shall write you because after this I should get home just as soon as a letter will.

My weekend was taken up with Secretary Marshall and I

wrote for him the press conference that you will have seen. I was surprised that he followed my notes so carefully and I was rather flattered, too. I went with him to Korea and we flew in light planes on the worst flying day that I have ever experienced. When we got to I Corps the General suggested that we better give up and go back by jeep and call off the rest of the trip. General Marshall asked the General whether he would turn back if he were alone. Ridgway said, "No" and the Secretary said let's go. The pilots shuddered, as did we, and off we went into squalls and rain and wind, bouncing all over the sky in light planes. I always ride with the phones on and the pilots were swearing and sweating but agreed that if the Old Man could do it so could they. It was so dangerous it was silly but Generals are like that. They think they always have to be braver than anyone else and they get away with it. We were glad to get back to Yongdungpo and into the Constellation that could go up over the weather.

General Marshall is a remarkable man with the finest mind that I have ever known, even greater than Ridgway. When the General assured him that I was just a member of the family, he had two Old Fashioneds and we had a good lunch at the Ridgways. He was most appreciative of my press conference notes. I sure have been operating on a high level. It will seem easy to start worrying about stand cards and house ads again.

I guess I am a perpetual adolescent because I cannot get used to people taking my opinion and advice seriously. I have forced a new psychological warfare policy, have completely changed the whole policy on military censorship, have argued many a high level matter like the rearming of Japan, the depurge and many others but I am always a little surprised that people listen to me with any respect. I do get a lot here and have left some mark on this command with a lot of people. I come home with nothing to be ashamed of.[17] Maybe I can leave as big a mark on the *Philadelphia Inquirer.* I know this is a way of bragging a little bit but this has been a successful venture from the standpoint of accomplishment.

I love you and will see you soon. Get ready and good night. (12 June 1951, Tokyo)

During the course of General Marshall's visit, he proposed ending the Korean War by giving the Communists "a taste of the atom.[18]" The upshot of that proposal is detailed in the Afterword. On July 10, 1951, truce talks began. A formal cease-fire was signed on July 27, 1953.

Chapter Five: Between Wars
1951–68

Colonel Jim Quirk arrived home at 30th Street Station in late June 1951. We met him at the train. It had been a historic six months, one that Elizabeth was intensely proud of, one that their son understood only dimly. My father's Legion of Merit, shown off proudly at school the previous month, had made an impression. Nobody in my second grade was quite sure what it meant, but it looked important. James's picture in Life *magazine with General Ridgway added a certain gravitas to his absence. He had lost weight during the six months overseas, Elizabeth noted with concern. It took her a while to tell him that their son had experienced a flare-up of the almost-forgotten fevers and had missed twenty-seven school days during his absence.*

The next month was a whirlwind of welcome-home salutes and newspaper stories: "Colonel Quirk Back from Korean Duty"; "Colonel Quirk Terms Korean Cease-Fire Potential Boon"; "Hardships of War in Korea Described by Special Assistant to General Ridgway." The city's Poor Richard Club honored him at a luncheon, which was highlighted by a message to the club from Tokyo adding General Ridgway's praise for "service to the nation of great value at a most critical time." Upon James's return to work in July, there was more good news. He was named promotion manager of the Philadelphia Inquirer. *In November, we moved from the small apartment to a large house on Bryn Mawr Avenue.*

The next two years fulfilled my parents' World War II dreams. They were financially secure for the first time. The family, having endured two wars and two separations over a seven-year

span, was together. Two of the perks of James's new job that re-
dounded to the benefit of me and my classmates were the annual trip to the Inquirer pressroom to watch the printers and editors put together the next morning's paper, and spending New
Year's Day wedged onto the huge windowsills high in the white-
towered Inquirer building, the best seats in the city for the annual Mummers Parade.

In April 1953, my fellow Cub Scouts in Pack 104 got to see the
artistic side of Elizabeth. For the annual Play Night—which rarely
rose above the level of tacky hand puppets or amateurish dance
routines—our den presented The Crusades, an ambitious six-
scene play, which Elizabeth researched, wrote, produced, and directed. When she first broached the idea, we Cubs were cool to
the concept. Not only wasn't it going to be a Three Musketeers-
Errol Flynn sword fight, we were going to have to memorize
speaking parts. Elizabeth stuck to her guns. During the four
months of rehearsal, we fashioned tunics out of old pillowcases
and emblazoned them with red crosses, then converted our football helmets to knightly headgear with aluminum foil. Meanwhile, Elizabeth wheedled, cajoled, and flattered her young cast,
winning us over by ones and eventually in our entirety. On the
big night, we were boffo. From the opening tableau of Crusaders
in silent contemplation on the evening before battle to the final
victorious "God wills it," the audience, long conditioned to more
lowbrow performances, sat raptly. At the final curtain, the church
hall erupted into appreciative cheering and clamoring for the author. From the wings we spiritedly pushed Elizabeth to center
stage, where Chuckie Schonders from our den handed her a bouquet of flowers, and she blushed with embarrassed pride.

That was the spring we found Icarus, a fledgling who had
fallen out of a nest in one of the trees in our front yard. The bird
was hobbling along the concrete walkway, one wing in mangled
disarray, while its distraught mother shrieked from the depleted
nest above us. I brought the bird inside and handed it to my
mother. The Darwinian approach would have been to scoot it
back outside. Charles Darwin had never met Elizabeth Wolstencroft. Rebuffed by a haughty veterinarian when she called,
Elizabeth first fashioned a splint for the injured wing out of

tongue depressors. When that proved too weighty an apparatus for Icarus (the name was another Elizabethan touch), she tried popsicle sticks. For the next month, we nursed the uncomprehending bird back to health, hydrated it with water from an eyedropper, and fed it raw hamburger (Elizabeth reasoned that it looked like worms) with eyebrow tweezers. As the wing mended, we took the bird out back and watched it lumber about the yard like the Wright brothers pre–Kitty Hawk, until one day it flew away. When I got home from school the next day, I spied Icarus on the front walkway. He had swooped down, apparently not to see me but to say thanks to Elizabeth. She came out to receive his appreciative chirps.

Although James thought he had walked away from the army for good, the army beckoned from time to time. He was asked to return to Korea in late 1951 and step back into his old job. When General Ridgway was named Army Chief of Staff in 1953, he made a final pitch to bring James back on board in a brigadier general's slot. In the spring of 1954, as Roy Cohn and Senator Joseph McCarthy ramped up their jihad against the army for treating their buddy Pvt. G. David Schine like any other private, James made a hurried trip to Washington, then mulled over with Elizabeth the offer to come to the Pentagon. The answer to all of the offers was a reluctant no.

By then, James had the make-or-break opportunity he had been seeking since his return from the war. In 1953, Walter Annenberg, always looking to move Triangle into new areas, launched a national magazine covering television. A common editorial section, printed in Philadelphia, would be shipped around the country to accompany local television listings, which would be printed locally. The hybrid product would be sold in regional editions. It would be small enough to display at supermarket checkout counters, so customers could toss it into their shopping carts, yet hardy enough to withstand a week of being thumbed through by reader-viewers.

Other publishers and Annenberg's own financial people told him the idea was crazy. Their objections contained a certain logic: Faced with the realization that television was not going to *go away, newspapers throughout the country were starting their own Sunday television supplements, which meant that TV viewers would get the local listings for nothing with their Sunday paper. In addition, several cities were already served by independent local guides, which were doing quite nicely (and whose owners could be induced to sell them to Triangle only at a premium), and readers conditioned to cut-rate home magazine subscriptions could hardly be expected to pay the full fifteen-cent cover price at the supermarket checkout. One senior Triangle employee dismissed the concept as "tenement journalism," and was summarily fired.*

Annenberg assembled the management team from within Triangle. Some jumped at the opportunity; others were less enthusiastic (one requested assurance in writing that he could have his old job back after the magazine bellied up). Most had no experience in their designated fields. It was, in the words of an Annenberg biographer, "a motley executive crew that struck others as the officers of a new Titanic." The name of the new venture was TV Guide. *To be the Ahab of this ship, Annenberg tapped a true believer in the concept, the* Inquirer's *promotion director, Jim Quirk.*

TV Guide was launched in April 1953. Years later, when the magazine had become a publishing phenomenon, people tended to forget that it had given initial signs of proving the Cassandras right. At the end of the first year, there were only ten regional editions. Circulation was 1.5 million. Advertising was slim—slightly more than 200 pages for the year, most of it local (the big national accounts found the upstart publication beneath them). In a year when advertisers were paying out $667 million for magazine space elsewhere, TV Guide's revenues were an unspectacular $760,000. (In contrast, the Saturday Evening Post *boasted 1954 advertising revenues of $78 million, nearly 3,700 pages of advertising, and a circulation of 4.6 million.) TV Guide's losses were compounded by the handsome buyouts (totaling an estimated $2.7 million) that Triangle had paid for the independent guides.*

In 1954, TV Guide came under direct attack from a well-heeled opponent. Curtis Publishing Company, awash in profits from the Saturday Evening Post *and the* Ladies' Home Journal, *announced publication of* TV Program Week, *a head-to-head competitor. It was the only time I saw my father visibly sweat the future of the magazine. I tried to reassure him by doing my own informal market research, trekking to Dake's Drug Store on City Line Avenue each afternoon and counting the number of* TV Guides *and* TV Program Weeks *on the newsstand. Based on my limited sample (the stack of* TV Guides *kept getting smaller),* TV Guide *was winning the newsstand war. My father feigned great relief at my numbers. As it turned out, they weren't bad. As Dake's went, so went the nation.* TV Guide's *newsstand circulation jumped 400,000. Curtis folded* TV Program Week *after eight issues, the first in a series of financial reverses that led to the company's eventual implosion a decade later. With Curtis gone and the independent local guides gone as well,* TV Guide *had a clear field.*

In the summer of 1954, the tenth anniversary of D day, James and Elizabeth sailed to England ("Someday you'll get to use them," he had told Elizabeth when he'd given her the fancy luggage), then went on to the D-day battlefields, Mont St. Michel, and Paris. Before leaving England for Normandy, James kept one other promise, taking a detour to Bristol and stopping in unannounced on an elderly British couple who had housed him in the period before D day and had sat up and had tea with him that final weekend before the convoys were loaded. "You came back!" Mrs. James exclaimed with delight.

When my parents got home, we made what had become the annual vacation trek to the seashore. The only disquieting note came on the final weekend when a neighboring family had to leave early. Their daughter, a playmate, had come down with a fever that wouldn't break. Elizabeth, a veteran of nursing childhood fevers, tried to reassure the concerned family. I thought nothing of it until the following summer when they weren't back. They appeared briefly for one weekend that summer. Their daughter was heavier by then, her legs encased in metal braces and beyond the reach of Jonas Salk's new miracle vaccine. The weekend was awkward for everyone. Activities involving mobil-

ity—bikes, bats, and balls—were avoided out of concern that she would feel excluded. Board games—Monopoly and Clue—were played and replayed. We were glad when the weekend was over and Monday came so we could get back to our normal routine, glossing over the fact that for her there were no Mondays.

Our family spent increasing amounts of time together. Scouts with my mother, summers at the seashore, and playing a made-up baseball game called Wireball with my best friend, Charlie Greeley, in which we tried to hit the overhead phone wires with a rubber ball, then advance imaginary runners around imaginary bases. (We caused unknown havoc with local telephone calls.) We also took September trips to the ballpark with my father to watch Robin Roberts win his twentieth game of the season (an event you could set your watch by in Philadelphia). Winter nights were at the Palestra in what was the golden age of Philadelphia basketball, with Tom Gola at LaSalle, Guy Rodgers and Hal Lear at Temple, and a seven-footer at Overbrook High School named Chamberlain who made the game look easy.

In sixth grade, I experienced a daunting rite—altar boy tryouts. We were herded into the church and put through our genuflection and related paces by the assistant pastor, who berated us with his best Marine Corps drill instructor imitation ("Head down," "Back straight," "You look like an old man"). Having culled out the round of shoulder, the insufficiently pious, and the attitude cases, the assistant pastor assembled the survivors in the front pews and handed out the Latin liturgy, which we were expected to memorize. We thumbed silently through the responses in the strange language, emitting groans when we got to the Declaration of Independence–length confiteor. The assistant pastor set a patently arbitrary and unreasonable deadline for full memorization and sent us on our way. Although Elizabeth had no grounding in the Roman liturgy—she was an Episcopalian, and a thoroughly lapsed one at that—she stepped me smartly through my paces to the point that when I returned on the appointed day, my Latin was top drawer. Everyone assumed I had a built-in advantage, because James had been a seminarian. That's what the nuns thought. Elizabeth sagely suggested that we keep the truth hidden. *Spiritual benefits aside, moving to the front ranks of the altar boy corps meant Saturday weddings, which were good for at least a twenty-dollar spot from the groomsman, which our three-man crew split. (Weekday funerals netted no dollars but got us out of math.)*

My triumphs as an altar boy offset one of the major disappointments of seventh grade. I had emerged over the years as the spelling bee champion of my class at Saint Matthias School. The bees, a biweekly staple of the SMS curriculum, served a twofold purpose: Spelling proficiency was secondary; with a teacher-student ratio of 1:47, the bees enabled the embattled nun to fill two afternoon hours. In spring, the top spellers from each grade assembled onstage in the school auditorium for a sort of spelling Super Bowl. The winner proceeded up the road to Norristown for the next round of play-offs, culminating months later with a state champion. For the school-based round, aspirants were provided with lists of words that the judges would draw from. With Elizabeth quizzing me, I spent the weeks leading into the bee working on the toughies: occurrence, minuscule, irresistible. I entered the contest confident and ready, only to belly up in the second round on delicatessen. As my classmates groaned, I left the stage feeling like Brando's Terry Malloy: I could have been a contender.

With the advent of the 1956 election, I learned that James and Elizabeth were a rare (and vaguely suspect) species in my neighborhood—Democrats. The part of Bala Cynwyd in which we lived was (James grumbled) dyed-in-the-wool nouveau Republican—like us, former members of the Roosevelt coalition who had fared well thanks to the New Deal and moved to the suburbs, but who (unlike us) expressed their gratitude by turning on the Democrats with a middle-class vengeance. I learned this during a straw poll. The nun (still smarting, I suspected, from the demise of Joe McCarthy, and no fan of Democrats—the lamented Alfred E. Smith excepted) asked for a show of hands. How many families were for General Eisenhower? Forty-odd hands shot up. And (distasteful pause) how many for Stevenson? Two hands were raised. I drew solace from the kinship of the one other dis-

favored Democrat (although it occurred to me later that he may have misunderstood the question). The overwhelming sentiment for Eisenhower spawned a bit of schoolyard doggerel (sung to the Snow White tune): "Whistle while you work / Stevenson's a jerk / Eisenhower has more power / Whistle while you work." My Democratic colleague and I were unable to fashion a suitable riposte, which would have to have been a duet. On election night, my parents watched the election results in glum silence.

By the mid-1950s, television had come of age. There were TV sets in 32 million U.S. homes—a tenfold increase in just five years. With circulation booming, the marquee advertisers finally discovered TV Guide. In 1956, the back cover was sold for the first time to a national advertiser. The following year, the entire operation moved out of the cramped Philadelphia offices over a popcorn distributor to a large, new national headquarters on eight acres in suburban Radnor, on the Philadelphia Main Line. To celebrate jumps in circulation, a staff member would roam the Radnor halls ringing a schoolyard bell with a loud clapper every time circulation increased by 100,000. "It did not take long," a TV Guide historian noted, "for the bell to applaud itself into disrepair." The publishing Titanic had silenced even its most caustic critics.

My father found himself increasingly on the road, putting out fires at the thirty-five regional editions and making presentations to national advertisers, convincing them that their advertising dollars were best spent in what was to become the largest-selling weekly magazine in the world. He tried to bundle the presentations and condense his time on the road. But it wasn't that simple or that manageable. Many a Sunday night was spent taking him to the Philadelphia airport, then picking him up on Friday evening when he came back, exhausted. Air travel was still a rarity. He would return from these forays with souvenirs from the flights, usually the little salt and pepper packets that came with in-flight meals. I saved them for a while, but the novelty quickly wore off.

We lived in a community where most of the fathers were nine-to-fivers, who willingly picked up the carpool slack while my father was gone. His absences were most telling at youth sporting events, which tended to draw a sizable number of parents in our sports-crazy community. Not that he missed memorable achievements. I was a middling athlete (so much so that when I unexpectedly won a rowboat race at summer camp, my father exclaimed in joyous disbelief, "This is the greatest moment since the four-minute mile"). My only athletic achievement of note came in my final year of grammar school, in 1957. With my friend Charlie Greeley pitching and the tying run on second base, I ran down a well-hit fly ball in left-center field to preserve one of our few wins of the season. Afterward I experienced what for me was new—the congratulatory back thumps of teammates as we celebrated the win. My teammate Jimmy Colman's dad came over and said, "I wish your old man had been here to see that." It was an idle wish; my father was on the road.

In the summer before I started high school, my parents built a house on three acres well west of Philadelphia in rolling farmland: two bedrooms to three acres in six years. We were situated smack dab in the middle of nowhere. The only commotion was the monthly hunt. Horses, impeccably dressed gentry, and yapping dogs assembled in Currier & Ives fashion in the meadow behind our house on the appointed day, a ritual that we unreconstructed city slickers came to look forward to. It was a good place for James to decompress on weekends, which he did primarily by reading and by taking walks along the country lanes with Elizabeth. (We watched little television, a heretical practice which for reasons of economic survival went unmentioned.) Along the wall of one room, James had installed bookcases, which overfilled rapidly. Elizabeth would fuss at him to weed out his holdings, which he would—but with clear regret. James was the Will Rogers of books.

As an unintended result of his collecting, he seemed to know something of just about everything. Part of it was his innate curiosity. The greater part stemmed, I concluded later, from the fact that at no point in his education had he actually walked across a stage and been handed a diploma. He used to joke that with *seven years of grammar school, three of high school, and three-fourths of a college degree, he'd never graduated from anywhere. The self-deprecation was the sock on his Achilles' heel. So he read voraciously and retained it in his Grand Canyon of a memory. The breadth of his knowledge was driven home one weekend while my friend Dick and I were watching the television program College Bowl. Rhodes scholar wannabes, buzzers at the ready, waited anxiously to flaunt their knowledge. Dick and I sat in humbled silence, modern know-nothings. My father, his nose in a book, would look up at the screen from time to time and answer the arcane questions. When one of the know-it-alls hit the buzzer and blurted out an incorrect answer, my father said to no one in particular: "No, it's Heraclitus." The quizmaster, echoing my father, graciously corrected the intellectual miscreant. Dick looked at me disbelievingly: "It's Heraclitus? Does he always do this?" To which I replied candidly, "Yeah, pretty much."*

By the time I was in high school, my father's wars had receded to the historical margins with San Juan Hill and the Wars of the Roses. At our house, the only vestiges were framed photographs on the den wall: the V-E Day group shot with Patton (the one in which James had warned Elizabeth that his helmet was crooked, which it was); a photograph with Ridgway in the dead of a Korean winter, the icy landscape punctuated only by the palpable chill; and a formal photograph of Ridgway inscribed with the general's thanks for my father's service.

The rest he kept to himself. The "Colonel" Jim Quirk moniker had lasted all of two weeks following his return from Korea, which was how long it took him to tell everyone to cut it out. He never bellied up to a VFW bar, wore a Legionnaire's cap, or strutted in a Fourth of July parade. Nor was he much of a talker. He would allude obliquely to his wartime service, and only when provoked. If some loudmouth spoke ill of Patton or Ridgway or belittled the performance of their armies, my father would inquire of the armchair commando: "Is that so? What outfit were you with?" The mumbled response—a trick knee or equally specious disqualifying malady—would draw my father's dismissive end-of-conversation stare.

Everything tangible from his wars was consigned to a large wooden crate in the attic and was off-limits to the rest of the family. I made my only foray into that dusty archive after James remarked offhandedly that he had squirreled away a piano key from Hitler's charred Berchtesgaden piano and gave me the go-ahead to search for it. After much digging, I located it in a yellowed envelope at the bottom of the box, along with photographs taken at one of the abattoirs that had been the cultural cornerstone of the Reich. The grainy snapshots bore a similarity to the grim newspaper and magazine photographs of the era, but were unspeakably worse.

"Where is this?" I asked, proffering the snapshots. "Buchenwald," James replied. "Where did you get these?" I asked. "I took them," he said. "Why would you want them?" I asked indignantly. He was silent for a moment. Then his voice rose in a tightly controlled fury that I had never observed before. "Because someday people are going to say it wasn't all that bad, and I'm going to say, 'Yes, it was, and I have proof.'"

He handed me the photographs and walked away. I realized then that I had crossed an unspoken line, blundered into a sanctum where I was forever unwelcome, and that I'd best never venture there again. And I never did.

As his time on the road increased, he tried to get back for major high school milestones, with varying success. In the winter of my senior year, I was wrestling in the final citywide tournament of the year, held on the University of Pennsylvania campus. James had made a special point of adjusting his schedule so he could get back to Philadelphia for my Friday match. As I warmed up, I scanned the bleacher seats and spotted my mother (her first-time presence was a huge concession; she equated wrestling with bullfighting) but not my father. After the match, Elizabeth and I rode home. Shortly after we arrived, James appeared in a cab from the airport. His plane had been delayed somewhere in the Midwest. At least, he said, he could watch me in the Saturday matches. After an awkward silence, I told him that I had lost that afternoon and had been eliminated from the tournament; there would be no Saturday match for me. The next day, trying to put the best face on our shared disappointment, we drove into Philadelphia and went through the motions of dutifully cheering for my teammates who were still participating in the competition. We both feigned isn't-this-great? cheerfulness, failing mightily and feeling relieved when it was finally over.

As TV Guide grew, my father became an increasingly hot property. Board memberships and club memberships beckoned. James T. Quirk, publisher, became a trustee at Villanova. When the university president learned that its distinguished alumnus and trustee was not a graduate, he sought to rectify things. There was talk of an honorary degree (talk my father encouraged; it was the only award I actually saw him actively seek). The proposal somehow got derailed onto a slow track. Then the president moved on, leaving James degreeless.

The wooing by the old-line clubs, on the other hand, he found incongruous. A feeler came from one particularly august organization. Having a forebear who served as Meade's aide-de-camp at Gettysburg wasn't a prerequisite for membership, but it or something of comparable societal pedigree certainly helped. As the screening luncheon progressed, the screener ran through a perfunctory checklist: name, rank, serial number, Republican Party affiliation. To the last James said, "There might be a bit of a problem: I'm a lifelong Democrat." By the club's standards, it beat being a Communist, but not by much. The membership went untendered, to his great delight.

By 1960, more than 50 million families owned a television. TV Guide's circulation exceeded 7 million copies a week. By September 1962, it had become the largest selling weekly magazine in the world. With the magazine a fixture in American homes, TV Guide launched the annual "TV Guide Awards," a nationally televised prime-time variety special from Hollywood. Bob Hope, Carol Burnett, Loretta Young, Andy Griffith, and other television entertainers selected as the year's best would troop out onstage to receive their gleaming Tiffany bowls from the magazine's publisher (and onetime host of You Tell Me), who served *as both master of ceremonies and presenter. The show, weeks in production, drew good prime-time ratings and garnered respectable reviews from television critics in the nation's newspapers (as did the host, which pleased James more than he let on in public).*

As Elizabeth and I sat in the comfortable family room of our comfortable house watching James in a smartly tailored tuxedo banter with television stars on national television on a stage three thousand miles away, the fruits of his success were all around us. As I looked at the big chair empty in the corner ("You and the big chair and the radio and a book and a quiet drink," he had written to Elizabeth of his postwar dreams), I saw that the costs of that success were there as well. We were proud of him. But Hollywood (and Denver and Dallas) suffered from the same infirmities as the Reich (and Suwon and Seoul). He was there and we weren't. We wanted him home with us. But as we well knew, home and road were inextricably linked in a Gordian knot of success.

In early 1963, after Elizabeth died, James came down to see me at college and spend the weekend. It was the kind of Washington day that should have suggested spring but didn't. We spent the morning tramping about in the chill, visited the house that he and Elizabeth had lived in on New Hampshire Avenue before he had shipped out to North Africa, and drove along the Mall so he could point out the falling-down wartime buildings. We had a late lunch at a coffee shop and talked about his work and my school until the conversation dwindled to nothing at all. He checked his watch, not that there was any danger of his missing the train home but rather to figure out how much unfillable time remained.

He said he was sure I had some studying to do so he might as well take the early train. I looked at him in his finely tailored suit, a well-preserved man just past fifty, on top of his game at TV Guide. Just two months before he had stood at midfield in a packed stadium in Philadelphia introducing with practiced ease the 1962 All-America football team to President Kennedy and a national TV audience during halftime of the Army-Navy game. As he headed for the earlier train, I felt a great respect for my father, and a great sorrow for him at the same time.

When I graduated from college in 1965, he came down. On the night before we received our diplomas, he took me to dinner. Late in the evening, some of my friends in the college singing group repaired to an old stone building on campus for a farewell sing. The long first-floor hallway, thick walls, and vaulted ceilings were an a cappella group's dream. As the group went through its repertoire, some outlanders chimed in. On this night, the singers wanted the floor to themselves. The tone deaf and monotones were gingerly moved aside. To James's delight, the group encouraged him to stay. I had heard him hum an occasional tune but had never heard him sing before. He was good, blending in well on the standards (wisely eschewing some of the doo-wop numbers). For the finale, the singers formed a small circle, placed their arms around one another's shoulders, and finished with gusto. In that charmed circle was James Quirk, almost Villanova Class of 1932. When they were finished, the singers came up to him, complimented him for hitting the high note, and shook his hand.

And my father, whose middle name should have been Intensity, did something rare. He broke into a wide grin.

Chapter Six: A Family at War
1968–69

In April 1968, I came home to say so long.

James and I had seen each other only occasionally in the intervening three years. I had enlisted in the army the winter after college graduation and received my commission the following November. James had come down to Fort Benning for my commissioning. Afterward, we went to a reception at the officers' club. While we were there, an officer came over to James, introduced himself, and said he believed that they had served together in Korea. They had, and swapped reminiscences. The officer introduced James to other members of the Fort Benning cadre, explaining that "Colonel Quirk" had been with Matt Ridgway in Korea and had served with Bradley and Patton in the Big War, too. My father looked a little awkward and a little flattered. To me, the long-ago generals were artifacts. To the professional soldiers surrounding the long-ago soldier, they were icons. I imagined a New York Yankees spring training with the younger players gathered around the old-timer, listening to tales of DiMaggio and Gehrig and Ruth.

I spent the next year and a half at Fort Myer with the Old Guard, the army's ceremonial unit headquartered adjacent to Arlington Cemetery. In peacetime, it was a plum assignment, with White House welcoming ceremonies for visiting heads of state, a summertime pageant at the Jefferson Memorial, and the occasional burial of a World War II veteran or spouse in Arlington. But by 1967, peace and grave sites were in short supply. As Vietnam grew, the burials became more numerous. Cemetery space, already at a premium, became scarcer. To handle the increased demand, the cemetery converted a grassy divider on one of the service roads to burial space, but that began to fill up, too. The war was brought home starkly when we bade farewell to one of our second lieutenants as he shipped out to Vietnam, then buried him the next month when his coffin was shipped back.

In the spring of 1967, my father called. He was in Washington for a presentation to some major advertisers the following day and invited me to join him and them for dinner. I did. It was instructive and impressive. Seated around the well-appointed dinner table were a half dozen or so men whose names meant nothing to me but whose companies were household words. My father orchestrated the meal and the conversation the way a symphony conductor rehearses the woodwinds and strings, all as the precursor to the presentation the next day. After coffee, there were handshakes all around. I went back with my father to his suite. We had a beer and I watched him visibly decompress. The appearance of effortlessness had been just that. He had worked hard, and he needed to wind down so he could do it again tomorrow. Before I left, he was reviewing notes for the next day's presentation. I thought admiringly, so this is what he does.

That summer, I bought my first car, a Volkswagen. Amenities were few: There were no seat belts, not even a sun visor on the passenger side. Whem my father saw the car for the first time, he looked disapproving. I sought to assure him, crackerbox appearances aside, that the car was indeed safe. He was unmoved. Safety, I sensed, had nothing to do with his disapproval. "Why," he asked softly, "would you buy a German car?" He can't be serious, I thought; how long is he going to hold it against them? For a long time, as it turned out. For as long as he lived.

On Armistice Day 1967, I was assigned to escort a small group of World War I veterans to ceremonies at the Pershing grave site in Arlington. The members of the group were old and stooped, many were deaf, several shuffled unsteadily on canes, one was in a wheelchair. They had come in their service caps and Sam

Brown belts with their faded medals pinned to their suit jackets. It was moving and more than a little sad—this dwindling group of survivors come to a little plot of cemetery to say thank-you to their long-dead commander and their deceased colleagues. The group leader, eyeing my mere lieutenant's bars, asked if anyone else would be joining them. I told him no, I was it. He said with an air of resignation and I thought a tinge of bitterness: Lieutenant, it was a long time ago. No one cares.

That month I got my orders for Vietnam. ("Rory can miss his generation's war," James had written Elizabeth during the first of his two wars.) When I called him with the news, he took it well and said he looked forward to seeing me in March when Ranger training was complete.

We hooked up in March 1968 at his office. I had not been there in some time. It exuded the kind of confidence that only the white shoe law firms, Wall Street investment banks, and other really successful enterprises manifest. With good reason. In a decade in which some three hundred newspapers and magazines had gone out of business, TV Guide, the publishing Titanic, was still on top. The staffer back in 1953 who had asked for written assurance that he could have his old job back when the magazine cratered had hedged his bets unnecessarily.

James took me to lunch at his regular spot, at what amounted to a power table in those pre-power table times, and we got caught up. I told him that I had met a girl and that we were going to be spending a lot of my thirty-day leave together before I left, but I would be back to spend time with him. He brightened at that. His mind was still sharp. The trip-hammer brilliance and intensity were still there. But a lifetime of two packs of cigarettes a day was beginning to take its toll. He hacked incessantly, and his complexion looked almost jaundiced. When coffee came, he spilled as much of it in the saucer as he managed to drink. He was fifty-seven, but an old fifty-seven.

Midway through my leave, I stopped home to see him. He was in a good mood. The Sunday morning New York Times had a fifteenth anniversary profile of TV Guide featuring an interview with the publisher, who was pictured prominently. The article walked through the staggering revenue and circulation num-bers, contrasting them with the paltry figures of the start-up in 1953, and cited the magazine's personalized presentations to ad-vertisers as the key. The article noted that James had made 140 of them himself in the past year.

A few nights later, while James was sitting in his big chair reading, the news flash came from Memphis—Martin Luther King Jr. had been shot and killed. When he heard the news, my father stiffened, then seemed to physically deflate. "I suppose," he had written enthusiastically to Elizabeth after describing the racially integrated army he'd encountered in Korea, "that it could be done in civilian life if people put their minds down to it." He had seen the paradigm and had embraced it. On this night, that paradigm and his long-ago optimism bore little rela-tion to the ugly present. As I headed out of the room, I asked if he wanted me to leave the radio on. He said it didn't matter. With a defeated sigh, he sank deeper into his chair.

I spent the next two weeks in Florida with the girl I had met. We spent a lot of time talking about the past and the future, avoiding the looming present. When she took me to the airplane for Philadelphia, we said all the right things about writing and how quickly a year would pass. It was a scene at variance with the cynical marching song sung at army training centers about every soldier's nemesis: "Jody," the lowlife civilian stay-behind who steals girlfriends ("Ain't no use in goin' home / Jody's got your girl and gone / Ain't no use in feelin' blue / Jody's got your car keys, too").

I came home the final weekend to see my father. We went to dinner. The dining room was full, a festive Saturday night crowd. People stopped by the table to say hello to us and ask what brought me to town. "He's going to Vietnam on Monday," James would say with forced cheerfulness. People's reactions were stark—a monosyllabic "Oh" or a Sands of Iwo Jima *pep talk. The evening was a disaster. Sunday was spent moving the detritus of childhood and sundry clothing to the attic.*

The next day, a steel-gray mid-April Philadelphia Monday, we headed for the airport, a route I knew by heart from the Sunday evening drives with Elizabeth to see James to his plane, except now the roles were reversed. Before we left the house, he had presented me with a small tape recorder and some blank tapes, so we could keep in touch. We rode most of the way in silence. When the boarding announcement was made, I hugged him hard. He did something he had never done before: He bridged the respectful distance that had characterized our relationship and kissed me on the forehead. ("I always have a lurking fear he will break my heart completely," he had written to Elizabeth about me in the long-ago spring of 1945. In the almost-spring of 1968, I surely had.)

He told me to take care of myself. Then he did something I had seen him do only once before, when Elizabeth died—he wept.

• • •

The Huey hovers just off the airstrip. I jump the short distance to the ground. As it climbs, I give the pilot an appreciative thumbs-up on this decidedly thumbs-down day. He returns the signal, banks hard into the sunset, and heads back to the war that has no back or front.

I sling my rucksack over my shoulder and jog across the airstrip. I am heading home, to bury my father next to my mother.

• • •

He had died on a Saturday night of a massive coronary in the very Philadelphia airport where nine months before he had said good-bye, hugged me, and turned away crying. He had died in harness, changing planes for a business trip out west.

The funeral was on a bright, bone-numbing January day. The chapel on the campus of Villanova University, his almost alma mater, was filled to overflowing. My father was not one for ceremony, especially when the focus was on him. He had always said, only half jokingly, "When I die, just prop me up under a tree somewhere." We did a little better than that.

It was a simple ceremony. We fulfilled his one request: An American flag was draped over his casket so he could have a proper veteran's burial. I accompanied his flag-draped casket into the chapel, past pew after pew of the many people who had known him—as Jimmy Allan, as Col. Jim Quirk, as James T. Quirk, Publisher, the local boy who made good, then better than good.

As we left the chapel and were waiting for the cars to load for the trip to the cemetery, a man in his midseventies, yet with regal bearing, walked up, apologized for being late, and explained that his plane from Pittsburgh had been delayed. I recognized the aquiline face from long-ago photographs, the ones with the signature hand grenade taped to his battle harness, but struggled to come up with a name for this old man who had obviously taken great pains to come hundreds of miles to help me bury my father. "I am Matthew Ridgway," he offered helpfully. "Your father and I served together in Korea. I felt I should come and say good-bye."

We buried my father in the family plot, a stone's throw from his childhood haunts. I had been there last in 1962 when we buried my mother. As I scanned the gravestone bearing the names of the generations of Quirks, their spouses, and their children who had preceded my father to this place, I realized why he had lived his life in overdrive and shown little interest in pensions or retirement; he had known intuitively that longevity was not his strong suit. His grave was roughly equidistant from the house in which he was born and the Philadelphia airport where he died—a symmetrical anomaly in an asymmetrical life. As the crow flies, my father had not come very far in his fifty-seven years. But what does the crow know?

In the days following, I reflected hard about my father. The obituaries—front page in the Philadelphia papers, prominently played in the New York Times—*hit the high points:* TV Guide, *Ridgway, Patton, Bradley. I put away the obituaries with his letters. The magazine that had been his life said as much, celebrating his achievements in a gracious editorial. The final trip to his office, to bring home the mementos and knickknacks he had accumulated over the years, was more painful for his staff than for his son. I had been there last on the day of our final lunch, when James couldn't keep the coffee in the cup. Col-*

leagues wept openly. His desktop, always full of materials, was clean. The big ashtray, the size of a dinner plate, in which he snubbed out his two-plus packs of cigarettes each workday, was empty. I decided then to stop smoking.

In trying to sort it all out, I realized that his was a truly American story. His leadership and management skills had been forged in the crucible of two wars. Like so many men of his generation, he had been given responsibilities, in Europe and then in Korea, for which there was no template. And like so many men of his generation who found themselves in those circumstances, he had learned by doing—found that his reach was greater than he had thought and that his untested grasp was the equal of that reach. "This experience has been very valuable," he had written Elizabeth in the dying days of World War II. And indeed it had been.

Although he had seen the worst of man, on the killing fields and in the murder factories of the Reich, he had retained an innate optimism. As he had written to Elizabeth:

> War may do bad things to men, but it does seem to move them beyond, if not above, many of the little pettinesses and greeds that we are used to. We have to hope that some of the evil geniuses of our day will not twist the shapeless ideal that men are fighting for into some mad scramble for power and money. Everyone has to get at least a glimpse of a picture bigger than themselves and bigger than America. There is so much of the rest of the world that is not America, but all of it could find the best of what we have if it were only given a chance. The Arabs that American soldiers beat on the Suez docks and the Indians that starve in Bombay could have enough to eat if the people weren't misguided or misinformed—more by stupid people than by evil ones. There must be someone in the world big enough to move the people with him toward something more decent, and it may be that this war will reveal him.

The war changed my father's generation. Then they came back and changed America, transformed it in marvelous mate-

rial ways but transformed it also into something more decent—
far short of my father's ideal to be sure, but something appreciably closer to that ideal than it had been before.

"I hope that Rory will be proud of his father," James had written to Elizabeth as his landing craft had headed to the Normandy beaches. I was, in midwinter 1969, every bit of that; how
could I not be? I think he knew it, although I never came right
out and said it. There was in our time together some of the little boy in the father-son photograph keeping a respectful distance from the strange man in uniform who materialized into
my life on Christmas night 1945. I never fully bridged that respectful distance, never came right out and said a lot of things
I wanted to say to him. I would have gotten to it in good time.
But the good time ran out before I did.

James T. Quirk was at peace, which made one of us. Ten days
later, I went back to Vietnam.

On the April day two months later when I left Vietnam for the
second time, this time for good, the plane was late. The unvar-
iegated lot of us—gathered from throughout the Republic of
South Vietnam for shipment back to The World—was left to
while away the time, seeking shade on wooden benches under
open, roofed shelters along the periphery of the landing strip.
The shelters would have been ideal at a roadside park in the
States. This being Vietnam, the roofs shielded the sun but
trapped the heat, silently baking the people beneath.

Going home had the same impersonality as arriving in country. We were an amalgamation of strangers, thrown together by
chance and a flight manifest, antithetical John Donne—every
one of us an island.

While we were waiting, a helicopter landed from up north
and disgorged a general and his entourage—like us, headed for
home. A microphone had been set up on the edge of the strip
so the general could give his farewell speech to his staff, which
stood respectfully in the heat while he droned on. The troops
lolling under the roofs eyed the proceedings with sleepy-eyed
indifference. A few read. Some dozed. Most just sat looking off

into the monotonous middle distance. There was a sameness to them—lean, hard, with the New England lobsterman's look of too much sun and too little sleep. "Rode hard and put up wet," cowboys would have said.

Looking at them, I realized that underneath the weathered tans and wary, weary eyes, they were kids; they just weren't young anymore. If a dog year is the equivalent of seven human years, what, I wondered, is a Vietnam year's equivalent? Reflecting on that scene years later brought to mind the line in the Warren Zevon song: "They were too old to die young, and too young to die now."

In the distance, we could see the airliner making its final approach to the airfield in the shimmering heat. Its appearance was greeted with whistles, claps, and a few murmurs of "about time." We really were going home. The plane landed and taxied to a stop a short distance from us. After a brief interval, the portable stairs were wheeled out to the plane, and the stewardess inside popped the door. The troops on the ground shifted impatiently on the wooden benches, anxious to board.

From out of a building adjacent to the airstrip, metal shipping containers were taken to the plane. As the dead were loaded in the belly for shipment home, an apprehensive, untanned, fearful face appeared in the airplane door. This first of the planeload of replacements from the States surveyed the scene. The hard-eyed troops on the periphery looked silently at the face looking silently at them. In that moment, the new guy had his future at his feet—and the stark, mutually exclusive outcomes.

The new guys started down the stairs, wide eyed, recoiling at the tropical heat. Looking young and scared and pasty white in the bright midday sun, they shuffled self-consciously through the silent gauntlet of men-children to the edge of the strip. There they would be fed into the maw of the half-million-man machine that the deep thinkers on the banks of the Charles River had assembled here, just as the deep thinkers on the banks of the Seine had done a generation before. In 364 wake-ups and a duffel bag drag, many of them would be right back here, staring down the next group of new guys. Some would go home earlier, staring down nobody.

We got ready to board, but there was another delay as the general and his party boarded the plane. They grabbed the best seats, in front. Or so they thought. They'd seated themselves so far forward that they were behind the screen for the in-flight movie and would miss John Wayne intrepidly fighting oil-well fires. When it was our turn to board, we formed up in Noah's ark fashion, trooped across the strip, climbed the metal stairs, and were greeted by the perky shtick of the smiling stewardesses: "Hi, how are ya? How y'all doin'? Where y'all from back home?" Bad idea. They didn't get a lot of chitchat back.

As we settled in, troops fidgeted with their seat belt clasps and squirmed in their seats, waiting anxiously for the pilot to put the airborne show on the road. As a departure gift, each of us had received a publication titled "Tour 365," a year-by-year history of the war, which at this tenuous point in the conflict had exhausted the talents of even the most relentlessly upbeat word merchants in the Military Assistance Command Vietnam (MACV) stable. How many variations are there on "the light at the end of the tunnel"? Most of the troops set the publication aside; they didn't need anyone to tell them about their year in Vietnam.

I thumbed through my copy, past the photograph of a firm-jawed President Kennedy and accompanying kick-ass quote ("the United States is determined to help Vietnam preserve its independence"), an unprophetic relic from the heady early days when everybody figured that Vietnam was a counterinsurgency piece of cake, back before the whole thing turned sour. I scanned the congratulatory letter on the back page: "Now you are going home to rejoin your family and friends. They are proud of you and are anxiously awaiting your return."

We could hope.

As we flew east from day into night and into day again, people picked at the succession of proffered meals and a few watched the movie; most slept. When the plane finally approached the States, the pilot came on the intercom to tell us to *look out the windows. Below us the Pacific was lapping against the California coastline. There was desultory applause, a few hoots, then silence.*

We deplaned, which was delayed again to permit the general and his entourage to exit leisurely, then were loaded on buses for final processing elsewhere on the air base. Our bus ride took us along a street past the base public school, which was letting out for the day. Some of the teenagers flashed us the peace sign; most ignored us.

Later, in a taxi, when the driver tried to engage me in a discussion about the San Francisco Giants, I allowed as how I wasn't as up on the 1969 baseball season as I'd like to be. Eyeing me warily in the rearview mirror—the tan, the haircut, the uniform—he asked me where I was coming from. I told him. He looked at me as though I was from Mars, which was how I was beginning to feel.

When I got to New York, the girl I had said good-bye to in Florida a year and a seeming lifetime before was waiting at the foot of the escalator at Kennedy airport, a welcoming committee of one. The Kennedy-Johnson Vietnam Brain Trust was conspicuously absent; Rostow and the Bundys must have gotten stuck in traffic.

She hugged me, a tight, little, undramatic hug—not like the one in the photograph of the sailor and the pretty girl in an off-balance embrace in Times Square at the end of World War II. Different war, that: big-hug war.

We grabbed my duffel bag at the baggage claim, walked out into a warm New York evening, and hailed a cab. Time to move on, time to get going with the rest of our lives. Except we didn't have the foggiest idea where—or how.

Chapter Seven: A Family at Peace

In the years afterward, I worked for a newspaper, went to law school, and married the pretty girl at the foot of the Kennedy airport escalator. I thought about my father, his wars and mine, very little.

When I did, it was with the sense that my father's third war had been one war too many. Friends would confide awkwardly over a few drinks that he had aged badly during that last year, had fretted, had begun to question the war. I thought back to the accordion file in his briefcase and the phone number he'd clipped out of a newspaper to order detailed military maps of Vietnam, the phone number he couldn't bring himself to call. Years later, I would come across a letter from that period from Walter Annenberg to my father, obviously in response to my father's inquiry about his future. "I fully expect that you will remain with this organization until you reach the retirement age of 65," Annenberg wrote, which must have been reassuring to a man of fifty-seven who sensed that he had lost a half step and feared losing another. Annenberg had added, "I am worried about the state of your health."

Vietnam intruded on occasion. In the winter of 1971–72, "Hire the Vet" posters appeared in the New York City subway depicting a fresh-faced GI in dress uniform, back from the war, eager for work. "He's home," the poster proclaimed cheerfully, "with experience and skills." A freelance editorialist had taken a black marking pen to one of the posters, etched dark circles under the vet's eyes, stuck a hypodermic in his arm, and expanded the ad copy so it read: "He's home with experience and skills . . . and a $200 a day habit." The people in the university community where I spent that winter chuckled at the derisive addendum, which pretty much summed up the feelings of twenty-one year olds ensconced in academe toward the nineteen year olds half a world away.

When the POWs came home, I misted up a little at the photo of the mom and the fresh-faced, miniskirted daughters bounding joyously across the tarmac, arms outstretched, to hug their POW dad. I recalled a fragment from the "Tour 365" booklet: "They are proud of you . . ."

I got angry only once. As South Vietnam imploded, I was summoned to a roomful of assignment editors planning their coup de grace coverage. They were, said one, kicking around a terrific story idea and wanted to bounce it off me: How about sending a writer over to the wards at Walter Reed Army Hospital to ask the wounded Vietnam veterans for their reaction? There was a faux poignancy to the proposal, one that masked the final opportunity for the journalistic picadors to stick their barbs in the shattered warriors of the war they loathed. I said: "It's a dreadful idea; leave them the hell alone." There was an awkward silence and some paper shuffling, then I walked out. A few days later, with the flag of the revolution firmly planted on the former U.S. Embassy grounds in Saigon, Vietnam and the Walter Reed veterans were yesterday's news. The incident was forgotten by everybody. Practically everybody.

In time, my grief over my father's death eroded into resignation and ultimately into nothingness. I squirreled it away in the deepest recesses of memory. Having erased the past, I attacked the present with a vengeance. As my children were born, I tried to rectify my father's absences in life and his loss in death, volunteering at schools, coaching youth teams. Other parents marveled at my apparent altruism. It was more complex. Part of it was to enrich my offsprings' childhood. A large part was to reinvent my own.

As my children became more aware of time and memory and mortality, they asked basic childlike questions about my family *and my past, and were unartfully brushed off. To them, I had no past, at least not one beyond yesterday or last month.*

One night in 1990, on a family vacation in New Hampshire, we went into the nearby village to the movies. The film was Field of Dreams. *At the end, when Kevin Costner played catch with his long-dead dad in the cornfield Valhalla, I cried. My children had never seen me cry. We rode home in embarrassed silence.*

In the spring of 1991, my family and I were walking through Dulles airport to catch a plane. Approaching us from the other direction along the broad concourse were two soldiers in camouflage gear, their Desert Storm duffel bags bouncing jauntily on their shoulders. They looked young and confident, like the winners they were. From my right, a woman, her teenage daughter in tow, cut across in front of us and intercepted the soldiers. The woman said something to the two strangers and shook their hands. Then her daughter shook their hands. The soldiers smiled modestly and reshouldered their duffels as the woman and her daughter rushed to make their plane. It reminded me of my father's account of the Brits coming out to meet the convoys heading for the D-day ports, saying, "Good luck, lads," and offering them cups of hot tea. The girl at the foot of the Kennedy airport escalator watched me as I took in this concourse scene, and she had the good sense to say nothing.

In 1992, my daughter was looking for something to bring to show and tell at school, something with a family connection. I came up empty. She excused herself for a moment, routed about in a desk drawer, and came back with an oblong blue case.

"What about this?" she asked. "The thing that Grandfather got from the general, what is it?"

It was my father's Legion of Merit from Korea. We took out the medal and I started to read her the yellowed citation he had folded neatly in the box. Her eyes glazed. So I told her a story about her grandfather instead, of how proud he had been of the medal the general gave him. It was the first order he'd ever published in his new job, he'd written proudly to Elizabeth. I could see that my Elizabeth was proud, too. The medal was a big hit at her school the next day, as it had been at mine forty years be-

fore. She'd forgotten most of the details I'd primed her with, but she remembered the part about it coming from a general. Her friends were impressed with that, and with the colors; it had really pretty colors.

In the weeks thereafter, it was as though we had opened a large memory vault. We began in fits and starts to peel the leaves of the familial artichoke, going back in time to my childhood and my parents. Elizabeth and her brother listened with rapt attention when I recalled some event or other. It was the first time for them, and a long time for me. In revisiting those times, I came to see my father and mother through an objective prism, unblemished by separation and early death.

Together—through their letters—they had experienced great events, had worked with great men, had helped defeat the metastasized evil of the Reich, had decided the Cold War in Korea (a stretch maybe; maybe not), had helped launch a publishing miracle where cynics predicted a newsstand Titanic. Together, they had given to their son much of what their childhood and the Depression had denied them.

I came to realize in those reminiscences with my children that all my life I had viewed my parents through the wrong end of the looking glass, rendering them smaller than life. When I looked at them in the proper perspective, I came to appreciate them for what they were, see in them what others had seen: Elizabeth pushed by her cast of Cub Crusaders to center stage, where Chuckie Schonders gave her the bouquet of flowers as the applause and cries of "Author" rained down; James catching his commanding officer in a moment of weakness (and what greater weakness than V-E Day?) to push through a promotion for one of his officers; Elizabeth going to her classmate's home to reprise her graduation speech and right an unintended wrong; James on the trip to Europe when he was on his way to becoming a big shot, but not too big to take a side trip to Bristol to introduce his bride to an old English couple who had taken him in during that long-ago spring of 1944, and Mrs. James exclaiming: "You came back!"

These were not necessarily momentous things. They were fundamentally gracious things. And for that reason they were important things.

As I stopped being angry about the fact that there had been no final acts in their lives—that for them the theater had gone dark after the first intermission—I celebrated instead the pieces of the unfinished mosaic and what they had done in the time they had. "It may be that these are the years the locusts have eaten," James had written at the end of the war in Europe. The locusts never had a chance. My parents had captured lightning in a bottle, and it had glowed incandescently.

Incandescence, I came to learn in those months of reminiscence and reflection, is like the Fourth of July fireworks: Things burn intensely and arc across the sky, but turn your head for just a moment and suddenly they're gone—which is why you can't measure them in years, only moments. And for James and Elizabeth there had been those.

"It may be," James had written in the spring of 1945, "that we shall never be able to say that the war ended at any given time on any particular day."

And it may be that we can.

My daughter had from time to time asked to go to the Vietnam Veterans Memorial, a place I had never visited and for inarticulable reasons never wanted to. I resisted. She persisted. So on Veterans Day 1992, we made the short trek. I didn't know what I would find there, or if I would find anything at all. When we got back, I wrote this:

Veterans Day. November 11, 1992
5:30 p.m. The Vietnam Veterans Memorial

The large crowds that gathered earlier in the day for the tenth anniversary of the Vietnam Veterans Memorial have gone. The television crews are breaking down the last of their equipment. Darkness creeping in.

John Donne said that any man's death diminishes us.

Here, in the shadow of The Wall, the diminution is over-whelming. The names run out endlessly to the east, toward the Capitol; to the west, toward the Lincoln Memorial. Steven Sparks . . . Richard Garcia . . . Ezekiel Page . . . Hanson . . . Adkins . . . Nugent . . . Beauregard . . . Woolridge . . . and 58,000 others.

The enormity of it. And at my feet the small American flags, the handwritten notes and yellowed photographs wrapped in protective plastic against the scudding rainclouds. And around me the whispered cries of recognition as a name is identified on the massive granite slabs ("See? There!"), the choked-back sobs as people touch The Wall, trace the letters etched in the granite, trying to reach beyond the inanimate surface, to reconnect with a time long ago.

In my hand I hold a scrap of paper bearing three names. With my seven-year-old daughter at my side, I begin my search. Here in this place of grief, and loss, and might-have-been.

Don's twenty-first birthday party was held in the summer of 1965 in New York City, at the Carlyle or the Plaza or one of those grand New York hotels. It was black tie. There was a trendy rock band that played Motown. And if we didn't dance 'til a quarter to three, we came close. When you're twenty-one, you think: This is just about as good as it gets.

When I saw him next, it was 1967, a Sunday night in Clyde's. I had ragged him about his white sidewall haircut. He was a marine lieutenant, stationed at Quantico, getting set to ship out to Vietnam.

"How are you going to find it, Dad?" my daughter asks as we look at The Wall. "There are so many names."

So many. Then I see it, on Panel 36E, Line 81:

Donald D. Perkins Jr.
First Lieutenant, United States Marine Corps. Winnetka, Illinois. Killed in the Republic of South Vietnam on February 2, 1968. Age: 23.

He was buried at Arlington National Cemetery. When I returned to Washington, I visited his gravesite—a lovely setting on a slight rise in the tranquility of Arlington. A fine site for a picnic. Not a great place to bury a twenty-three year old. Then, there are no great places to bury a twenty-three year old.

Vietnam scholars will debate when it was that the United States crossed the Rubicon into Vietnam. Maybe it was in 1963 in the delta at Ap Bac when Viet Cong guerrillas stood and fought well against an overwhelming force of South Vietnamese, who, to the rage and disbelief of their American advisers, did not fight well at all, portending a longer and different war. Maybe it was in 1965 in the Ia Drang Valley of the Central Highlands, when elements of the Air Cav, possibly the finest fighting force ever assembled by an American army, engaged North Vietnamese regulars in the first full-scale battle of the war, at a cost of 230 U.S. killed, and Westmoreland said that the troop level would have to go way up, and it did. Maybe it was at some other point in time, some other Rubicon. The truth, as Oscar Wilde noted, is rarely pure, and never simple. But crossed it was. And this Wall is testament to the enormity of that crossing.

There's an oil painting of Joe in one of the buildings at his college, the one named in his memory. It was dedicated shortly after his death, and created a bit of a stink. So riven by the war was our generation that the naming of a building after a dead Vietnam soldier could provoke angry dissent. There was concern that there would be a disruption at the naming ceremony. Friends feared that the family, having endured one heartbreak, would now be subjected to another. The event passed without disruption, and everyone let out a sigh of relief. I find his name near the apex of the Wall, high up on Panel 14W, so I have to crane my neck to read it:

Joseph M. Lauinger
First Lieutenant, United States Army. Tulsa, Oklahoma.
Killed in the Republic of South Vietnam on
January 8, 1970. Age: 24.

Some years ago, I learned that a group of students was interested in placing a small Vietnam memorial stone on the campus listing the names of students who had died in Vietnam. They were aware of the building named after Joe but wanted more—a memorial. To these students, it was not a question of politics but of fairness. For them, Vietnam was a historical memory, like Normandy or Belleau Wood or Antietam. A committee was set up to look into this idea. Maybe it will happen someday. In the meantime, the oil painting of Joe hangs in the building bearing his name, his likeness frozen. Joe would have been forty-seven last July. But he will always be twenty-four.

It is dark now. To the east, the Capitol dome stands brightly lit against the autumn sky. It was from that building that the Congress gave the carte blanche thumbs-up to the Vietnam War in August 1964, passing the Tonkin Gulf Resolution in about as much time as it takes to shine a pair of shoes. It was to be a limited war. The wrongness of that assessment is etched in this Wall.

Bill was one of the first people I met at college. We found that we had a great deal in common. Neither of us had gotten around to reading some dreary tome assigned to incoming freshmen for one of the orientation seminars. Both of us liked baseball, and the conversation turned to the weighty matter of whether Roger Maris would hit sixty-one home runs and break Babe Ruth's record. We remained good friends over the years. I last heard his voice in February 1969. We had exchanged voice tapes sporadically throughout the previous eight months. On the last one, he was looking forward to getting back to the States, possibly going to law school, maybe calling the girl he'd dated in college, getting on with his life. But that was before his chopper went down.

William G. Scott Jr.
First Lieutenant, United States Army. Scarsdale, New
York. Killed in the Republic of South Vietnam on
February 12, 1969. Age: 26.

My daughter is at my side, holding a small red rose someone has given her. "I'd like to put this on your friend's grave," she says. And she does, at the base of Panel 32W, where the path in front of The Wall begins its gradual rise to the west.

As we walk along the path, small green hand-held lights flicker in the hands of the silently moving crowd. To my left, two men embrace tearfully, their torsos a little thick for their faded jungle fatigues. Time has a way of doing that. "Qui Nhon," one says tearfully of a long-ago grid square, a place that time has not erased.

I have finished what I have come to do. As I take one last look, I try to think of something to say. To Don. To Joe. To Bill. To all of them. But what? That the price they paid was well worth it? I have tried for a long time to believe that. And for a long time I succeeded. But I don't believe it anymore. I say, "I'm sorry."

And I turn to go. My daughter asks me if all the people named on The Wall are buried behind it. I start to say no but stop myself. For in a sense they are. "What do you think this place means?" I ask. She thinks for a moment, then says: "I think I know but I'm not sure how to say it." Nor do I.

It's raining hard now. The raindrops are falling on my cheeks, bringing to mind the fine old Temptations song about rain, the one where David Ruffin sings:

My eyes search the skies
desperately for rain
Cause raindrops will hide my teardrops
and no one will ever know.

I take my daughter's hand. She snuggles against me to
ward off the autumn chill. We head away from this hallowed
place of grief, and loss, and memories.

Epilogue: On a Green Field in the Sun
June 12, 1995

Jelleff Boys and Girls Club Field in Georgetown is a Norman Rockwell sliver of green against a cloudless azure sky. It's the Yankees versus the Rockies for the Northwest Washington Little League championship.

I am standing in the third-base coaching box, talking to my runner, a towhead named Chris.

Five minutes earlier, our team, the first-place Yankees, had trailed in this the final inning of the decisive final game by a score of 6 to 2. Our storybook season (overachieving smoke and mirrors and a left-handed pitcher named Bayard with a whip for an arm) was poised to end on a sour "close, but" note. The championship trophy lying in the trunk of my car in anticipation of a victory was about to go unpresented, along with my DEWEY DEFEATS TRUMAN championship talk. Then, with two outs, the Yankees rallied improbably, scoring three times and now trail by just one run. Any hope of a championship comes down to somehow moving Chris the last sixty feet from third base to home.

As the Rockies change pitchers, Chris and I mull our limited options.

"What would you think about trying to steal home?" I ask. Pause. "Okay . . . I guess . . . yeah, sure."

"If you don't think you can make it, well . . ."

"I can make it."

"Then let's go for it first chance we get."

Nervous swallow. "Okay."

Two pitches later, the ball squirts away from the catcher and dances just out of his reach along the first-base line. With the window of opportunity cracked ever so slightly, Chris breaks for home. The Rockies' catcher, sensing him in homeward motion, lunges to recover the ball, then dives catlike back toward the plate as Chris slides to avoid the fatal tag. Ball, catcher, and Chris converge at the plate simultaneously in a variegated heap of Yankee gray, Rockie white, and dusty ball-field brown.

As the dust settles, the home plate umpire eyes the zero-sum scene carefully, sorts it out un-Solomonically, and swipes his hands parallel to the ground.

Chris is safe at home.

Bedlam. The exuberant Yankees rise up off their bench, swarm around Chris, and snow him under in a human avalanche mixed with whoops of boyish joy and disbelief.

As I watch from third base, feigning nonchalance at the bedlam sixty feet away, I think back to another game, to my running catch in left field that saved Charlie Greeley's win, to Jimmy Colman's dad saying afterward, "I wish your old man had been here to see that."

Chris's old man is here to see this. I am feeling very proud of my son.

The umpire allows the impromptu celebration to go on a bit, then gently reminds everyone that the game is only tied, not over. But the Yankees know otherwise. And so do the Rockies. And they're both right. Final score: Yankees 11, Rockies 6. The Yankees win the championship.

This being Little League, we don't go to Disney World. We go next door, to Pizza Hut.

At the joyous victory celebration, the once-despaired-of championship trophy sits ceremoniously on the table amid pizza detritus and spilled soda. Surveying the scene, my cocoach Dale leans over to me and says, "You know, coach, it doesn't get a whole lot better than this."

I try to freeze the scene indelibly in my mind, pleased that Chris's mom and sister are on hand, wishing that James and Elizabeth could share in it, too.

Later, after the good-byes, thanks coach, and see you next year, I gather up our family and head out into a thumbs-up evening on a decidedly thumbs-up day.

We walk home in the June dusk. The soft clatter of Chris's cleats on the weathered brick sidewalk is the only sound punctuating the stillness. The old globed streetlights wink on, casting their champagne glow. Up ahead, I can see a neighbor taking his dog for its evening walk. Off in the distance, the Healy Tower clock at Georgetown University bells the hour. In a few moments, when we get to our house, our next-door neighbor Cherie will lean out her kitchen window and ask, as she has all season, "Well Chris, how'd we do today?"

We are walking single file now, channeled where the sidewalk narrows. Chris's sister is carrying the trophy, the one that rose Lazarus-like from the car trunk. His mom carries his first baseman's glove in her free hand, the one I am not holding tightly. Chris walks ahead, his bat bag slung across his shoulder, a batting glove dangling from his back pocket, the dust still visible on his uniform pants from the safe-at-home slide.

A family safe at home.

Dale is right. It doesn't get a whole lot better.

Afterword: The Atomic Bomb and the End of the Korean War

The Korean War ended with a whimper because the United States was about to end it with a bang.

During the course of General Marshall's visit to Korea in June 1951, with Colonel Quirk the only other person present, General Ridgway and General Marshall candidly reviewed the situation in Korea. Ridgway asked Marshall for his impressions of the war, now that he had the opportunity to see it firsthand. Marshall replied that it was bad. Worse than he'd anticipated? Ridgway asked. Worse, much worse than he, or anyone in Washington, could appreciate, Marshall replied, and it couldn't be permitted to continue.

Marshall went on to say that he knew Chinese premier Chou En-lai pretty well from his time in China during the civil war and had a good relationship with the premier; Chou trusted him. Marshall said that if he were to take a message from the president, Chou would believe him.

When Marshall got back to Washington, he said, he was going to suggest to the president that he send him to China to see Chou and tell him that unless there was an end to the fighting, "we [the United States] are going to give them a taste of the atom."

My father told me this story in 1967. It occurred, he said, after General Marshall's press conference in Tokyo, just prior to my father's return to the United States. He said that he had recorded the Marshall visit in a letter home to my mother, but (for obvious reasons of national security) he had not memorial-

ized the specifics of the subsequent Ridgway-Marshall conver-
sation. My father said that with Marshall dead and Ridgway the
only living witness other than himself, he thought he would con-
tact Ridgway and see that the event was memorialized, because
it was of historical significance. My father died shortly thereafter
without taking any action.

In 1968, while reviewing my parents' correspondence, in the
letter of June 12, 1951, I came upon the reference to the Mar-
shall-Ridgway discussion. In 1976, I contacted Marshall's biog-
rapher, Forrest Pogue, who was then in residence at the Smith-
sonian Institution, where he was completing the final volume of
his Marshall biography (encompassing the Korea period). I
shared with him my father's account and the letter of June 12.
Pogue said he intended to contact General Ridgway for corrob-
oration.

A few months later, I received back from Pogue the file of my
father's Korea letters along with a copy of a letter from General
Ridgway to Pogue dated November 16, 1976, the relevant part
of which read:

Dear Forrest,

Your good letter, dated 08 Nov, reached my desk only
yesterday, as I had been in Florida . . .

I do not recall the conversation which Jim Quirk reported
to his son, but I would have implicit confidence in Jim's ac-
curacy. He would not have reported it unless it was true,
and I do think it was quite in accord with General Marshall's
thinking and his frankness when talking to those he trusted.

The second incident you relate is as you state it. There
was a high wind with a low ceiling, and flying in our light
planes—a pilot and one passenger—over those rugged
mountains was hazardous. I did not want to expose Gen-
eral Marshall to such hazards, and told him so. He said:
"Ridgway, would you go on if you were alone?" I replied:
"Yes, sir. I have been flying this terrain for an average of
over two hours daily since I came, and I am used to it." So
General Marshall replied: "We'll go." I do not remember

a rougher ride, particularly when we came over the rim of the famous Punchbowl in the eastern mountains. Though strapped in, my head banged hard against the roof of the plane, but the helmet prevented injury.

    Faithfully,

    M. B. Ridgway

I saw Forrest Pogue the next and last time at a book signing in Washington in June 1987 upon the publication of the final volume of his Marshall biography, George C. Marshall: Statesman 1945–1959. *Thinking it likely he would remember neither me nor our 1976 meeting, I introduced myself. To my surprise, Pogue immediately recalled our meeting, my father's letter, and his subsequent correspondence with General Ridgway, then told me of the Marshall-Ridgway discussion: "It's in the book."*[18]

    Here is the rest of the story.

    What transpired upon Secretary Marshall's return to Washington in June 1951 is intriguing. On June 12, Marshall, coming directly from his plane, which had landed a half hour before, met immediately with President Truman at the White House. Two days after the meeting, Marshall prepared an eyes only message to Ridgway. On June 20, Ridgway sent an eyes only message back to Marshall.

    On June 23, in a dramatic turnabout, Soviet ambassador to the United Nations Jacob Malik called for a Korean cease-fire and armistice. In response, the Joint Chiefs instructed Ridgway to seek a negotiated settlement; the Chinese and North Koreans agreed to talk; and truce negotiations began on July 10.

    While the talks dragged on for another two years, the nature of the war changed dramatically. There were no more human wave attacks by the Communists and no further efforts to drive Eighth Army into the sea. In the space of three weeks in June 1951, a war that seemed to have no end saw the end come into view.

    The reason has its genesis in the Marshall-Ridgway "taste of the atom" discussion three weeks before.

    Did Marshall and the president discuss the use of atomic weapons in Korea on June 12? The answer is most assuredly yes.

Records at the Truman Library confirm the Marshall-Truman meeting, but the president's papers provide no details of what was discussed. Records at the George C. Marshall Library, where Marshall's personal papers are housed, contain nothing regarding the Marshall-Truman meeting (although Marshall, the consummate gentleman, did send a thank-you note to Mrs. Ridgway for her hospitality in Tokyo). Marshall's official correspondence as secretary of defense is housed at the National Archives in College Park, Maryland. There is nothing in the Marshall "Korea" file regarding the Marshall-Truman meeting. However, there are two eye-catching entries in the declassified index of Marshall-Ridgway correspondence in the aftermath of the Marshall-Truman meeting:

> *19 Jun 51—SENSITIVE FILE (Sealed Envelope contains EYES ONLY message from Gen. Marshall to Gen. Ridgway of 14 Jun 51. CD313.2 (SF)*
> *20 Jun 51—SENSITIVE FILE (Sealed Envelope contains EYES ONLY message from Gen. Ridgway to Col. Carter [Marshall's senior aide] dtd 20 Jun 51. CD313.2 (SF)*

In discussions with one Marshall historian who has worked closely with Marshall's papers, I learned that Marshall secured documents in sealed envelopes in two instances, where the material dealt with Ultra code breaking during World War II and with atomic weapons.

What is contained in the Marshall-Ridgway eyes only messages that followed the Marshall-Truman meeting?

Archives file CD313.2 (top secret) is available to researchers in highly sanitized form. It contains summary descriptions of documents filed in a "sensitive file" in "Restricted Data Safe #229." Where document summaries have been removed from the file for security reasons, withdrawal notices to that effect are inserted in their stead, except in the case of the two Marshall-Ridgway documents. Oddly, there is no reference whatsoever in File CD313.2 to the two eyes only Marshall-Ridgway documents listed in the index. Not only are there no documents in the file, there are no summary descriptions and no withdrawal notices alerting the researcher to the removal of the documents.

In July 1998, I filed a request for the two documents, pursuant to the Freedom of Information Act (FOIA), citing the declassified index entries, the references to Restricted Data Safe #229, the background of the Marshall-Ridgway discussions in Tokyo regarding atomic weapons, the Pogue-Ridgway correspondence on the matter (and Pogue's subsequent publication of it in his Marshall biography), and my belief that the June 14 eyes only document (dated just two days after the Marshall-Truman meeting) advised Ridgway of the result of Marshall's discussion with the president on the subject of atomic weapons and that the June 20 eyes only document was Ridgway's acknowledgment-response.

In August, the archives responded. Their search had come up empty; the two eyes only documents could not be found. "Our guess is they never got to us," the archives FOIA specialist told me. He suggested that I contact the Pentagon.

In September, I submitted an FOIA request for the two documents to the Pentagon's Directorate for Freedom of Information and Security Review. On the chance that General Ridgway had retained copies for his files, I also submitted a request for the documents to the Archives Branch of the U.S. Army Military History Institute, where the Ridgway papers are housed.

In November, the Military History Institute advised me that there was nothing in the Ridgway papers.

In December, the Pentagon advised me of the results of their search: The records of the Office of the Secretary of Defense (OSD) are housed at the Federal Records Center in Suitland, Maryland, pending periodic review by the National Archives. Documents deemed to have historical significance pursuant to the archives review are then "accessioned" to the archives. (Documents deemed to have no archival value are not accessioned and are discarded at the Suitland site.)

With respect to the two June 1951 eyes only documents I was seeking, the Pentagon advised me that their search had come up empty, too. The oldest existing OSD records at Suitland date *back to 1959; there is nothing prior to that date. I was advised by the Pentagon FOIA specialist that if the eyes only documents on Secretary Marshall's index had ever made it out of the OSD, they would now be at the National Archives. But my previous FOIA request at the archives had confirmed that they were not there. The paper trail that began in the Marshall index ended there—I believe, with good reason.*

What did happen in late June 1951? What was the nature of the Marshall-Ridgway eyes only sealed-envelope communications? What became of the documents? An educated conjecture based on the record, and the gaps, follows.

When Secretary Marshall met with President Truman on June 12, the "taste of the atom" option was dicussed. The president authorized Marshall to instruct General Ridgway that in the event of another CCF offensive, Ridgway was permitted to use atomic weapons.

An eyes only sealed-envelope communication to that effect was prepared by Marshall for Ridgway on June 14 (with instructions to make no copies and to return the document to Marshall by sealed envelope). On June 20, Ridgway responded in an eyes only sealed-envelope communication to Secretary Marshall (through Marshall's senior military aide, Col. Marshall Carter). Ridgway confirmed receipt of Marshall's communication, advised Marshall that he was prepared to carry out Marshall's instructions, and returned the original of the secretary's communication in the sealed envelope.

The gist of the Marshall-Ridgway communications—that a nuclear trip wire had been authorized and set in Korea—was shared with the Communists, most likely the Russians. On instructions from Stalin (who had soured on Korea and we now know was prepared to write it off[19]), Ambassador Malik then called for a Korean cease-fire and armistice without preconditions. The Chinese and North Koreans, under pressure from the Russians, reluctantly acceded. Truce talks began on July 10, 1951. After two years of tortuous negotiations, a formal cease-fire was signed on July 27, 1953.

The U.S. decision to play the nuclear card was closely held by Truman, Marshall, Ridgway, and perhaps Marshall's aide, Colonel Carter. Only two copies of the eyes only document authorizing the use of atomic weapons were prepared by Secretary Marshall. One was transmitted to General Ridgway and returned; both were retained by Secretary Marshall in his files. When Marshall prepared to step down as secretary of defense later in the year, he had indexes of his files prepared. Upon review by the secretary for eventual shipment to the archives, the two eyes only documents were destroyed. Corresponding deletions were not made in the index sent to the archives. Perhaps it was an oversight; more likely there was no perceived need to make deletions because there was no description in the index of the contents of the documents, which take on historical importance only in the context of the Marshall-Ridgway discussion in Tokyo.

Against this background, the abrupt end of the Korean War comes into definitive focus. The United States, embroiled in a war with no extricable end, in a place that was sapping men and materiel from European reconstruction, against an enemy with inexhaustible reservoirs of troops, quietly laid down the nuclear marker.[20]

The war, as the secretary of defense had told the Supreme Commander in the Far East in June 1951, was not going to continue as it had; rather it was going to end in one of two ways: diplomatically or, failing that, atomically.

Confronted with these stark choices, the Communists chose half a Korean loaf over "a taste of the atom." The Korean War, although far from finished, was over.

End Notes

1. On August 1, General Bradley moved up from First Army to direct 12th Army Group (comprising Hodges's First Army and Patton's Third Army). Major Quirk moved from First Army to 12th Army Group with General Bradley as his PRO.

2. "At the end of his triumphal march down the Champs Elysses he was greeted not only by the cheers of the people massed in the Place de la Concorde but also by a hail of bullets from the surrounding rooftops." Schoenbrun, *The Three Lives of Charles de Gaulle* (1965), p. 171.

3. Sergeant Mauldin's cartoons in the *Stars and Stripes* were a GI favorite. Patton loathed them and had threatened to ban the paper in Third Army if it didn't drop Mauldin's cartoons. The meeting settled nothing. SHAEF backed Mauldin; Patton backed off.

4. Apparently for getting caught up in the middle of the bullion controversy. In April, XII Corps of Third Army had uncovered the German gold reserve (approximately $58 million, plus millions more in currency, paintings, and gold and silver dental fillings wrenched from the mouths of the concentration camp dead) hidden in an underground cavern in the Merkers salt mine. Patton ordered the story embargoed, but the story leaked and was then passed by a SHAEF censor. Patton, infuriated, ordered the censor (over whom he had no authority) out of the Third Army sector. Several correspondents wrote critical articles about Patton's performance. Eisenhower intervened and the matter faded.

5. Pyle, forty, had covered the war in Europe from Normandy through the liberation of Paris. He was killed on April 19 in the Pacific, on the island of Ie Shima, west of Okinawa.

6. The French decoration was the Croix de Guerre for the Paris operation.

7. A well-intentioned but poorly chosen remark by Patton in Boston that was intended to honor the war dead provoked protests from Gold Star parents of men killed in action. They believed it insensitive and demanded an apology. To ensure that there were no further gaffes, a Patton press conference held subsequently in Washington was chaired by none other than Secretary of War Stimson.

8. Supreme Court Justice Robert Jackson, appointed by President Truman in May 1945 as chief U.S. prosecutor at Nuremberg, had been on FDR's vice presidential list in 1944.

9. General Bryant Moore was the IX Corps commander whose helicopter crashed into the Han River. He died shortly thereafter of a heart attack.

10. The Massacre Valley story is discussed in the Quirk-Ridgway memorandum of March 17. The U.S. 2d Division casualties were 1,448 killed, wounded, and missing.

11. Blair, *The Forgotten War: America in Korea 1950–1953*, pp. 743–44.

12. Leckie, *Conflict: The History of the Korean War 1950–1953*, pp. 266–67.

13. James, *The Years of MacArthur: Triumph & Disaster 1945–1964*, p. 583; *Foreign Relations of the United States 1951, Volume VII (Korea and China)*, Part I, pp. 229, 244.

14. Van Fleet, appointed without Ridgway's knowledge, was not a Ridgway favorite.

15. For "exceptionally meritorious service" with Eighth United States Army in Korea during the period February 1–April 13, 1951. He was promoted to full colonel shortly thereafter.

16. Ridgway's primary mission as Supreme Commander for the Allied Powers (SCAP) was the defense of Japan. The invasion of Japan by the Soviet Union while the Eighth Army was engaged in Korea was a matter of concern.

17. On July 9, Ridgway wrote the following to the Adjutant General of the Army:

Having been specially recommended by reason of his high professional standards and competence as well as his character and personality, I requested an effort be made to secure the services of Colonel Quirk. Without hesitation, Colonel Quirk, from purely patriotic motives and to his own distinct financial disadvantage, volunteered to come to Korea as my special advisor on public relations.

He served with me in that capacity from 30 January 1951 to 22 June 1951.

During this period of service, I had opportunity for almost daily observation of Colonel Quirk, and my opinion expressed herein is the result of that intimate contact.

In integrity, high principled competence in his own field, breadth of view, loyalty, initiative, devotion to duty and ability to work in harmony with others, both in the military service and among the large group of war correspondents in this theater, Colonel Quirk rendered conspicuous superior service.

Originally agreeing to serve for approximately 90 days, he voluntarily, again to his own disadvantage, remained for an additional like period because of the evident need for his services here. I would welcome the opportunity to share service with him again.

18. The "taste of the atom" conversation is described by Pogue in *George C. Marshall: Statesman 1945–1959* (1987), p. 488 (and p. 582, notes 25 and 26).

19. Previously classified Soviet documents reveal that Stalin had "few, if any" nuclear weapons at the outbreak of the Korean War and "no feasible means of delivering them upon American targets." The United States, in contrast, had a growing nuclear stockpile approaching three hundred. Stalin did not share the parlous state of the Soviet nuclear capability with the North Koreans or the Chinese. However, the nuclear imbalance presumably tempered his bullishness. Although he gave the green light to the North Korean invasion, Stalin hedged his bets, telling the North Koreans that they would have to look to the Chinese, not the Soviets, for military assistance if the United States intervened. Stalin later informed the Chinese, in the wake of the Inchon landing, that Russia was unprepared to risk a third world war in Korea. Gaddis, *We Now Know: Rethinking Cold War History* (1997), p. 104.

20. This would not have been the first time that Marshall sought to force a silent showdown through extraordinary measures. In the fall of 1941, he attempted to derail the impending war with Japan in similar fashion. As Army Chief of Staff, he began a surreptitious, massive shift of pilots and warplanes from throughout the United States to the Philippines, then unveiled his plans at a secret November briefing in Washington for newsmen:

> When he had their attention Marshall announced calmly that the United States and Japan were on the brink of war. . . . If the United States were allowed to complete the build-up, he said, the President would then suddenly reveal to the moderate leaders of Japan the extent of the vast air force that menaced them. Perhaps, if they were allowed to save face, they would desist from their aggression. Pogue, *George C. Marshall: Ordeal and Hope, 1939–1942* (1966), p. 202.

A Note on Sources

Although much of this book is drawn from memory, I have relied as well on interviews, research, and a range of public sources in understanding the wars, the leaders who fought them, and the home front. The following books were helpful.

Omar N. Bradley: Bradley's World War II memoir, *A Soldier's Story* (1951), and his more expansive autobiography (with Clay Blair), *A General's Life* (1983), were useful.

George S. Patton: There is a kaleidoscopic quality to Patton that is not easily captured. Patton's *War As I Knew It* (1946), published posthumously with annotations by his deputy chief of staff, Paul D. Harkins, was informative. Martin Blumenson's excellent work *Patton: The Man Behind the Legend* (1985) and the two volumes of *The Patton Papers* (1972–1974), which he edited, were particularly helpful. Patton biographers Carlo d' Este, *Patton: A Genius for War* (1995), and Ladislas Farago, *Patton: Ordeal and Triumph* (1963) offered further insight into a complex figure.

Matthew B. Ridgway: Ridgway is one of the major military figures of twentieth-century America. His performance in Korea has no equal in American military annals. He warrants a definitive biography. The best portrait can be found in two excellent books by Clay Blair: *Ridgway's Paratroopers: The American Airborne in World War II* (1975) and *The Forgotten War: America in Korea 1950–1953* (1987). *Soldier,* Ridgway's memoir (with Harold H. Martin) (1956), provides a useful (albeit guarded) overview.

World War II: I found Russell Weigley's *Eisenhower's Lieutenants: The Campaigns of France and Germany, 1944–1945* (1981) to be the best

one-volume history of the war in Europe, and I drew from it exten-
sively. I also found helpful the volumes of the U.S. Army's official history *United States Army in World War II: The European Theater of Operations*, especially Forrest C. Pogue, *The Supreme Command* (1952), and
Charles B. MacDonald, *The Last Offensive* (1972). I relied heavily on
them, as well as on Stephen E. Ambrose's excellent *Citizen Soldiers:
The U.S. Army from the Normandy Beaches to the Bulge to the Surrender of
Germany* (1997).

Two excellent day-by-day chronologies were helpful in pulling together the story of the war: Mary H. Williams, *Chronology 1941–1945*
(1958), which is part of the *United States Army in World War II* series;
and Cesare Salmaggi and Alfredo Pallavisini, *2194 Days of War*
(1977).

Dwight Eisenhower, *Crusade in Europe* (1948); Stephen E. Ambrose, *The Supreme Commander: The War Years of General Dwight D. Eisenhower* (1970); and Harry Butcher, *My Three Years With Eisenhower*
(1946), provided insight on the Supreme Command and its commander.

Two accounts by wartime correspondents—Andy Rooney's *My
War* (1995) and *Ernie's War: The Best of Ernie Pyle's World War II Dis-
patches* (1986), edited by David Nichols—provided helpful ground-
level perspectives.

Joseph E. Persico's *Nuremberg: Infamy on Trial* (1994) was helpful
in understanding the pretrial period in 1945.

The Korean War: Clay Blair's previously cited *The Forgotten War:
America in Korea 1950–1953* is an excellent one-volume history of the
conflict. I relied on it as well as Ridgway's *The Korean War* (1967);
James F. Schnabel's volume in *The United States Army in the Korean War*
series, *Policy and Direction: The First Year* (1971); Roy Appleman, *Ridg-
way Duels for Korea* (1990); and D. Clayton James's extraordinary *The
Years of MacArthur: Triumph & Disaster 1945–1964* (1985). I also
found the following helpful: Bevin Alexander, *Korea: The First War
We Lost* (1986); Doris M. Condit, *History of the Office of the Secretary of
Defense, Volume II: The Test of War 1950–1953* (1988); Joseph C.
Goulden, *Korea: The Untold Story of the War* (1982); Max Hastings, *The
Korean War* (1987); Robert Leckie, *Conflict: The History of the Korean
War, 1950–53* (1962); and James L. Stokesbury, *A Short History of the
Korean War* (1988).

The tension between MacArthur and Ridgway, which was effectively hidden from public view during the early months of 1951, is addressed in the following previously cited works: Blair, *The Forgotten War;* James, *The Years of MacArthur;* Leckie, *Conflict* and *also Foreign Relations of the United States 1951, Volume VII (Korea and China)*, Part I.

On the relief of Douglas MacArthur, the following were insightful: the previously cited Ridgway, *The Korean War;* James, *The Years of MacArthur;* and Bradley, *A General's Life* (he was chairman of the Joint Chiefs at the time of MacArthur's relief); as well as Forrest C. Pogue, *George C. Marshall: Statesman 1945–1959* (1987), covering General Marshall's service as secretary of defense during Korea; Secretary of State Dean Acheson's excellent memoir, *Present at the Creation: My Years in the State Department* (1969); the second volume of President Harry S. Truman's memoirs, *Years of Trial and Hope* (1956); and William Manchester, *American Caesar: Douglas MacArthur 1880–1964* (1978).

On Korea and the atomic bomb, in addition to archival research detailed in the Acknowledgments, I found the following helpful: Forrest Pogue's *George C. Marshall: Ordeal and Hope 1939–1942* (1966), regarding Marshall's tactic of quiet buildup and confrontation; John Lewis Gaddis's excellent *We Now Know: Rethinking Cold War History* (1997), on Stalin's reluctance to confront the United States in Korea; and Robert Norris and William Arkin's "Nuclear Notebook: Estimated U.S. and Soviet/Russian Nuclear Stockpiles, 1945–94," *Bulletin of the Atomic Scientists,* Vol. 50, No. 6 (Nov.–Dec. 1994), on the nuclear imbalance during the Korean War.

Stateside in the 1940s and 1950s: Doris Kearns Goodwin's *No Ordinary Time: Franklin and Eleanor Roosevelt, The Home Front in World War II* (1994) is an excellent account of the wartime 1940s. John Morton Blum's *V Was for Victory: Politics and American Culture During World War II* (1976) was helpful. David Brinkley's *Washington Goes to War* (1988) is an informative chronicle of life in wartime Washington.

Joseph C. Goulden's *The Best Years 1945–1950* (1976) helped jog childhood memories of the postwar years, as did Goodwin's *Wait Till Next Year* (1997), a reminiscence of her childhood love affair with the Brooklyn Dodgers. (I was spared the late-season heartache that Goodwin's Dodgers caused her and all of Brooklyn; the Phillies were usually hopelessly mired in sixth place by the Fourth of July.)

Radio, Television, and *TV Guide:* For an understanding of the evolution of *TV Guide,* the following were helpful: Glenn Altschuler and David Grossvogel, *Changing Channels: America in TV Guide* (1992); John Cooney, *The Annenbergs* (1982); Gaeton Fonzi, *Annenberg* (1969); and Joseph C. Goulden, *The Curtis Caper* (1965).

On the early days of radio and television, I relied upon *Broadcasting Yearbook* for the years 1937–41 and 1945–51; Erik Barnouw's *The Golden Web: A History of Broadcasting in the United States (Volume II—1933 to 1953)* (1968); and Michael D. Murray and Donald G. Godfrey, *Television in America* (1997).

On the early days of television in Charleston, *Broadcasting in West Virginia: A History* (1989), published by the West Virginia Broadcasters Association, was especially helpful (and includes a group photograph of the Charleston TV pioneers, in which my father, seated in the second row, is one of "next three men unidentified." Sic transit . . .).

Acknowledgments

One of the unexpected pleasures of writing this book was finding out how willing people were to help. The book would never have happened without the early encouragement of Clare Amend, David Ignatius, and Michael Skube, who offered counsel and suggestions on shaping this project long before I hit the first keystroke.

Michael Galvin introduced me to Jed Lyons, who guided me to Presidio Press, a fortuitous match of publisher and subject matter.

I am especially grateful to Jim Cannon, who convinced me early on that I had a book when I seriously doubted it. This is a better book because of his interest and advice.

Grace Bateman, Marc Leepson, and Alex Ward reviewed the manuscript and offered helpful suggestions, and I thank them. John Quirk, my father's brother, a delightful raconteur with an archival, just-yesterday memory spanning his eighty-four years, filled in critical information about my parents, as did my cousins Anne Quirk and Win Quirk.

I am indebted to the many people in Philadelphia who helped me: Terri Chango, the assistant principal at Frankford High School, guided me to documents on my mother's high school years; Shawn Weldon, assistant archivist at the Archdiocesan Historical Research Center, unearthed material on my father's time in the seminary; at Villanova University, Mary Jane Morrissy in the registrar's office, university archivist the Rev. Dennis Gallagher OSA, and the staff of the Falvey Library went out of their way to help reconstruct my father's time there. Kristin Fetzer at the Philadelphia Historical Commission and Susan Hauser of the Delaware County Planning Department verified dates and guided me to helpful sources.

Jack Deacon, station manager of WSAZ-TV in Charleston, West Virginia, helped me better understand the early years of West Virginia television.

Wil Mahoney and the military records staff at the National Archives in College Park, Maryland, provided assistance in researching the Marshall visit to Korea and its aftermath, as did Randy Sowell at the Harry S. Truman Library in Independence, Missouri, and Larry Bland at the George C. Marshall Library in Lexington, Virginia.

David Lake, FOIA specialist at the National Archives; David Maier, FOIA specialist at the Pentagon's Directorate for Freedom of Information and Security Review; and Pam Cheney, at the U.S. Army Military History Institute at Carlisle Barracks, Pennsylvania, assisted in trying to ascertain the elusive nonwhereabouts of the Marshall-Ridgway eyes only correspondence.

Thanks to former director Benedict K. Zobrist and the staff of the Harry S. Truman Library for sharing my enthusiasm for my parents' letters and giving them a permanent home.

I did the bulk of my historical research in Washington—at Georgetown University's Lauinger Library and at the Palisades Branch of the District of Columbia Public Library. Thanks to Palisades reference librarians Lucy Thrasher and Liane Rosenblatt, who fielded my unending interbranch loan requests. Special thanks to Georgetown University archivist Jon Reynolds at Lauinger, who unearthed and secured many hard-to-find sources and offered encouragement throughout.

At Presidio Press, Richard Kane, Robert Kane, and my editor, E. J. McCarthy, took a big gamble on a three-page proposal and a handful of letters. I am grateful to them for their faith in this project. Barbara Feller-Roth copyedited the manuscript with competence and care—welcome qualities in this slapdash age.

Gail Ross and Susan Munsat provided valuable legal counsel and guided me through the labyrinth of the book contract.

The late Fred Friendly, my adviser at Columbia, once offered a terse assessment of my potential: "You can write." Those three words had a lasting impact on my career choices. I hope this book would not have caused him to reconsider.

James Quirk and Elizabeth Wolstencroft figure prominently in this book. In a sense, they are its coauthors. Without James's letters, there is no book. Without Elizabeth, whose love of the written word equaled my father's—she was a better writer than he, if that is possible—it is doubtful he would have written with the care and at the length that he did. James knew he had an appreciative and demanding audience in Elizabeth. I regret that I did not have more of Elizabeth's letters to work with. She was the real writer in the family. I am fortunate to be their editor, and their son.

My family has been enthusiastic and supportive throughout. Clare Amend, Chris, and Elizabeth encouraged me on good days, steered clear when I hit the authorial wall, and had the intuitive ability to discern the difference. They will be glad to get their word processor back.

Finally, for inspiration and the last word, my 1995 Yankees: Bayard, Coach Dale, Daniel, Duff, Duncan, Fitz, Jamie, John, Jon, JT, Peter—and Chris, who really was safe at home.

RFQ
Washington, D.C.

Index